WORKBOOK FOR
ELEMENTARY HARMONY

Theory and Practice

Fourth Edition

Robert W. Ottman
University of North Texas

Prentice Hall, Englewood Cliffs, New Jersey 07632

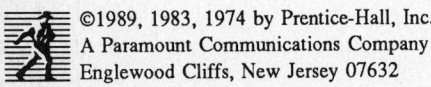©1989, 1983, 1974 by Prentice-Hall, Inc.
A Paramount Communications Company
Englewood Cliffs, New Jersey 07632

All rights reserved. No part of this book may be
reproduced, in any form or by any means,
without permission in writing from the publisher.

Printed in the United States of America
10 9

ISBN 0-13-257312-1

PRENTICE-HALL INTERNATIONAL (UK) LIMITED, London
PRENTICE-HALL OF AUSTRALIA PTY. LIMITED, Sydney
PRENTICE-HALL CANADA INC., Toronto
PRENTICE-HALL HISPANOAMERICANA, S.A., Mexico
PRENTICE-HALL OF INDIA PRIVATE LIMITED, New Delhi
PRENTICE-HALL OF JAPAN, INC., Tokyo
SIMON & SCHUSTER ASIA PTE. LTD., Singapore
EDITORA PRENTICE-HALL DO BRASIL, LTDA., Rio de Janeiro

CONTENTS

PREFACE   v

1   BASICS I: Pitch on the Staff and at the Keyboard; Scales; Key Signatures   1

2   BASICS II: Intervals; Chords; Staff Notation   6

3   BASICS III: Duration; Time Signatures   10

4   TONIC AND DOMINANT   16

5   TONIC AND DOMINANT: Part-Writing   37

6   THE SUBDOMINANT TRIAD   55

7   THE MELODIC LINE: I   64

8   C CLEFS; TRANSPOSING INSTRUMENTS   75

9   THE TRIAD IN INVERSION   85

10 HARMONIC PROGRESSION: Supertonic Triad and Leading Tone Triads   98

11 NONHARMONIC TONES I: Passing Tones and Neighbor Tones   118

12 NONHARMONIC TONES II: Suspensions and Other Dissonances   123

13 THE DOMINANT SEVENTH AND SUPERTONIC SEVENTH CHORDS   138

14	THE SUBMEDIANT AND MEDIANT TRIADS	152
15	THE MELODIC LINE: II	168
16	THE v AND VII TRIADS; THE PHRYGIAN CADENCE	181
17	HARMONIC SEQUENCE	194
18	SECONDARY DOMINANT CHORDS; MODULATION	200

PREFACE

This *Workbook* correlates with the author's *Elementary Harmony: Theory and Practice*, fourth edition (Englewood Cliffs, N.J.: Prentice Hall, 1989). It contains both music for analysis and appropriate written assignments for companion chapters in *Elementary Harmony*.

Correlation of Assignments. Most assignments from *Elementary Harmony* are found in the *Workbook*, with identical assignment numbers. However, although the numbering and intent of any individual assignment is the same in both books, the content in each case differs. This furnishes the student with additional practice material in each problem covered.

Assignments in *Elementary Harmony* which require only blank music manuscript paper for their completion are not repeated in the *Workbook*. On the other hand, new assignments for the *Workbook* have been included; these are identified by the chapter number plus a letter, e.g., Assignment 3A, 3B, etc. All assignments from both books are listed at the beginning of each chapter in order of their proper presentation, and with page number location in either or both books.

Writing Assignments. The writing assignments are of two varieties: those with answers given, and those without given answers. The former can be identified by the vertical line in the middle of the page separating the answer on the left side from the problem to be completed on the right side. The answers on the left should be covered while solving the problem, and uncovered for checking.

All assignments with given answers are followed by similar additional problems without given answers. These can be used for homework to be turned in to the instructor or for testing purposes.

Assignments in Analysis. Many chapters in *Elementary Harmony* include excerpts from standard compositions for purposes of analysis. The *Workbook* provides additional music for this purpose. These selections do not duplicate those in the companion chapters in *Elementary Harmony*, and cover a wide range of composers and of vocal and instrumental media.

Robert W. Ottman

CHAPTER 1

BASICS I: Pitch on the Staff and the Keyboard; Scales; Key Signatures

Chapters 1–3 present a brief review of basic materials already learned from previous experience. Students requiring additional study, including extensive drills and exercises, are referred to either of two texts designed to precede *Elementary Harmony*. They are (1) *Rudiments of Music*, second edition (Prentice Hall, 1987), and *Programmed Rudiments of Music*, (Prentice Hall, 1979), both by Robert W. Ottman and Frank D. Mainous.

In this text, EH refers to *Elementary Harmony: Theory and Practice*, fourth edition, 1989. equals

In Chapters 1–3, *Rud* refers to exercises in *Rudiments of Music* mentioned above where more complete coverage of the material under study can be found.

Before beginning these exercises, study *EH*, pages 1–5, through Figure 1.9.

Exercise 1.1. Name each pitch, using octave register symbols.

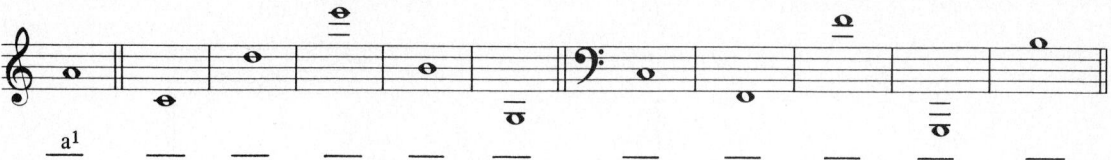

Exercise 1.2. Place each given note on the staff in its correct octave.

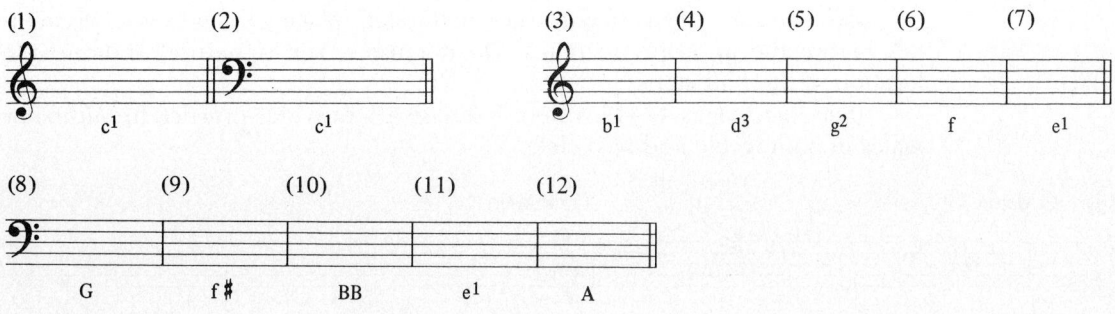

Exercise 1.3. Place the given pitch on both the treble and bass staves. See *EH*, Figure 1.6.

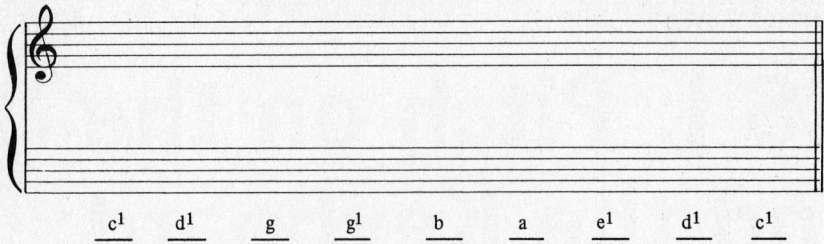

c^1 d^1 g g^1 b   a e^1 d^1 c^1

Exercise 1.4. Name the keys on the piano keyboard indicated by the arrows. The location of c^1 is given. Use octave register symbols.

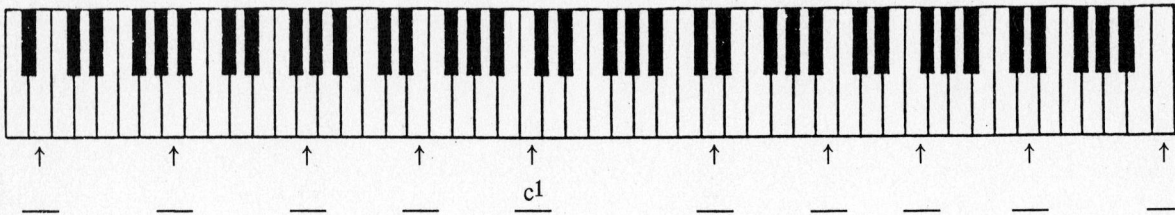

Exercise 1.5. (See *EH*, Figure 1.11).
a) Convert these whole steps to half steps by *raising* the *lower* note one half step. Write the new interval on the lower staff. *Note*: one of these intervals is already a half step; mark it with an **X**.

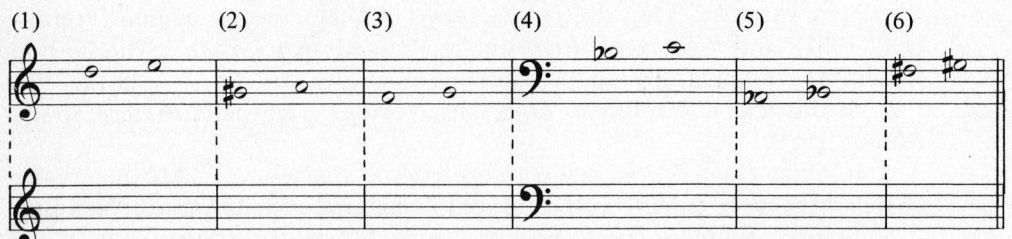

b) Convert these whole steps to half steps by *lowering* the *upper* note one half step. Again, one of these is already a half step.

Exercise 1.6. Write major scales on the staff, placing the necessary accidentals before the appropriate notes. Do not use a key signature. Indicate the location of the half steps.
(See *Rud*, pages 47–49, where Exercise 4.1 provides practice for *all* major scales in both treble and bass clefs.)

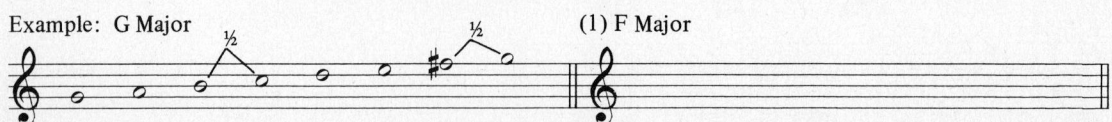

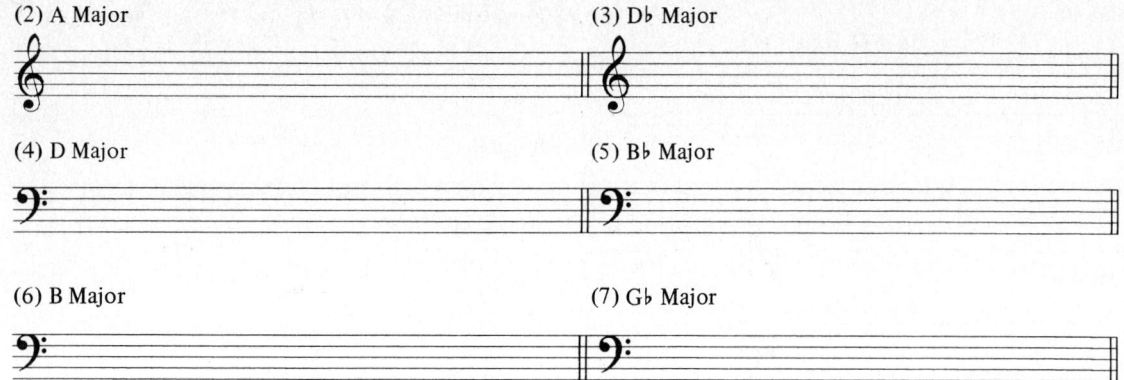

Exercise 1.7. Scale degree names. Place the scale degree number before each scale step name.

_____ Mediant   _____ Submediant

_____ Supertonic   _____ Subdominant

_____ Tonic   _____ Dominant

_____ Leading tone

Exercise 1.8. Name the major key indicated by each of these key signatures. (See *Rud*, pages 108–9, where Exercise 10.6 provides practice for recognizing all major key signatures.)

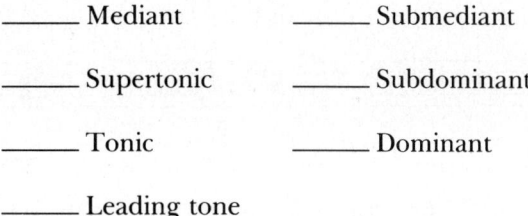

Exercise 1.9. Write these major key signatures on the staff. (See *Rud*, pages 109–10, where Exercise 10.7 provides practice for writing *all* major key signatures.)

Exercise 1.10. Write minor scales on the staff, placing accidentals before the appropriate notes. Do not use a key signature. Indicate the location of the half steps, and, in harmonic minor, the location of the step-and-a-half (1½). Write the melodic scale ascending and descending.

(See *Rud*, pages 149–56, where Exercise 13.1 provides practice for writing *all* minor scales in each of their three forms, in both treble and bass clefs.)

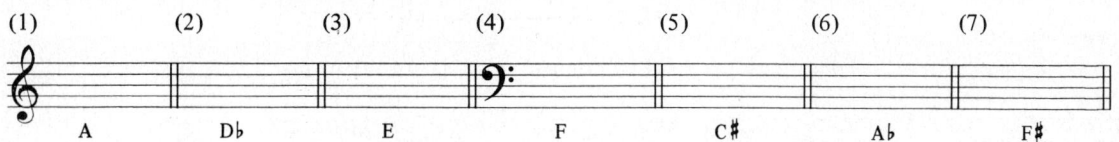

(3) E Natural   (4) C♯ Harmonic

(5) B Harmonic   (6) E♭ Natural

(7) G♯ Melodic

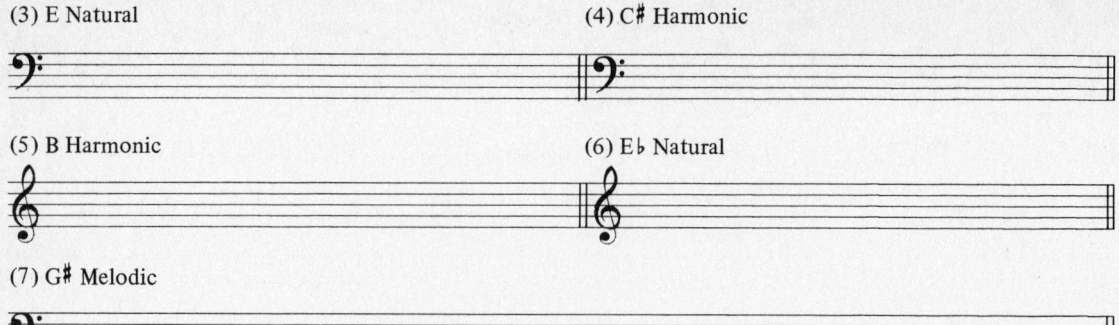

Exercise 1.11. Name the minor key indicated by these key signatures. (See *Rud*, page 184, where Exercise 15.6 provides practice for identifying *all* minor key signatures.)

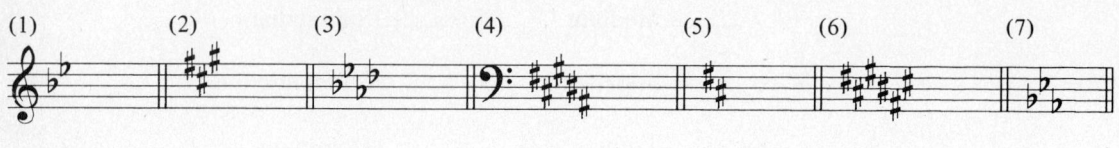

Exercise 1.12. Write the signature for the given minor key.

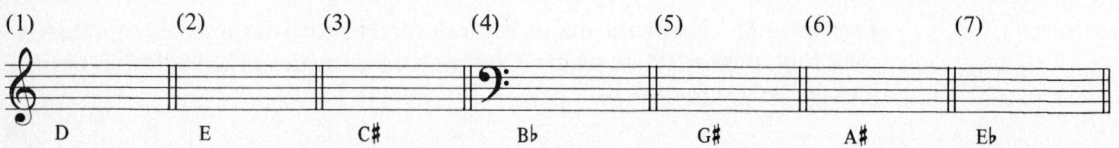

Exercise 1.13. Fill in either the key name or the number of sharps or flats in the key signature. Both major and minor keys are included.

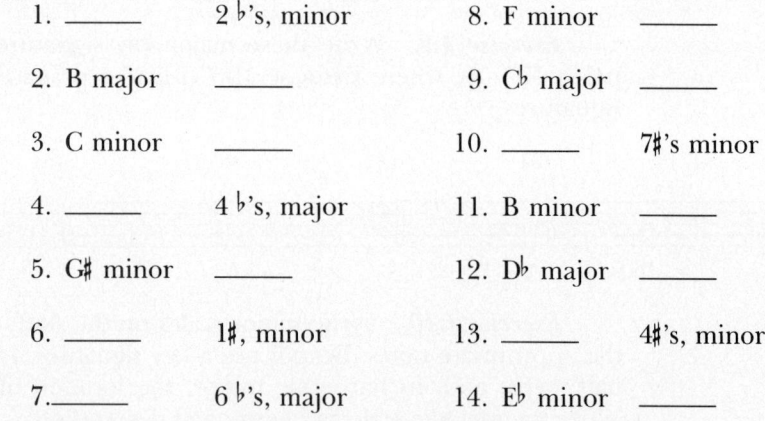

Exercise 1.14. Name the relative key and the parallel key to each of the given keys. Where no answer is possible, place an **X** in that space.

                                Relative Key   *Parallel Key*

1. B♭ major   _____   _____

2. C♯ minor   _____   _____

3. A♭ major   _____   _____

	Relative Key	Parallel Key
4. D♭ major	_____	_____
5. F♯ minor	_____	_____
6. G♯ minor	_____	_____
7. E♭ minor	_____	_____
8. F major	_____	_____
9. C♯ major	_____	_____
10. A♯ minor	_____	_____

Exercise 1.15. Name the key *enharmonic* with each of these keys:

1. C♯ major _____

2. E♭ minor _____

3. B major _____

4. G♯ minor _____

5. F♯ major _____

6. B♭ minor _____

CHAPTER 2
BASICS II: Intervals; Chords; Staff Notation

Exercise 2.1. Perfect and major intervals (see *EH*, Figure 2.4). (See *Rud*, Exercises 17.1 and 17.2 for extensive drills in these intervals.)

a) Name each of these intervals.

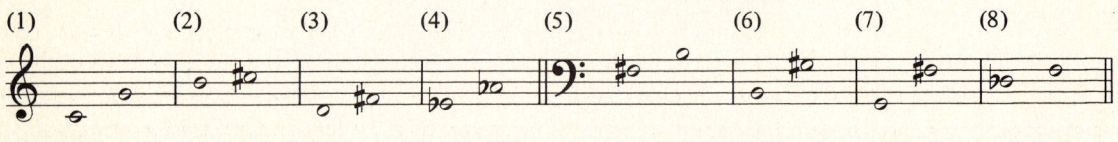

b) Write the second note of each interval above the given note.

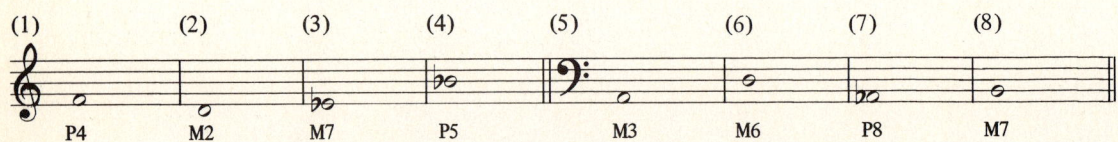

Exercise 2.2. Minor intervals (see *EH*, Figure 2.5). (See *Rud*, Exercises 18.1–18.3 for additional studies in m, d, and A intervals.)

a) Name each interval. Some intervals are major.

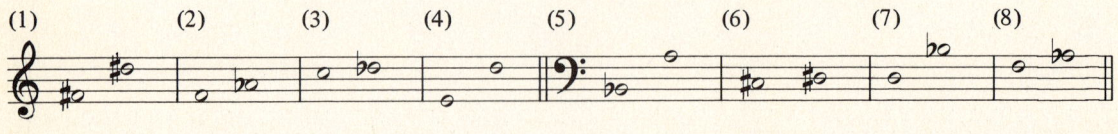

b) Write the second note of the interval above the given note.

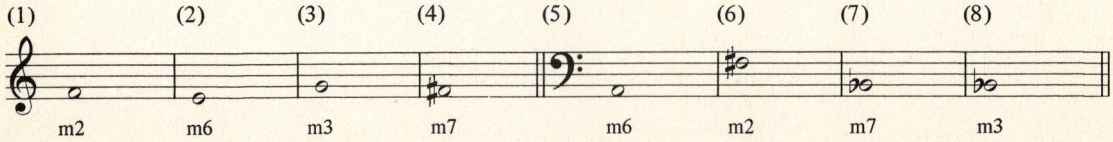

Exercise 2.3. Diminished and augmented intervals (see *EH*, Figures 2.6 and 2.7).

a) Identify these d and A intervals.

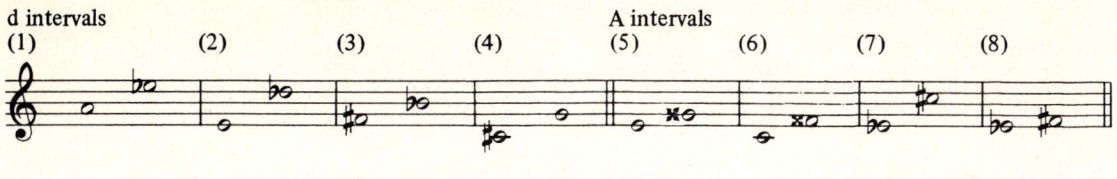

b) Write the second note of these intervals above the given note.

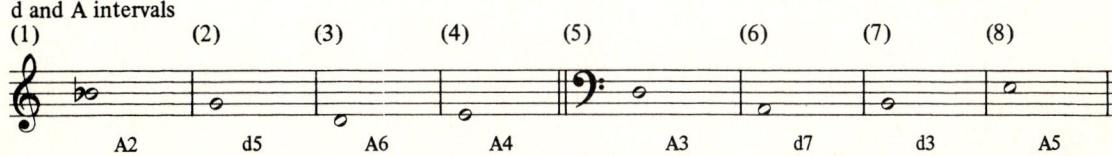

Exercise 2.4. Writing intervals above notes which cannot be tonic tones. Write the second note of the interval above the given note (see *EH*, Figure 2.8).

(See *Rud*, Exercises 18.6 and 18.7 for comprehensive practice in all types of intervals.)

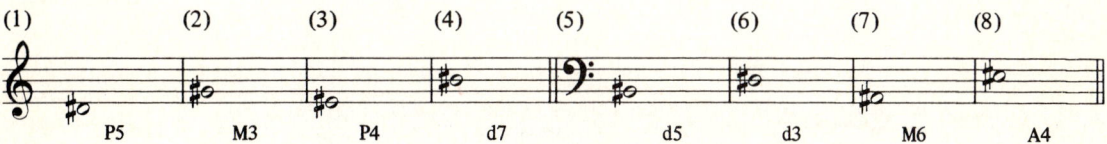

Exercise 2.5. Inversion of intervals (see *EH*, Figures 2.11 and 2.12). (See *Rud*, Exercise 18.9 for additional examples.)

Invert each interval twice: first by placing the *lower* note an octave *higher*, and second by placing the *upper* note an octave *lower*. Both inverted intervals should include the same pitches, although an octave apart, and hence each will carry the same name. Name both the given interval and the inverted interval.

Exercise 2.6. Writing descending intervals.

a) Write the second note of these descending *perfect* and *major* intervals. Use the inversion of the given interval to find the correct pitch name (see *EH*, Figure 2.14a).

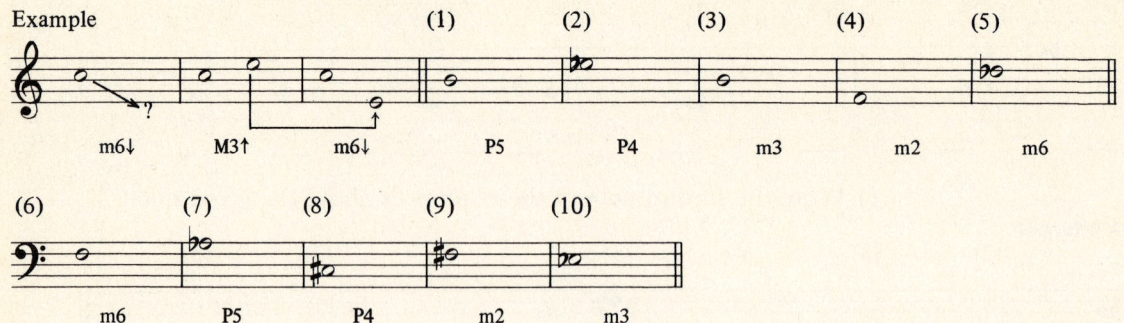

b) Write other types of descending intervals. First find the interval that is the inversion of the given interval, as in *EH*, Figure 2.14b.

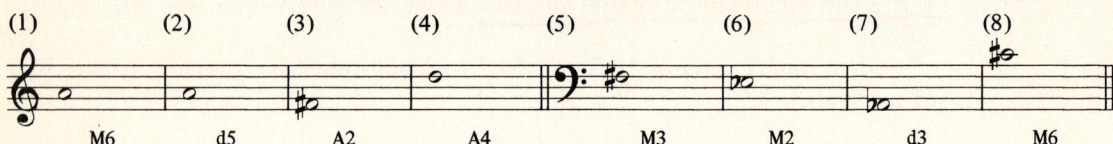

Exercise 2.7. Compound intervals. Reduce each compound interval to its simple form and name the interval (see *EH*, Figure 2.15).

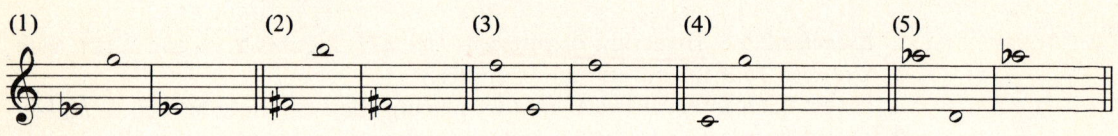

Exercise 2.8. Identify each triad as M (major), m (minor), d (diminished), or A (augmented) (see *EH*, Figure 2.17).

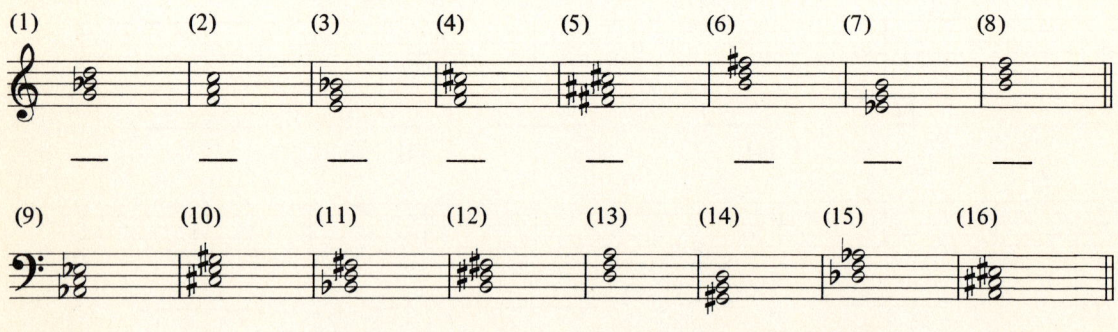

Exercise 2.9. Place the correct key name and Roman numeral number under each triad.

a) Each key signature indicates a major key (see *EH*, Figure 2.18).

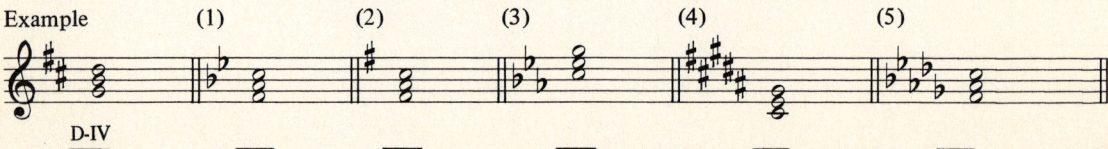

b) Each key signature indicates a minor key.

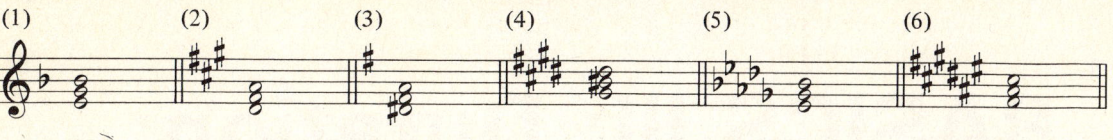

Exercise 2.10. Triad inversions. Write the given triad with its root as the lowest note, followed by its first and second inversions (see *EH*, Figure 2.22a).

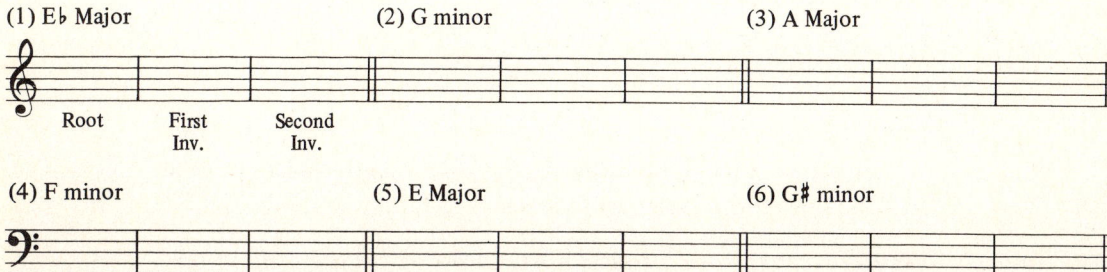

Exercise 2.11. Figured bass. Place one of these figured bass symbols below each triad. See *EH*, Figures 2.23 and 2.24.

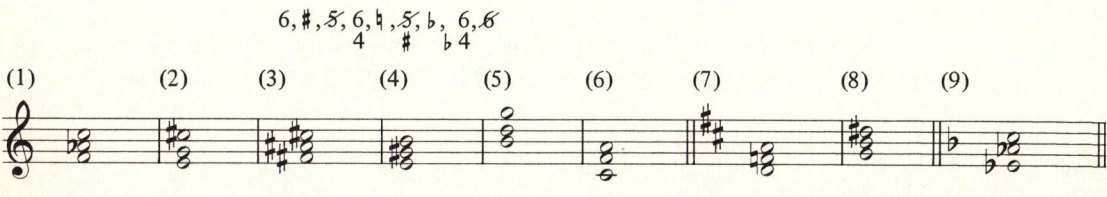

CHAPTER 3

BASICS III: Duration; Time Signatures

Exercise 3.1. Fill in each blank with the divisions of the given note or rest value. (See *Rud*, Exercises 3.3–3.8 for additional practice material.)

Example ♩ = ♫

1. 𝐨 = _____   6. _____ = ♩ ♩ ♩
2. _____ = 𝄾 𝄾   7. 𝄾 = _____
3. _____ = ♩ ♩   8. ♪ = _____
4. 𝄽 = _____   9. _____ = 𝄼
5. ♩. = _____   10. ♪ = _____

Exercise 3.2 is the first of a series of exercises in a "programmed" format, recognizable by the vertical center line. Cover the material to the left of the line and answer the question(s) to the right of the line. Then uncover the answer at the left to check your progress. Each such problem will be followed by a similar problem without answers given.

Exercise 3.2. Explain simple time signatures by description and by diagram.

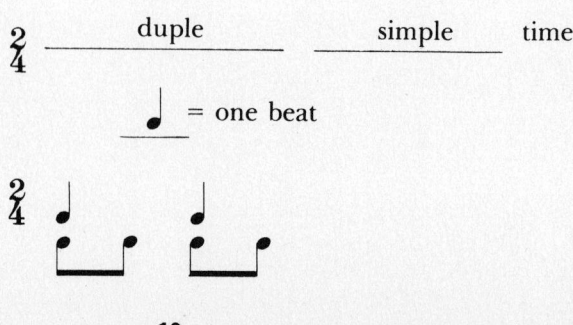

(1) 4/4 quadruple simple time

♩ = one beat

(2) 2/2 duple simple time

𝅗𝅥 = one beat

(3) 3/8 triple simple time

♪ = one beat

(4) 4/16 quadruple simple time

♬ = one beat

(5) 4/8 quadruple simple time

♪ = one beat

(1) 4/4 _____ _____ time
    ____ = one beat
    4/4

(2) 2/2 _____ _____ time
    ____ = one beat
    2/2

(3) 3/8 _____ _____ time
    ____ = one beat
    3/8

(4) 4/16 _____ _____ time
    ____ = one beat
    4/16

(5) 4/8 _____ _____ time
    ____ = one beat
    4/8

Exercise 3.3. Explain compound time signatures. Follow the directions in Exercise 3.2.

(1) $\frac{6}{8}$ duple compound time

$\textit{♩.}$ = one beat

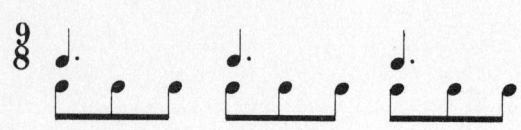

(2) $\frac{9}{8}$ triple compound time

$\textit{♩.}$ = one beat

(3) $\frac{12}{8}$ quadruple compound time

$\textit{♩.}$ = one beat

$\frac{12}{8}$ ♩. ♫♪ ♩. ♫♪ ♩. ♫♪ ♩. ♫♪

(4) $\frac{6}{16}$ duple compound time

$\textit{♪.}$ = one beat

(5) $\frac{12}{4}$ quadruple compound time

$\textit{𝅗𝅥.}$ = one beat

$\frac{12}{4}$ 𝅗𝅥. ♩ ♩ 𝅗𝅥. ♩ ♩ 𝅗𝅥. ♩ ♩ 𝅗𝅥. ♩ ♩

(1) $\frac{6}{8}$ _____ _____ time

____ = one beat

$\frac{6}{8}$

(2) $\frac{9}{8}$ _____ _____ time

____ = one beat

$\frac{9}{8}$

(3) $\frac{12}{8}$ _____ _____ time

____ = one beat

$\frac{12}{8}$

(4) $\frac{6}{16}$ _____ _____ time

____ = one beat

$\frac{6}{16}$

(5) $\frac{12}{4}$ _____ _____ time

____ = one beat

$\frac{12}{4}$

(6) $\frac{9}{2}$ triple compound time

   $\circ\!\cdot$ = one beat

$\frac{9}{2}$ $\circ\!\cdot$ $\circ\!\cdot$ $\circ\!\cdot$
♩ ♩ ♩ ♩ ♩ ♩ ♩ ♩ ♩

(6) $\frac{9}{2}$ _____ _____ time

   ____ = one beat

$\frac{9}{2}$

Exercise 3.4. Explain simple and compound time signatures. Follow the directions in Exercise 3.2.

(1) $\frac{3}{4}$ _____ _____ time

   ____ = one beat

$\frac{3}{4}$

(6) $\frac{9}{16}$ _____ _____ time

   ____ = one beat

$\frac{9}{16}$

(2) $\frac{4}{2}$ _____ _____ time

   ____ = one beat

$\frac{4}{2}$

(7) $\frac{4}{8}$ _____ _____ time

   ____ = one beat

$\frac{4}{8}$

(3) $\frac{9}{4}$ _____ _____ time

   ____ = one beat

$\frac{9}{4}$

(8) ¢ _____ _____ time

   ____ = one beat

¢

(4) $\frac{6}{4}$ _____ _____ time

   ____ = one beat

$\frac{6}{4}$

(9) $\frac{12}{16}$ _____ _____ time

   ____ = one beat

$\frac{12}{16}$

(5) $\frac{3}{2}$ _____ _____ time

   ____ = one beat

$\frac{3}{2}$

(10) $\frac{6}{32}$ _____ _____ time

   ____ = one beat

$\frac{6}{32}$

Exercise 3.5. Place a correct time signature before each musical example. The first measure of an example may be incomplete, in which case the last measure is also incomplete; the two partial measures equal one complete measure in time value. In a few cases, more than one correct signature is possible.

Exercise 3.6. Rhythmic transcription. Transcribe each melody below, using the time signature indicated. In *EH*, compare Figure 3.4 ($\frac{2}{4}$) with Figure 3.8 ($\frac{2}{2}$), and Figure 3.10b ($\frac{6}{8}$) with Figure 3.11 ($\frac{6}{16}$). In each pair, the melody is identical; only the rhythmic notation is changed.

CHAPTER 4

TONIC AND DOMINANT

Assignments in addition to those in *EH* are identified by a letter name, such as "Assignment 4A." All others, such as "Assignment 4.1," refer to the same numbered assignment in *EH*.

	Elementary Harmony	*Workbook*
Assignment 4.1	66	17
Assignment 4.2	66	18
Assignment 4.3	67	18
Assignment 4.4	67	19
Assignment 4.5	67	19
Assignment 4A	—	20
Assignment 4.6	70	21
Assignment 4.B	—	22
Assignment 4.7	74	24
Assignment 4.8	74	24
Assignment 4.9	78	27
Assignment 4.10	80	28
Assignment 4C	—	29
Assignment 4D	—	31
Assignment 4E	—	32
Assignment 4F	—	34
Assignment 4G	—	34
Assignment 4.11	81	35

Triad Spelling: Major & Minor

GROUP I
→ C F & G

Group One:
[3rd, fifth]
- E G
- A C
- B D

Triad Spelling. Although numerous major triad spellings are possible, only fifteen are needed to spell the tonic triad for each of the major keys in the circle of fifths (review *EH*, p. 8–10, Key and Key Signature, and Circle of Fifths). We will learn to spell not only these fifteen tonic triads, but many other major triads as well, in preparation for other uses of major triads in the chapters that follow.

The statement above applies equally to the study of minor triad spellings.

Assignment 4.1. (*EH*, p. 66). Spelling major triads from Group 1. Remember, each triad member in this group carries the same accidental (---); each note has no accidental, each note has a sharp, etc. After spelling the triad, place an "X" under the heading "Tonic?" if this triad is one of the fifteen tonic triads from the circle of fifths.

Review directions preceding Exercise 3.2 (pg. 10) for this and following assignments containing a vertical line.

Tonic? (X = "yes")

#	Triad	Tonic?
1.	C E G	X
2.	C♯ E♯ G♯	X
3.	C♭ E♭ G♭	X
4.	F A C	X
5.	F♭ A♭ C♭	(no)
6.	F♯ A♯ C♯	X
7.	G B D	X
8.	G♯ B♯ D♯	(no)
9.	G♭ B♭ D♭	X
10.	G♯ B♯ D♯	(no)
11.	G♭ B♭ D♭	X
12.	C𝄪 E𝄪 G𝄪	(no)
13.	F𝄪 A𝄪 C𝄪	(no)
14.	G♭ B♭ D♭	X
15.	C♭♭ E♭♭ G♭♭	(no)
16.	F♭ A♭ C♭	(no)
17.	C♯ E♯ G♯	X
18.	F♭♭ A♭♭ C♭♭	(no)
19.	F𝄪 A𝄪 C𝄪	(no)
20.	F♭ A♭ C♭	(no)

The 15 Scales:
1 – C
2 – G
3 – D
4 – A
5 – E
6 – B
7 – F♯
8 – C♯/D♭
9 – ~~G♯~~/A♭
10 – D♯/E♭
11 – A♯/B♭
12 – E♯/F♭
13 – B♯/C♭
14 – F♯/G♭
15 – C♯/D♭

#	Root	3rd	5th	Tonic?
1.	C	E	G	✓
2.	C♯	E♯	G♯	✓
3.	C♭	E♭	G♭	✓
4.	F	A	C	✓
5.	F♭	A♭	C♭	
6.	F♯	A♯	C♯	✓
7.	G	B	D	✓
8.	G♯	B♯	D♯	✓
9.	G♭	B♭	D♭	✓
10.	G♯	B♯	D♯	NO
11.	G♭	B♭	D♭	✓
12.	C𝄪	E𝄪	G𝄪	✓
13.	F𝄪	A𝄪	C𝄪	✓
14.	G♭	B♭	D♭	✓
15.	C♭♭	E♭♭	G♭♭	NO
16.	F♭	A♭	C♭	NO
17.	C♯	E♯	G♯	✓
18.	F♭♭	A♭♭	C♭♭	NO
19.	F𝄪	A𝄪	C𝄪	NO
20.	F♭	A♭	C♭	NO

not in group I

Group II:

Assignment 4.2. (*EH*, p. 66). Spelling major triads from Group II. In this group of triads, the third of the triad (middle note) carries an accidental one half step higher than the root and fifth (- ↑ -).

				Root	3rd	5th	Tonic?
				-	↑	-	
1. D F♯ A	X		1.	D			
2. A C♯ E	X		2.	A			
3. E G♯ B	X		3.	E			
4. D♭ F A♭	X		4.	D♭			
5. D♯ F𝄪 A♯	(no)		5.	D♯			
6. A♯ C𝄪 E♯	(no)		6.	A♯			
7. A♭ C E♭	X		7.	A♭			
8. E♭ G B♭	X		8.	E♭			
9. E♯ G𝄪 B♯	(no)		9.	E♯			
10. E G♯ B	X		10.		G♯		
11. E♭ G B♭	X		11.			B♭	
12. D♯ F𝄪 A♯	(no)		12.		F𝄪		
13. D♭ F A♭	X		13.		F		
14. D F♯ A	X		14.			A	
15. D♯ F𝄪 A♯	(no)		15.			A♯	
16. A♯ C𝄪 E♯	(no)		16.		C𝄪		
17. A♭♭ C♭ E♭♭	(no)		17.	A♭♭			
18. E♭♭ G♭ B♭♭	(no)		18.	E♭♭			
19. D♭♭ F♭ A♭♭	(no)		19.	D♭♭			
20. A♭♭ C♭ E♭♭	(no)		20.			E♭♭	

Group III:

Assignment 4.3. (*EH*, p. 67). Spelling major triads from Group III. There is only one triad in Group III; its third and fifth each carry an accidental one half step higher than the root (- ↑ ↑).

				Root	3rd	5th	Tonic?
				-	↑	↑	
1. B D♯ F♯	X		1.	B			
2. B♭ D F	X		2.	B♭			

			Root	3rd	5th	Tonic?
3. B♯ D𝄪 F𝄪	(no)	3.	B♯	___	___	___
4. B♭♭ D♭ F♭	(no)	4.	B♭♭	___	___	___
5. B D♯ F♯	X	5.	___	D♯	___	___
6. B♭ D F	X	6.	___	___	F	___
7. B♯ D𝄪 F𝄪	(no)	7.	___	D𝄪	___	___
8. B♭♭ D♭ F♭	(no)	8.	___	D♭	___	___
9. B♭♭ D♭ F♭	(no)	9.	___	___	F♭	___
10. B D♯ F♯	X	10.	___	___	F♯	___

Assignment 4.4. (*EH*, p. 67.) Spelling major triads when *a*) the root is given, *b*) the third is given, and *c*) the fifth is given.

a. 1. G ___ ___   *b.* 1. ___ E ___   *c.* 1. ___ ___ C
2. A♭ ___ ___   2. ___ A♯ ___   2. ___ ___ G♯
3. A ___ ___   3. ___ C♯ ___   3. ___ ___ A♭
4. C♭ ___ ___   4. ___ G ___   4. ___ ___ E♯
5. G♭ ___ ___   5. ___ D ___   5. ___ ___ E
6. D♯ ___ ___   6. ___ G♯ ___   6. ___ ___ F
7. B♭ ___ ___   7. ___ B♭ ___   7. ___ ___ F♯
8. B ___ ___   8. ___ D♭ ___   8. ___ ___ B♭
9. D♭ ___ ___   9. ___ A♭♭ ___   9. ___ ___ B
10. B♯ ___ ___   10. ___ F𝄪 ___   10. ___ ___ F♭

Assignment 4.5. (*EH*, p. 67). Spell the tonic (I), dominant (V), and dominant seventh (V^7) chords in each major key.

Key	Tonic triad	Dominant triad	Dominant Seventh chord
C	C E G	G B D	G B D F
G	G B D	D F♯ A	D F♯ A C
D			
A			
E			

	Tonic Triad	Dominant triad	Dominant Seventh Chord
B	_____	_____	_____
F♯	_____	_____	_____
C♯	_____	_____	_____
F	_____	_____	_____
B♭	_____	_____	_____
E♭	_____	_____	_____
A♭	_____	_____	_____
D♭	_____	_____	_____
G♭	_____	_____	_____
C♭	_____	_____	_____

Assignment 4A. Identifying authentic cadences. Circle the abbreviation below the staff that correctly identifies the cadence: perfect authentic (PA), imperfect authentic (IA), or half (H). Above the staff, write in the scale step numbers of the soprano line. Assume that each key signature is that for a major key.

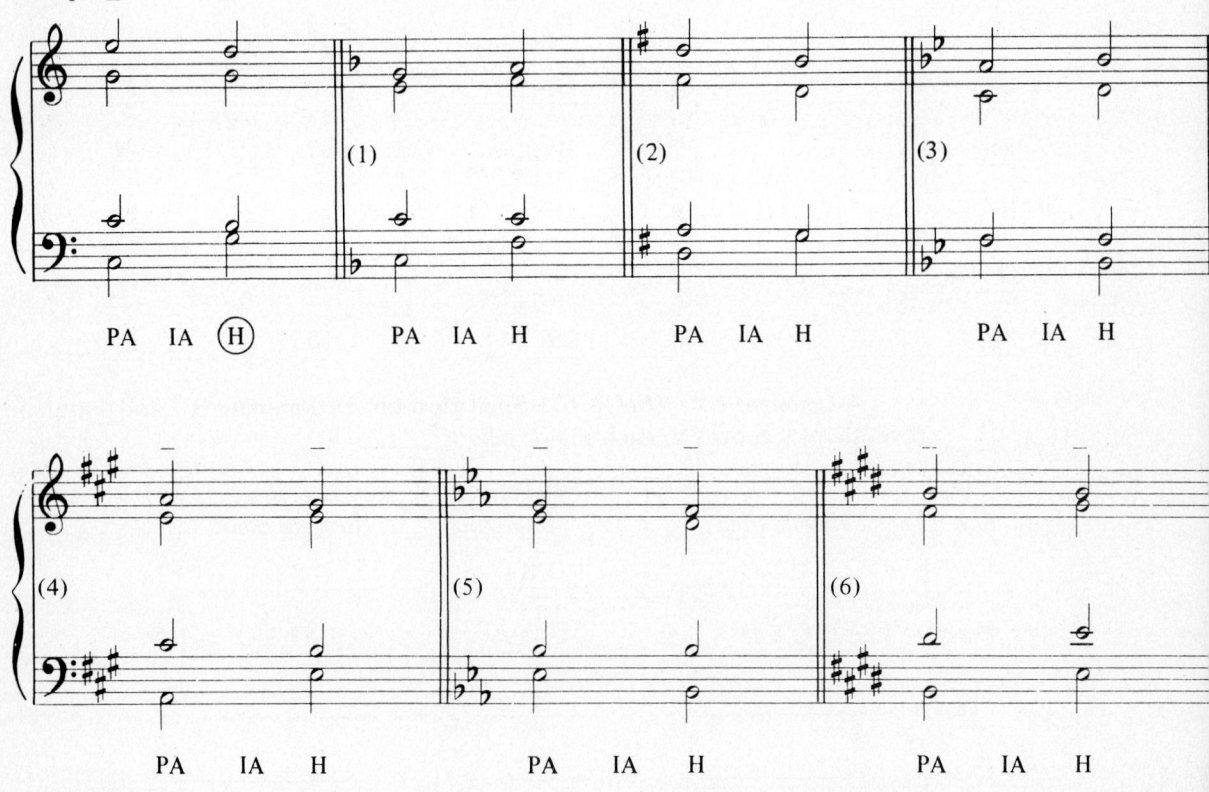

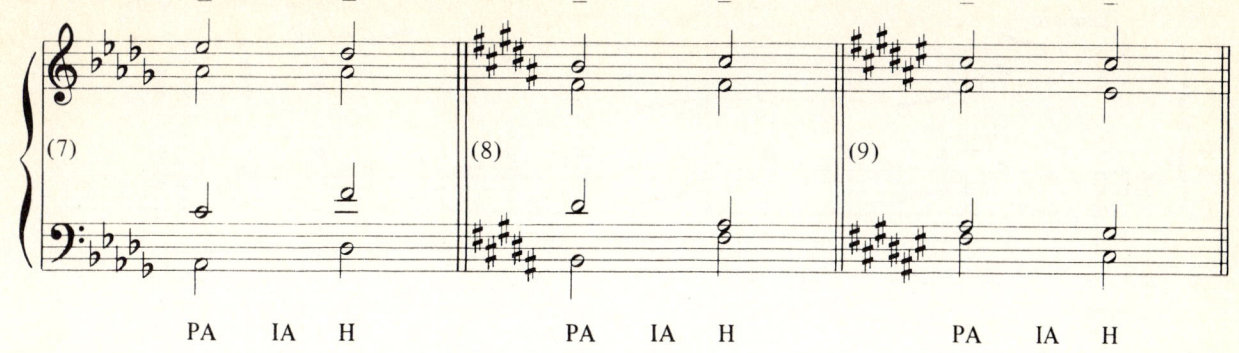

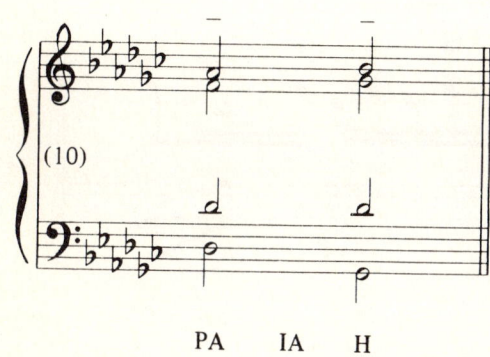

Assignment 4.6. (*EH*, p. 70). Locate the authentic cadence in each example, placing the numerals I, V, or V^7 at the appropriate places. Identify each cadence by name and indicate the scale step numbers of the soprano line.

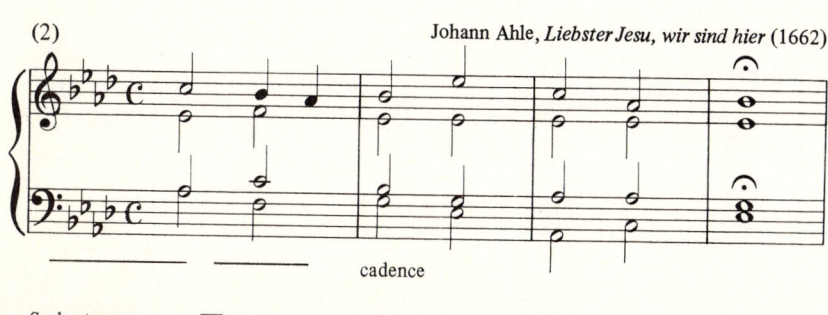

[1] The number refers to the location of the complete chorale in editions of Bach's *371 Chorales*. See *EH*, page 64, footnote 3.

(3) **Lebhaft**
Brahms, *Vergebliches Ständchen*, Op. 84, No. 4

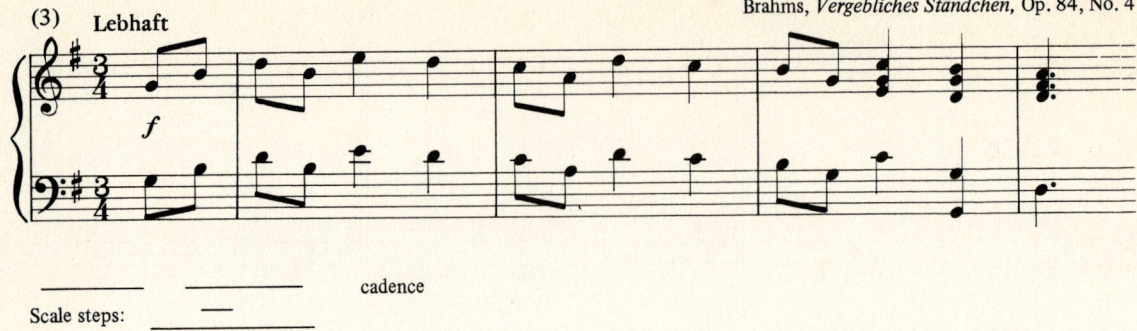

_____ _____ cadence
Scale steps: _____

(4) (♪ = 120)
Mozart, Sonata in A Major for Piano, K. 331

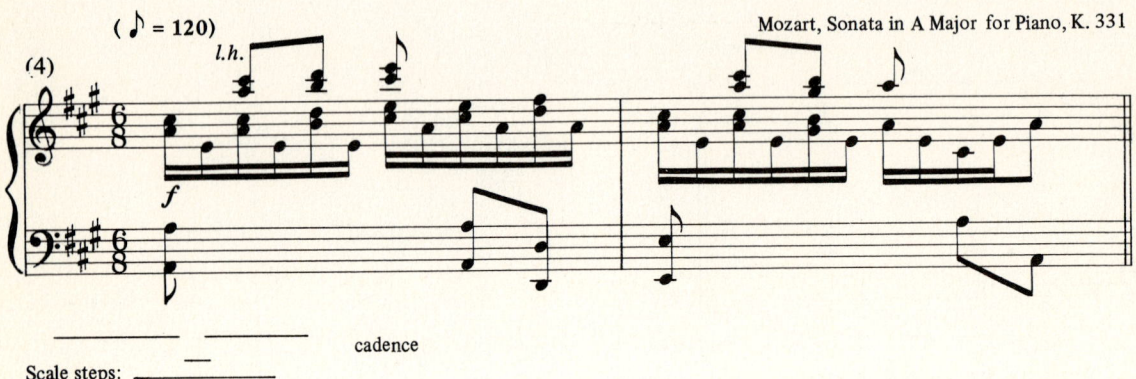

_____ _____ cadence
Scale steps: _____

(5) Vl. I, II
Beethoven, Quartet, Op. 74

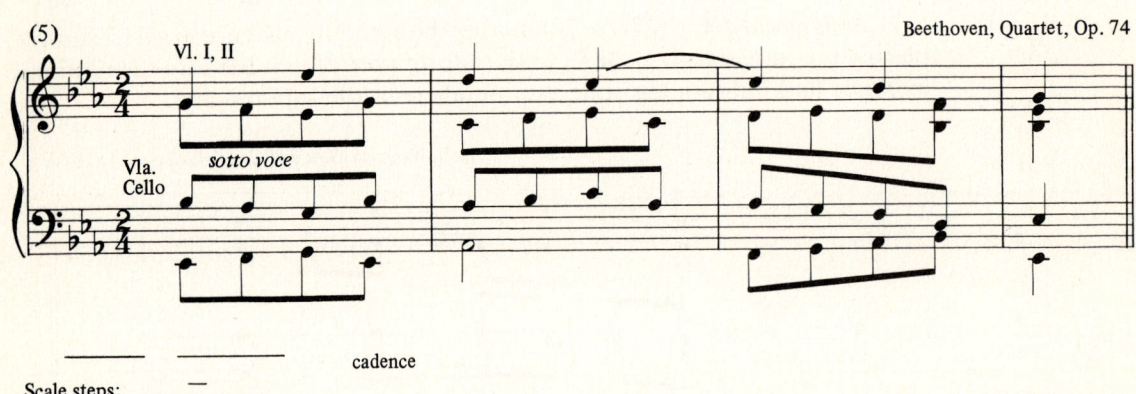

_____ _____ cadence
Scale steps: _____

Assignment 4B. Spelling minor triads. As with major triads, most of these minor triads can function as tonic triads in keys from the circle of fifths. After spelling each triad, indicate each possible minor tonic triad with an X.

  a) The root is given.

			Root	3rd	5th	Tonic?
1. G B♭ D	X	1.	G	___	___	___
2. A C E	X	2.	A	___	___	___
3. E G B	X	3.	E	___	___	___
4. E♭ G♭ B♭	X	4.	E♭	___	___	___
5. B D F♯	X	5.	B	___	___	___

			Root	3rd	5th	Tonic?
6. F♯ A C♯	X		6. F♯	___	___	___
7. G♯ B D♯	X		7. G♯	___	___	___
8. B♭ D♭ F	X		8. B♭	___	___	___
9. G♭ B♭♭ D♭	(no)		9. G♭	___	___	___
10. C♯ E G♯	X		10. C♯	___	___	___

b) The third is given.

			Root	3rd	5th	Tonic?
1. E G B	X		1. ___	G	___	___
2. A C E	X		2. ___	C	___	___
3. C E♭ G	X		3. ___	E♭	___	___
4. G B♭ D	X		4. ___	B♭	___	___
5. F A♭ C	X		5. ___	A♭	___	___
6. F♯ A C♯	X		6. ___	A	___	___
7. B D F♯	X		7. ___	D	___	___
8. B♯ D♯ F𝄪	(no)		8. ___	D♯	___	___
9. G♯ B D♯	X		9. ___	B	___	___
10. A♯ C♯ E♯	X		10. ___	C♯	___	___

c) The fifth is given.

			Root	3rd	5th	Tonic?
1. A C E	X		1. ___	___	E	___
2. E G B	X		2. ___	___	B	___
3. C E♭ G	X		3. ___	___	G	___
4. F A♭ C	X		4. ___	___	C	___
5. D♭ F♭ A♭	(no)		5. ___	___	A♭	___
6. C♯ E G♯	X		6. ___	___	G♯	___
7. E♭ G♭ B♭	X		7. ___	___	B♭	___
8. F♯ A C♯	X		8. ___	___	C♯	___
9. G B♭ D	X		9. ___	___	D	___
10. D♯ F♯ A♯	X		10. ___	___	A♯	___

Assignment 4.7. (*EH*, p. 74). Spell the tonic, dominant, and dominant seventh chords in each minor key.

	Tonic i	Dominant V	Dominant 7th V^7
A minor	A C E	E G♯ B	E G♯ B D
E minor	E G B		
B minor			
F♯ minor			
C♯ minor			
G♯ minor			
D♯ minor			
A♯ minor			
D minor			
G minor			
C minor			
F minor			
B♭ minor			
E♭ minor			
A♭ minor			

Assignment 4.8. (*EH*, p. 74). Harmonic analysis. Locate cadence(s) in minor keys. Furnish an analysis, using the symbols i (or **I** if a Picardy third), **V, and V^7**. Name each cadence and supply the scale step numbers of the soprano line.

In example (1), as in some of the others, the 7 of **V^7** appears on the second half of the beat. Identify these chords as **V^{87}**.

(1) Anonymous, 1535, *Durch Adams Fall ist ganz verderbt*
(Bach, No. 100)

Cadence _____ _____ ; scale steps _____

(2) In a chorale, the *fermata*(⌢) indicates the end of a phrase, rather than "to hold" as elsewhere. These phrases are the first, second, and eighth of the chorale.

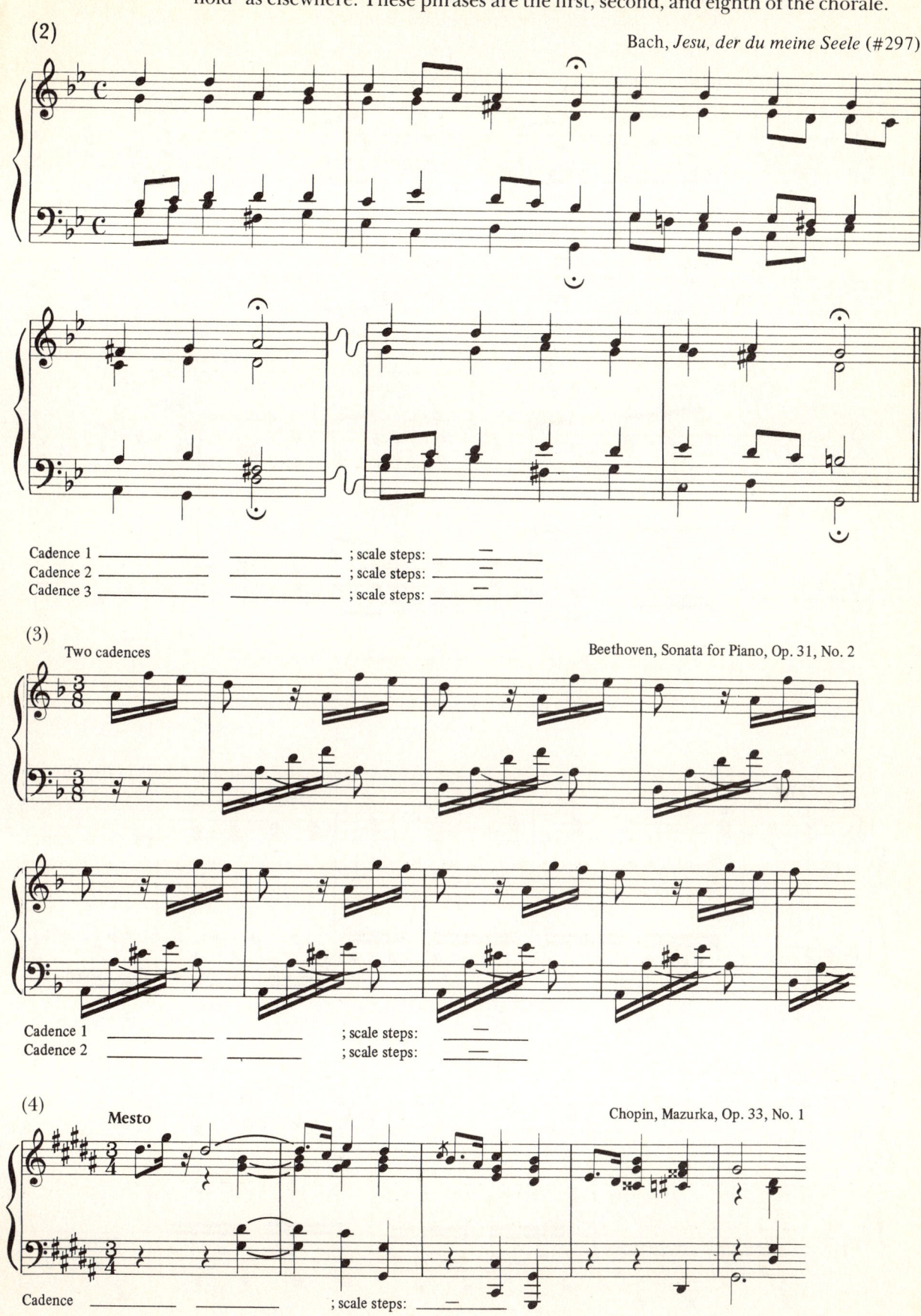

Bach, *Jesu, der du meine Seele* (#297)

Cadence 1 _____ _____ ; scale steps: ____
Cadence 2 _____ _____ ; scale steps: ____
Cadence 3 _____ _____ ; scale steps: ____

(3) Two cadences — Beethoven, Sonata for Piano, Op. 31, No. 2

Cadence 1 _____ _____ ; scale steps: ____
Cadence 2 _____ _____ ; scale steps: ____

(4) Mesto — Chopin, Mazurka, Op. 33, No. 1

Cadence _____ _____ ; scale steps: ____

Examples (5) and (6) each include cadences in two different keys, as indicated. Write in chord numbers only. (In number 5, measure 7, the D F♯ A–G B D progression is a secondary dominant usage, as described in Chapter 18.)

(5)

(Chorus, with piano) Brahms, *Liebeslieder Walzer*, Op. 52

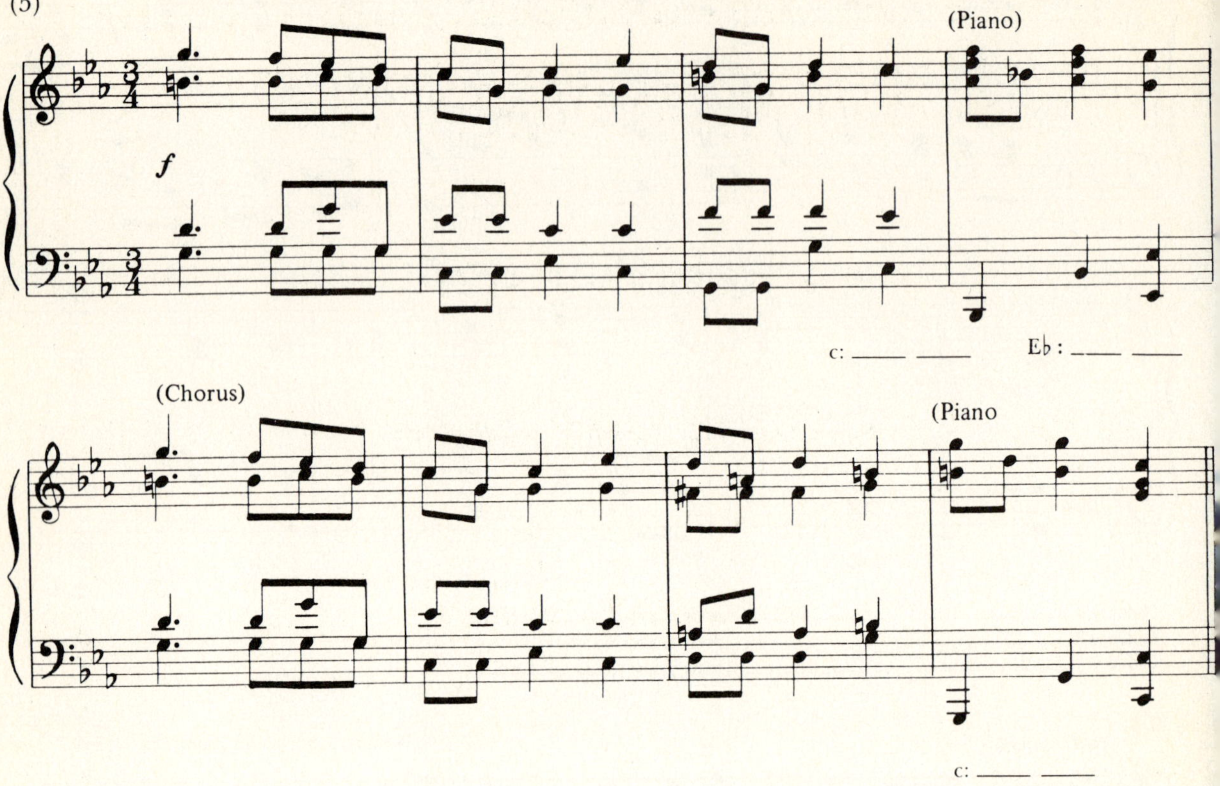

(6)

Haydn, Sonata in E Major for Piano (1776), Hob. XVI:31

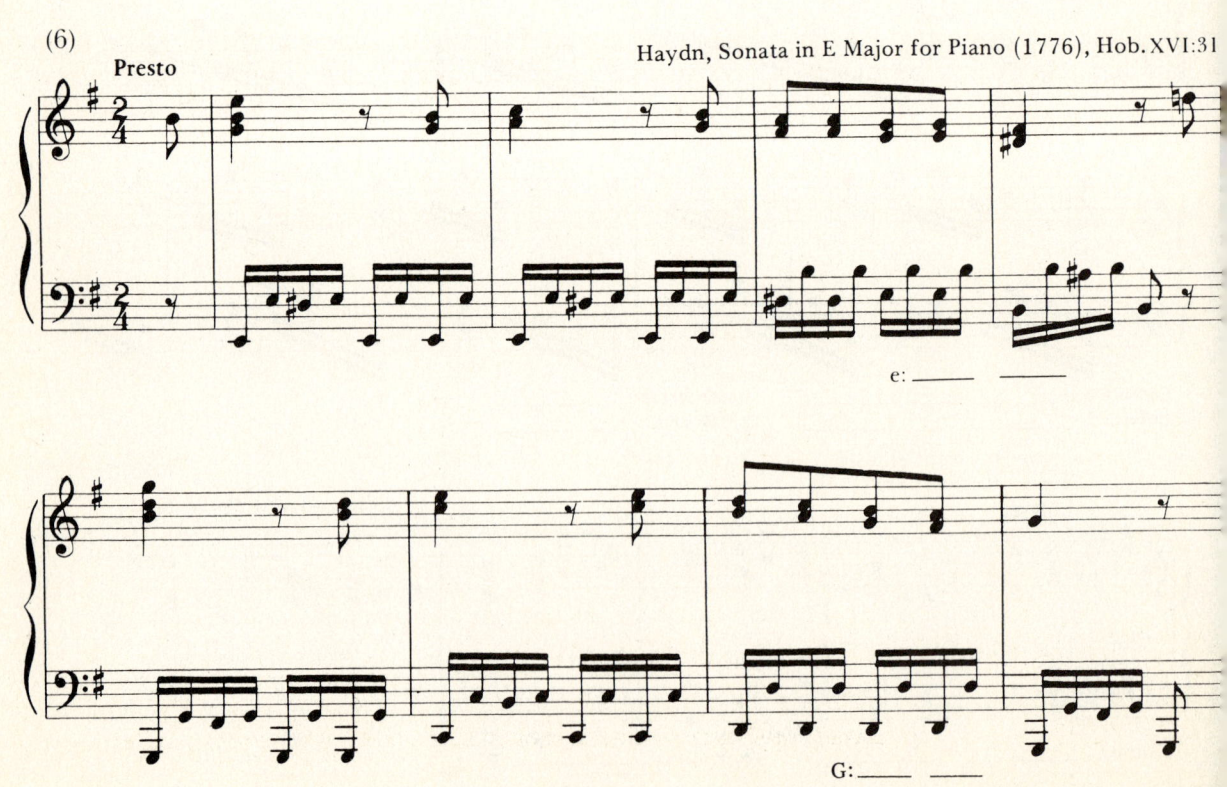

Assignment 4.9. (*EH*, 78). Harmonic analysis. Locate cadences and identify by chord numbers below the staff. Each cadence includes one or more nonharmonic tones. Circle each of these.

(1) Handel, *Messiah*, "Behold the Lamb of God"

(2) Bach, *Liebster Immanuel* (#194)

(3) Mozart, Sonata in D Major for Piano, K. 311

(4) Haydn, Sonata in G Major for Piano, Hob. XVI: 27

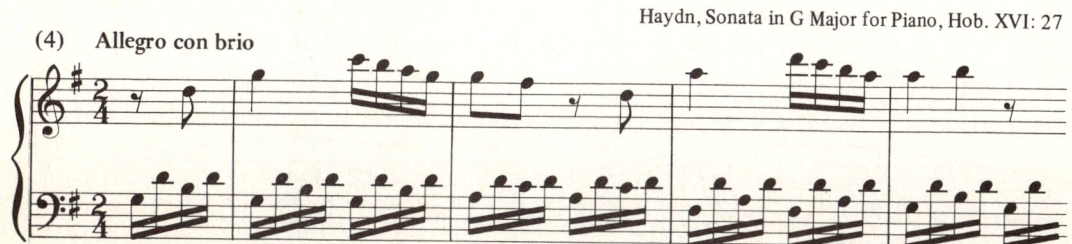

Beethoven, Symphony No. 6, Op. 68

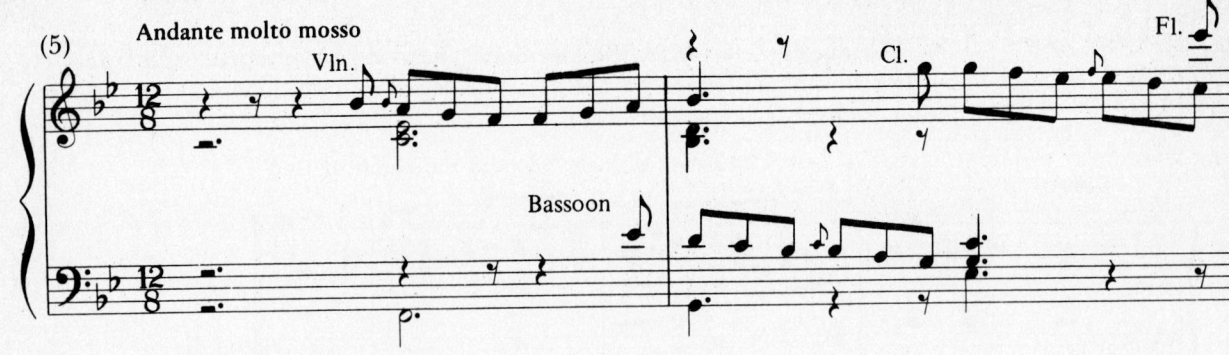

Chopin, *Valse brillante*, Op. 34, No. 1

Assignment 4.10. (*EH*, p. 80). Melodic analysis. Below each cadence, write in the chord numbers in the spaces provided. Fill in the blanks below each melody.

Giovanni Martini, *Plaisir d'amour*

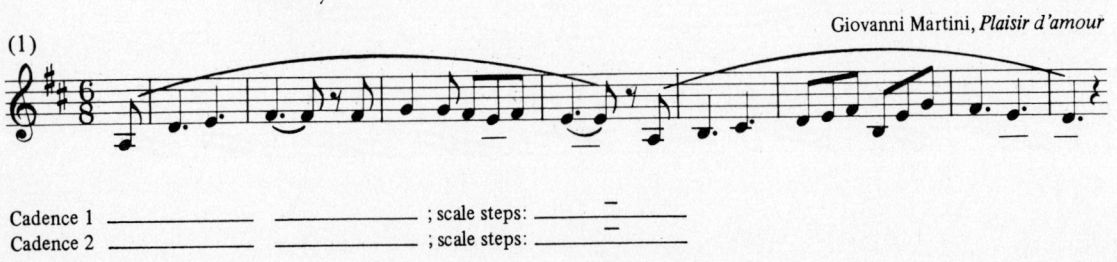

Cadence 1 _____ _____ ; scale steps: _____
Cadence 2 _____ _____ ; scale steps: _____

The following optional drills, Assignments 4C–4G, are based on the use of major triads as an aid to spelling intervals. Although intervals and drills were presented in Chapter 2, it should be noted that many students find that a harmonic approach is very helpful in achieving *rapid* and *accurate* spelling of intervals, especially the more difficult ones. The importance of this skill justifies the use of more than one means for its accomplishment.

Assignment 4C. (*EH*, p. 81). Naming and spelling intervals found in the major triad. Practice space is provided for drill in intervals from the G major, B♭ major, and E major triads. The same format may be used for any major triad. See *EH*, Figure 4.16, for a list of the intervals found in a major triad.

a)

G major	G major
1. M3	1. 1 up to 3 is a ___ ___,
G up to B	spelled ___ up to ___.
2. m3	2. 3 up to 5 is a ___ ___,
B up to D	spelled ___ up to ___.
3. P4	3. 5 up to 1 is a ___ ___.
D up to G	spelled ___ up to ___.

29

G major

4. P5

   G up to D

5. M6

   D up to B

6. m6

   B up to G

7. P8

   G up to G

b)

B♭ major

1. M3

   D down to B♭

2. m3

   F down to D

3. P4

   B♭ down to F

4. P5

   F down to B♭

5. M6

   D down to F

6. m6

   B♭ down to D

7. P8

   B♭ down to B♭

G major

4. 1 up to 5 is a ___ ___,

   spelled ___ up to ___.

5. 5 up to 3 is a ___ ___,

   spelled ___ up to ___.

6. 3 up to 1 is a ___ ___,

   spelled ___ up to ___.

7. 1 up to 1 is a ___ ___,

   spelled ___ up to ___.

B♭ major

1. 3 down to 1 is a ___ ___,

   spelled ___ down to ___.

2. 5 down to 3 is a ___ ___,

   spelled ___ down to ___.

3. 1 down to 5 is a ___ ___,

   spelled ___ down to ___.

4. 5 down to 1 is a ___ ___.

   spelled ___ down to ___.

5. 3 down to 5 is a ___ ___,

   spelled ___ down to ___.

6. 1 down to 3 is a ___ ___,

   spelled ___ down to ___.

7. 1 down to 1 is a ___ ___,

   spelled ___ down to ___.

c) Answer with triad numbers, 1 up to 3, etc.

E major

1. 1 up to 3

   M3

E major

1. E up to G♯ is ___ up to ___.

   The interval is a ___ ___.

E major

2. 3 up to 5
   m3

3. 5 up to 1
   P4

4. 1 up to 5
   P5

5. 5 up to 3
   M6

6. 3 up to 1
   m6

7. 1 up to 1
   P8

E major

2. G♯ up to B is ___ up to ___.
   The interval is a ___ ___.

3. B up to E is ___ up to ___.
   The interval is a ___ ___.

4. E up to B is ___ up to ___.
   The interval is a ___ ___.

5. B up to G♯ is ___ up to ___.
   The interval is a ___ ___.

6. G♯ up to E is ___ up to ___.
   The interval is a ___ ___.

7. E up to E is ___ up to ___.
   The interval is a ___ ___.

Assignment 4D. Spell all intervals from a given triad. Fill in the blanks with letter names.
Example: C major, M3: C up to E

a) A♭ *major*

M3: ___ up to ___
m3: ___ up to ___
P4: ___ up to ___
P5: ___ up to ___
M6: ___ up to ___
m6: ___ up to ___
P8: ___ up to ___

b) F♯ *major*

M3: ___ down to ___
m3: ___ down to ___
P4: ___ down to ___
P5: ___ down to ___
M6: ___ down to ___
m6: ___ down to ___
P8: ___ down to ___

Continue, using two additional triads, as assigned or self-chosen.

c) Triad: ___ *major*

M3: ___ up to ___
m3: ___ up to ___
P4: ___ up to ___
P5: ___ up to ___
M6: ___ up to ___

d) Triad: ___ *major*

M3: ___ down to ___
m3: ___ down to ___
P4: ___ down to ___
P5: ___ down to ___
M6: ___ down to ___

c) Triad:—major   d) Triad:—major

m6: ___ up to ___   m6: ___ down to ___

P8: ___ up to ___   P8: ___ down to ___

Assignment 4E. From a given note, spell all the intervals in the triad.
a) From the note C:

1. 1 up to 3

   E

2. 3 down to 1

   A♭

3. 3 up to 5

   E♭

4. 5 down to 3

   A

5. 5 up to 1

   F

6. 1 down to 5

   G

7. 1 up to 5

   G

8. 5 down to 1

   F

9. 5 up to 3

   A

10. 3 down to 5

    E♭

11. 3 up to 1

    A♭

12. 1 down to 3

    E

1. M3 is _1_ up to _3_

   M3 up from C is _E_

2. M3 is ___ down to ___

   M3 down from C is ___

3. m3 is ___ up to ___

   m3 up from C is ___

4. m3 is ___ down to ___

   m3 down from C is ___

5. P4 is ___ up to ___

   P4 up from C is ___

6. P4 is ___ down to ___

   P4 down from C is ___

7. P5 is ___ up to ___

   P5 up from C is ___

8. P5 is ___ down to ___

   P5 down from C is ___

9. M6 is ___ up to ___

   M6 up from C is ___

10. M6 is ___ down to ___

    M6 down from C is ___

11. m6 is ___ up to ___

    m6 up from C is ___

12. m6 is ___ down to ___

    m6 down from C is ___

b) From the note A:

1. C♯	1. M3: A up to C♯
2. F	2. M3: A down to ___
3. C	3. m3: A up to ___
4. F♯	4. m3: A down to ___
5. D	5. P4: A up to ___
6. E	6. P4: A down to ___
7. E	7. P5: A up to ___
8. D	8. P5: A down to ___
9. F♯	9. M6: A up to ___
10. C	10. M6: A down to ___
11. F	11. m6: A up to ___
12. C♯	12. m6: A down to ___

c) From the note B♭:

1. D	1. M3: B♭ up to ___
2. G♭	2. M3: B♭ down to ___
3. D♭	3. m3: B♭ up to ___
4. G	4. m3: B♭ down to ___
5. E♭	5. P4: B♭ up to ___
6. F	6. P4: B♭ down to ___
7. F	7. P5: B♭ up to ___
8. E♭	8. P5: B♭ down to ___
9. G	9. M6: B♭ up to ___
10. D♭	10. M6: B♭ down to ___
11. G♭	11. m6: B♭ up to ___
12. D	12. m6: B♭ down to ___

Assignment 4F. Spell all intervals from a given note.

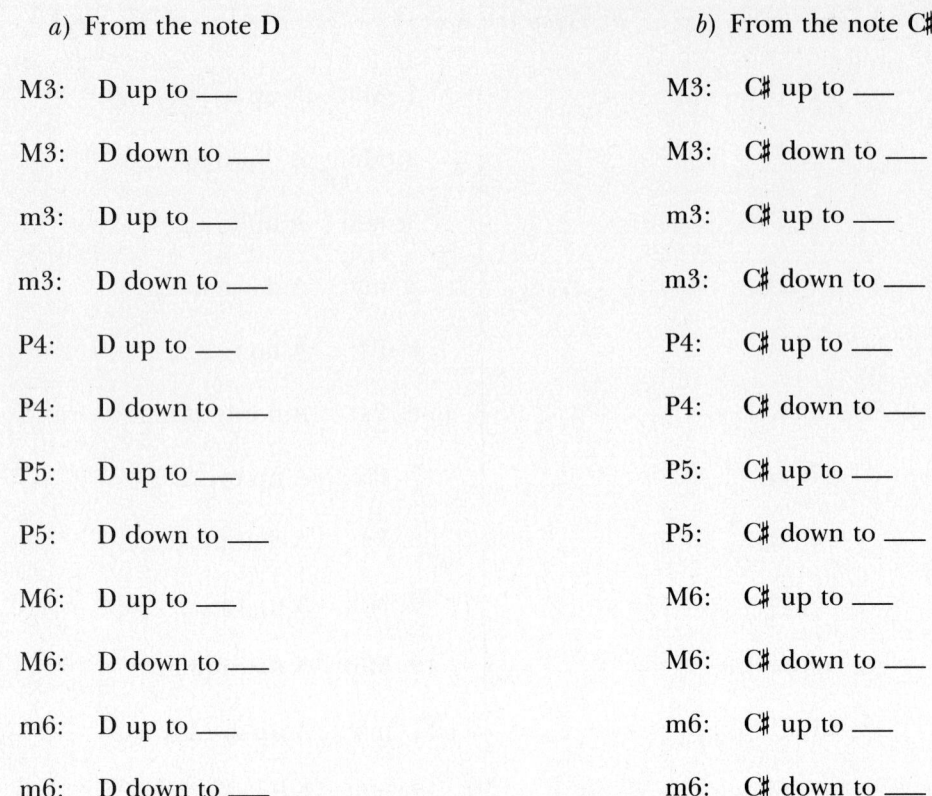

Assignment 4G. Writing intervals on the staff.
 a) Intervals from various tonic triads. Write the second note on the staff.

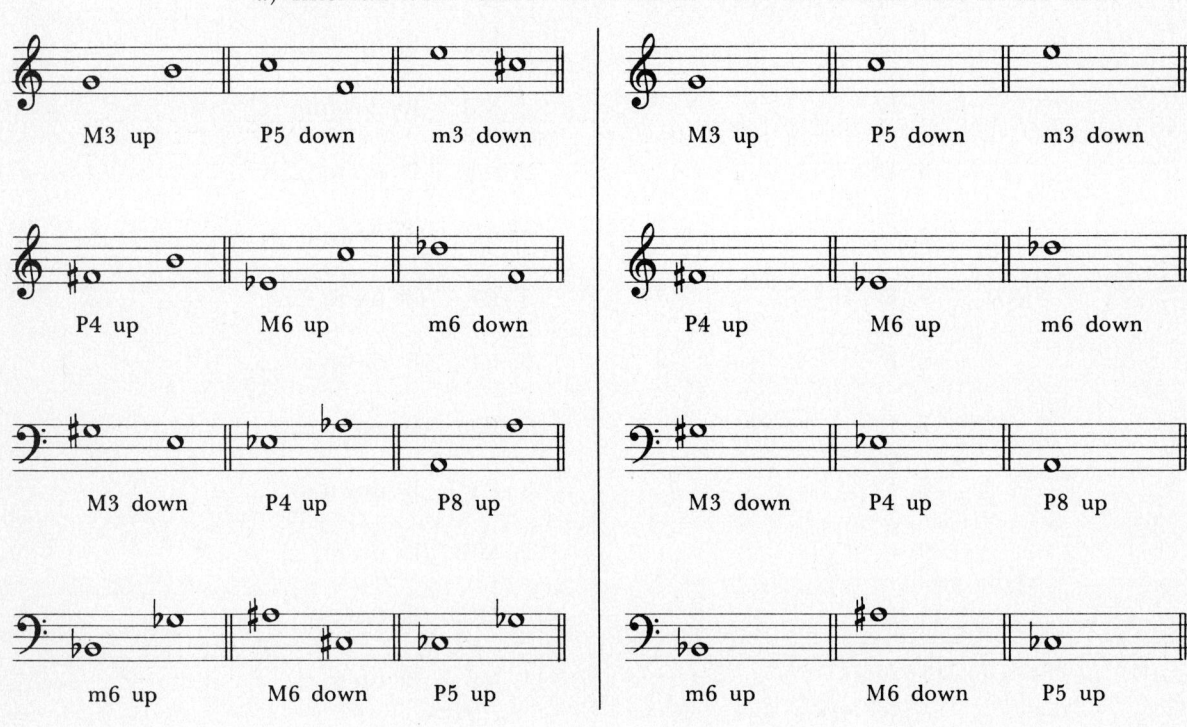

b) Intervals from other major triads.

Assignment 4.11. (*EH*, p. 81). Writing intervals. Place the second note of each interval on the staff.
 a) treble clef

b) bass clef

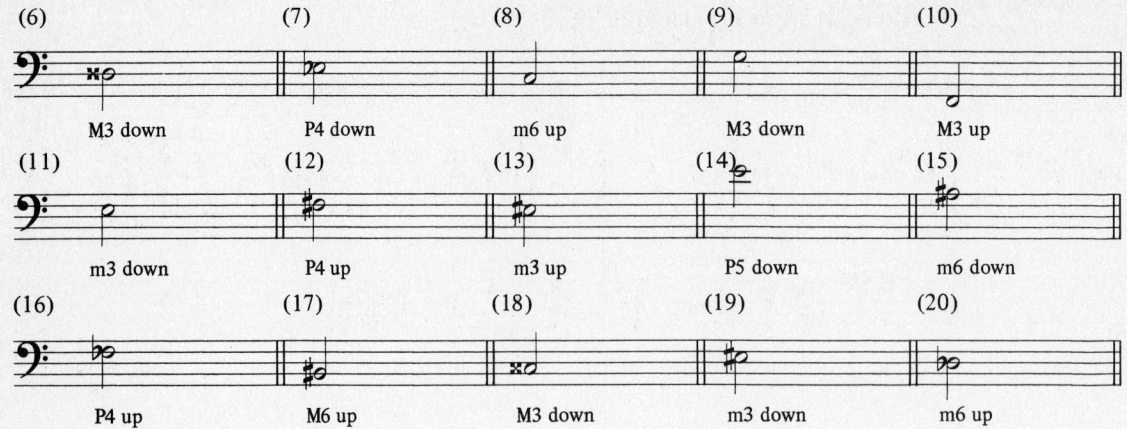

CHAPTER 5
TONIC AND DOMINANT: Part–Writing

	Elementary Harmony	*Workbook*
Assignment 5A	—	37
Assignment 5.1	92	40
Assignment 5B	—	41
Assignment 5C	—	42
Assignment 5D	—	45
Assignment 5.2	95	46
Assignment 5.3	95	46
Assignment 5.4	97	47
Assignment 5.5	98	49
Assignment 5.6	100	49
Assignment 5.7	101	51
Assignment 5.8	102	52
Assignment 5.9	104	53

Assignment 5A. Recognizing desirable factors in writing a single triad. Study *EH*, pages 91–92, *a*) range, *b*) doubling, *c*) position, and *d*) distance between voices.

a) Range. In each pair of triads below, one triad is written correctly, while the other has one voice out of range. Answer questions about each triad of the pair. For purposes of this exercise, consider the range within the whole notes of Figure 5.7 (*EH*) as acceptable.

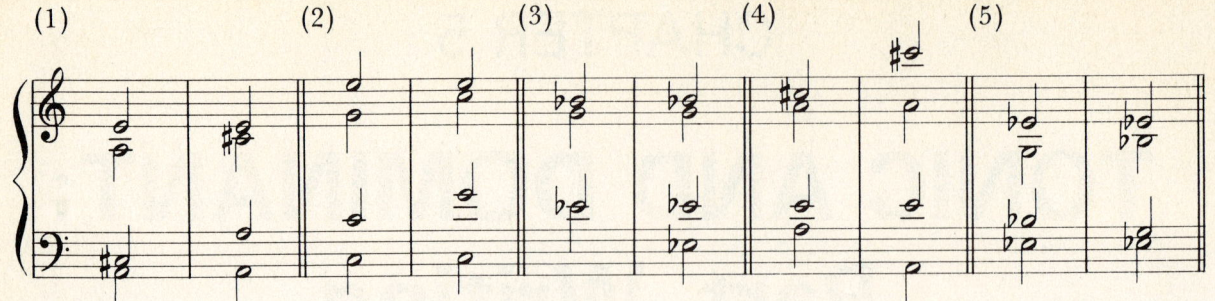

1. Measure 2 correct.

   In measure 1, the tenor voice is too low.

2. Measure 1 is correct.

   In measure 2, the tenor voice is too high.

3. Measure 2 is correct.

   In measure 1, the bass voice is too high.

4. Measure 1 is correct.

   In measure 2, the soprano voice is too high.

5. Measure 2 is correct.

   In measure 1, the alto voice is too low.

1. Measure ___ is correct.

   In measure ___, the _____ voice is too _____. (high or low)

2. Measure ___ is correct.

   In measure ___, the _____ voice is too _____.

3. Measure ___ is correct.

   In measure ___, the _____ voice is too _____.

4. Measure ___ is correct.

   In measure ___, the _____ voice is too _____.

5. Measure ___ is correct.

   In measure ___, the _____ voice is too _____.

b) Doubling. Write each triad with conventional doubling: two roots, one third, and one fifth. Answer questions about each of these triads: check that the doubling is correct, or indicate that the third or fifth is incorrectly doubled.

1. The fifth is incorrectly doubled.

2. The doubling is correct.

3. The third is incorrectly doubled.

4. The doubling is correct.

5. The third is incorrectly doubled.

1. ___ The doubling is correct, or, the _____ is incorrectly doubled.

2. ___ The doubling is correct, or, the _____ is incorrectly doubled.

3. ___ The doubling is correct, or, the _____ is incorrectly doubled.

4. ___ The doubling is correct, or, the _____ is incorrectly doubled.

5. ___ The doubling is correct, or, the _____ is incorrectly doubled.

c) Position. Identify the position (structure), close or open, of each of these triads.

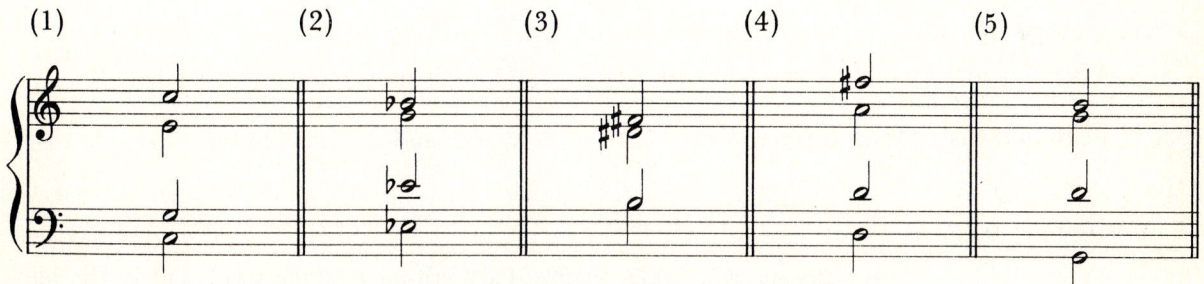

1. open position
2. close position
3. close position
4. open position
5. close position

1. _____ position
2. _____ position
3. _____ position
4. _____ position
5. _____ position

d) Distance between voices. In each of the triads below there are two adjacent voices more than an octave apart. Indicate which two voices, and whether or not this is correct.

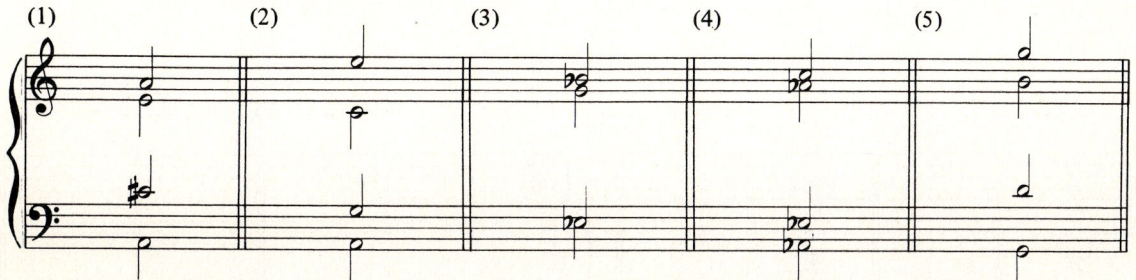

1. There is more than an octave between tenor and bass. This is correct.

2. There is more than an octave between soprano and alto. This is incorrect.

3. There is more than an octave between alto and tenor. This is incorrect.

4. There is more than an octave between alto and tenor. This is incorrect.

5. There is more than an octave between tenor and bass. This is correct.

1. There is more than an octave between _____ and _____. This is _____. (correct or incorrect)

2. There is more than an octave between _____ and _____. This is _____.

3. There is more than an octave between _____ and _____. This is _____.

4. There is more than an octave between _____ and _____. This is _____.

5. There is more than an octave between _____ and _____. This is _____.

Assignment 5.1. (*EH*, p. 92). Part-writing a single triad. Fill in the alto and tenor voices of each triad in both close position and open position, in that order. Use two roots, one third, and one fifth in each triad. Keep voices in correct pitch range. In this and succeeding exercises, ranges indicated by the black notes in Figure 5.7 (*EH*) may be used.

Example:

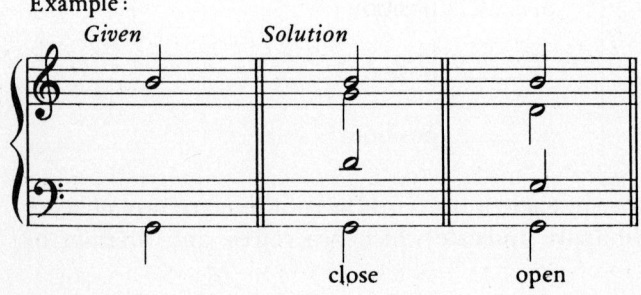

(1)   (2)

(1)   (2)

(3) (4)

(3) (4)

(5) (6)

(5) (6)

(7) (8)

(7) (8)

(9) (10)

(9) (10)

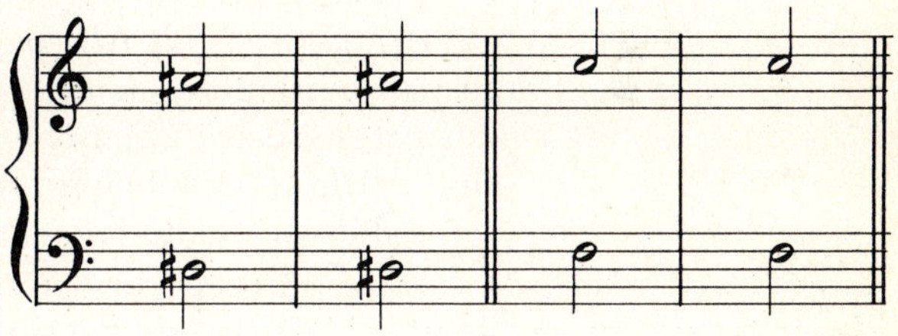

Assignment 5B. Part-writing a single triad. The root of the triad and soprano position is given. Write all four voices on the staff, first in close position, then in open position, as in Assignment 5.1. Observe all previous instructions. Example: G♭ (3) refers to the G♭ B♭ D♭ triad with B♭ in the soprano.

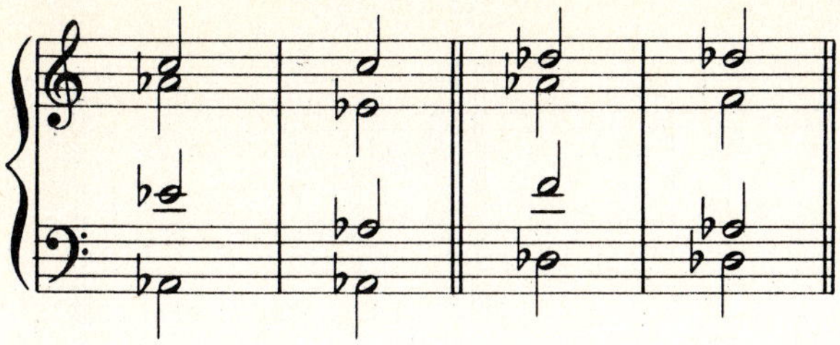

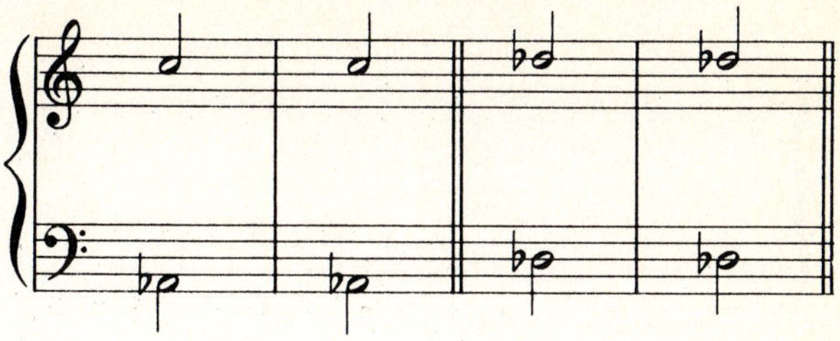

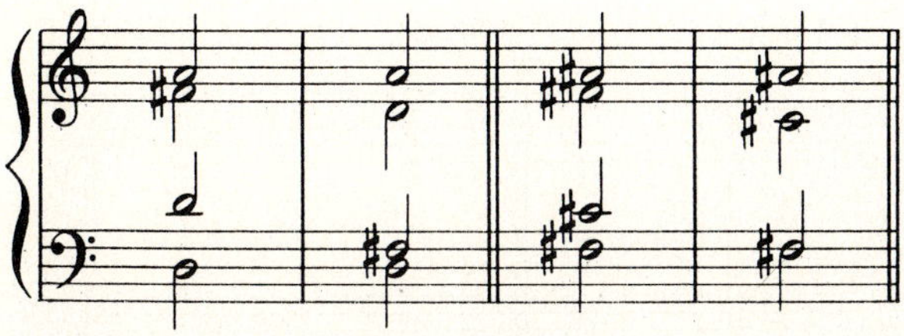

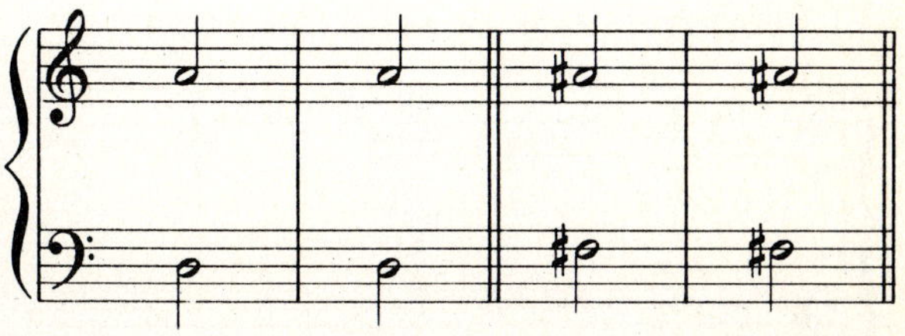

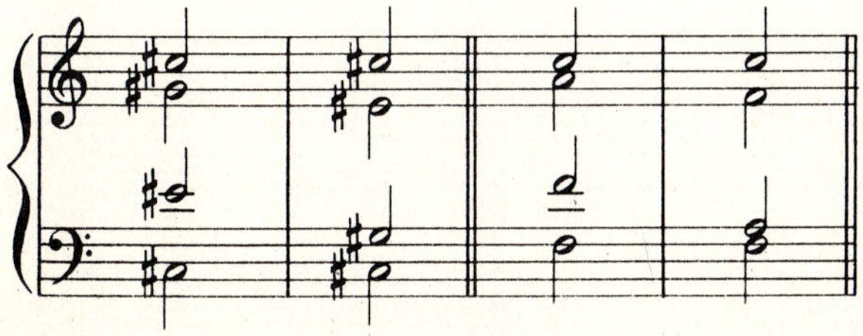

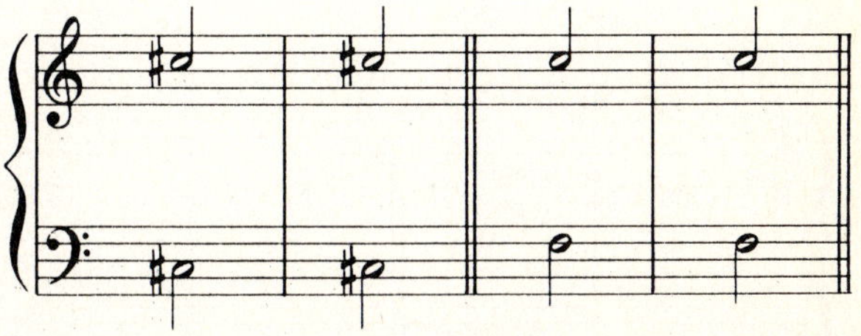

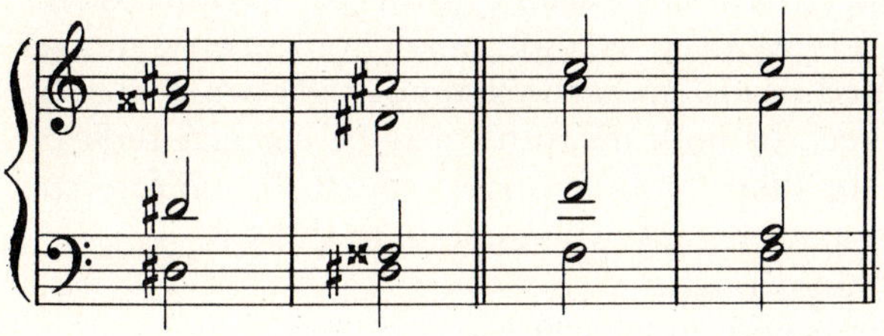

a) Major Keys

G♭(3)

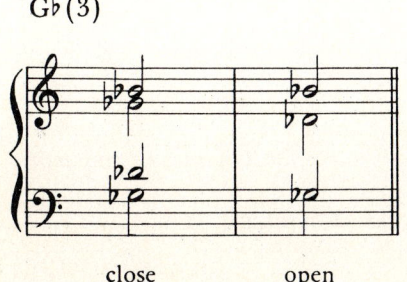

close open

a) major keys

(1) G (3)   (2) D (5)   (3) E (3)   (4) C♯ (5)

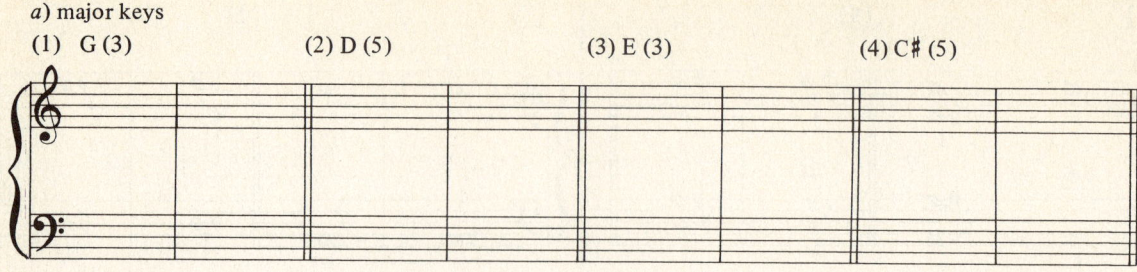

b) minor keys

(5) D♭ (1)   (6) B (1)   (7) g (1)   (8) b (5)

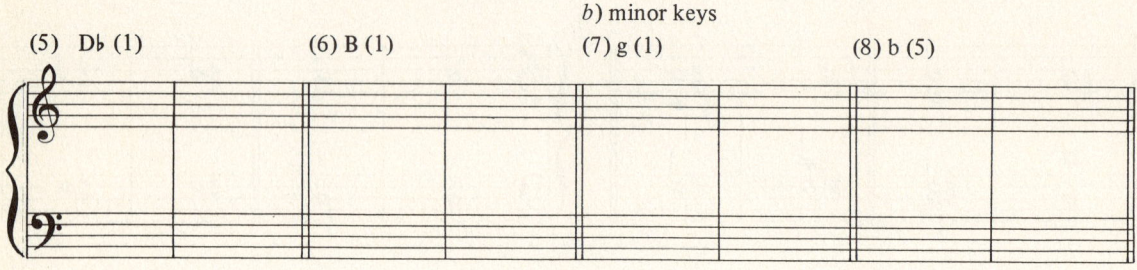

(9) c♯ (3)   (10) f (3)   (11) b♭ (1)   (12) e♯ (5)

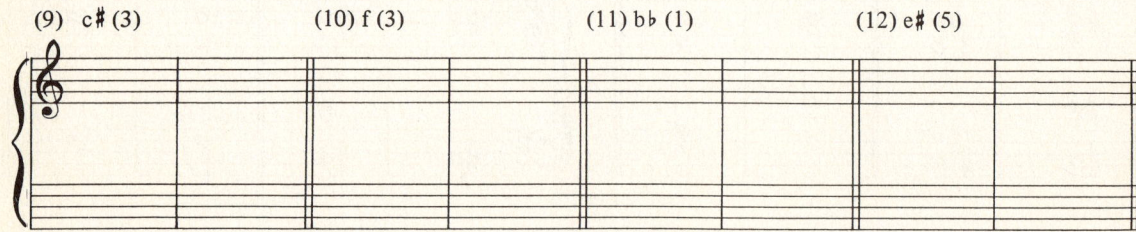

Assignment 5C. Recognizing desirable factors in the part-writing of repeated triads. Study *EH*, pages 91–92. Each example below shows two solutions to part-writing a pair of repeated triads. In each example, measure 1 may be correct, measure 2 may be correct, or both measures may be correct. Indicate one of these possibilities. Where there is an incorrect measure, indicate the type of error by the letter preceding the appropriate item in this list:

    A. voice or voices in poor range
    B. large leaps in one or both inner voices
    C. incorrect voice distribution

(1)

Measure 1 is incorrect for reason C.

(1)

___ Both measures are correct, or, measure

___ is incorrect for reason ___.

(2)

Measure 2 is incorrect for reason B.

(3)

Measure 2 is incorrect for reason A.

(4)

Measure 1 is incorrect for reason B.

(5)

Both measures are correct.

(2)

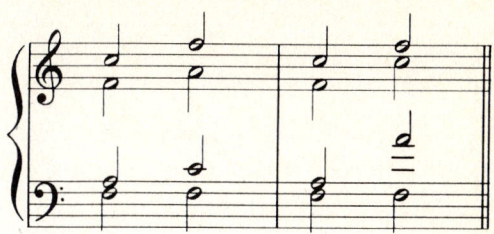

ㅡ Both measures are correct, or, measure ㅡ is incorrect for reason ㅡ.

(3)

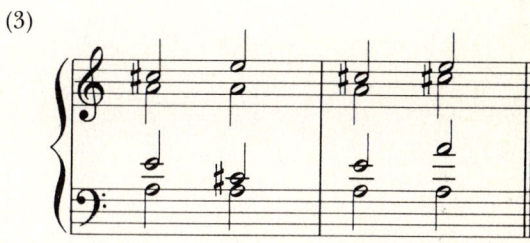

ㅡ Both measures are correct, or, measure ㅡ is incorrect for reason ㅡ.

(4)

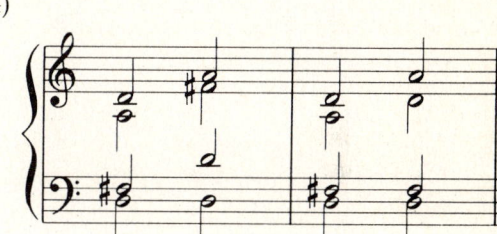

ㅡ Both measures are correct, or, measure ㅡ is incorrect for reason ㅡ.

(5)

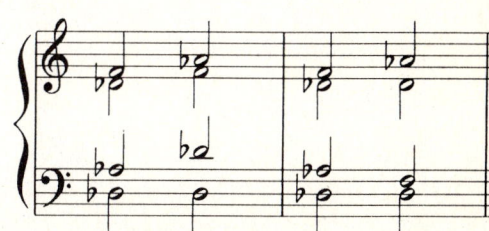

ㅡ Both measures are correct, or, measure ㅡ is incorrect for reason ㅡ.

(6)

Measure 2 is incorrect for reason A.

(6)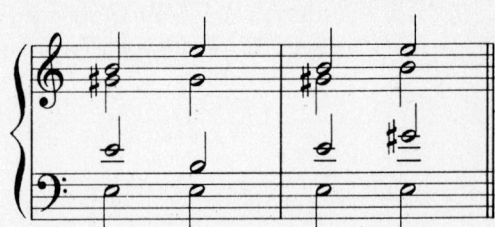

__ Both measures are correct, or, measure __ is incorrect for reason __.

(7)

Measure 1 is incorrect for reason C.

(7)

__ Both measures are correct, or, measure __ is incorrect for reason __.

(8)

Both measures are correct.

(8)

__ Both measures are correct, or, measure __ is incorrect for reason __.

(9)

Both measures are correct

(9)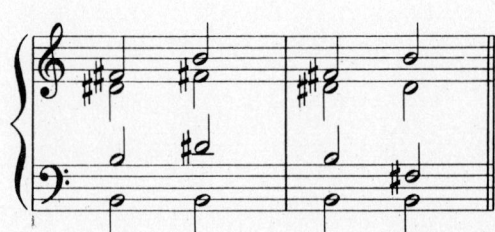

__ Both measures are correct, or, measure __ is incorrect for reason __.

Assignment 5D. Part-writing pairs of repeated minor triads.
 a) Answers given. Where possible, write two solutions. When not possible, place an **X** in the second measure.

Assignments 5.2–5.3. (*EH*, p. 95). Part-writing repeated triads. Write each pair of repeated triads using whichever method is appropriate.

1–10: First triad is given in full; fill in alto and tenor voices of the second triad.

11–20: Soprano and bass only are given; choose open or close position for the first triad. Observe figured bass (review *EH*, p. 32).

21–25: Second soprano note is omitted; choose a soprano different from the first soprano note and connect the two triads.

Assignment 5.4. (*EH*, p. 97). Writing authentic cadences. Write each cadence in close and open position, in that order, following the "first procedure" described in EH, p. 96. Use extended voice ranges where necessary and as indicated by the black notes in Figure 5.7 (*EH*). Identify each cadence as perfect authentic, imperfect authentic, or half.

a) Answers given.

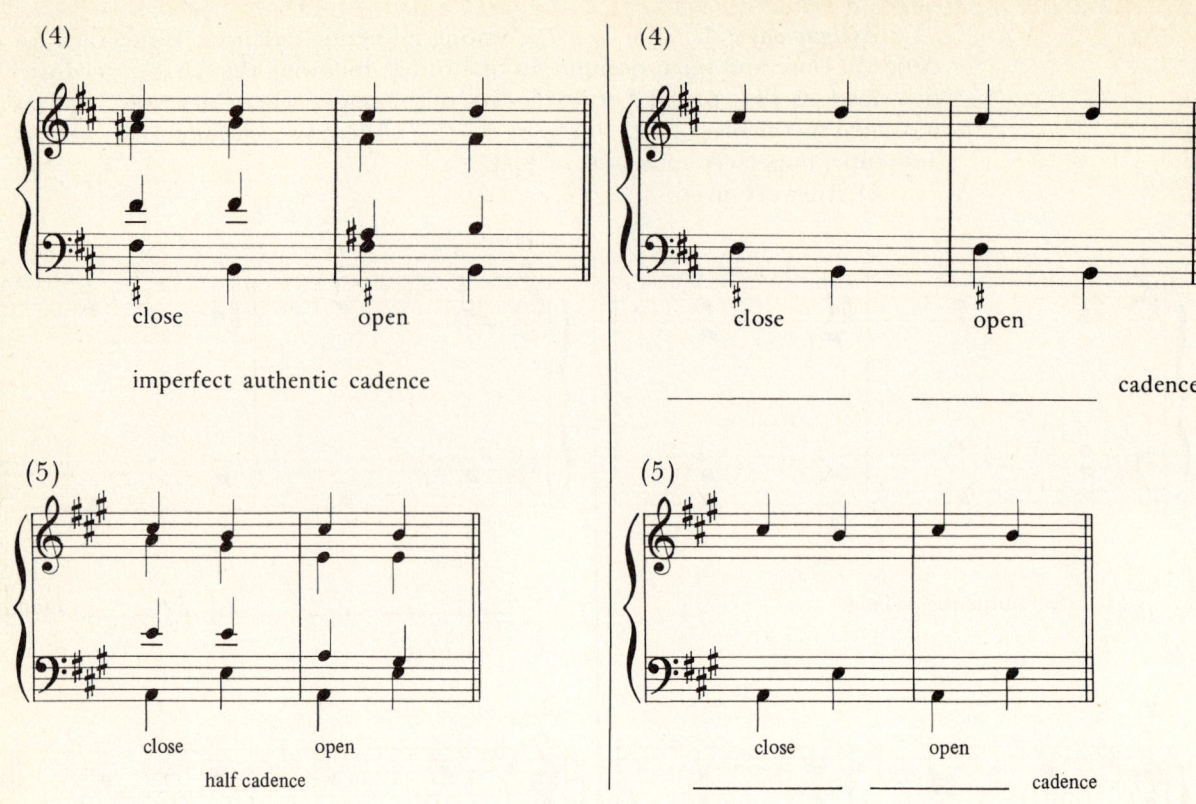

b) No answers given; use either close or open position as appropriate. Place chord numbers below staff.

Name the cadences. Use abbreviations, PA, IA, and H.

1. _____   3. _____

2. _____   4. _____

5. _____ 8. _____

6. _____ 9. _____

7. _____ 10. _____

Assignment 5.5. (*EH*, p. 98). Part-write cadences when soprano line only is given. Be sure the bass note is always the root of the triad. Place the chord number below each bass note.

a) Major Keys

b) Minor Keys

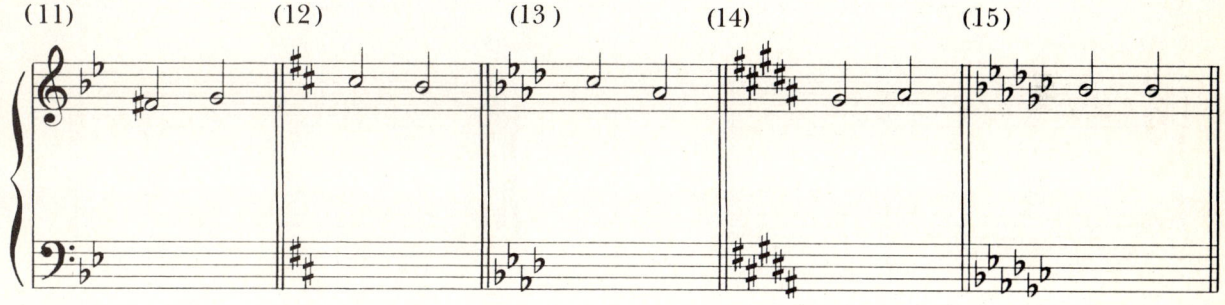

Assignment 5.6. (*EH*, p. 100). *a*) Write cadences in which the soprano line is 1̂–2̂ or 2̂–1̂. Include harmonic analysis.

b) Write cadences: (1) – (3): The third of V skips to the third of I. (4)–(5). Triple the root in the tonic triad.

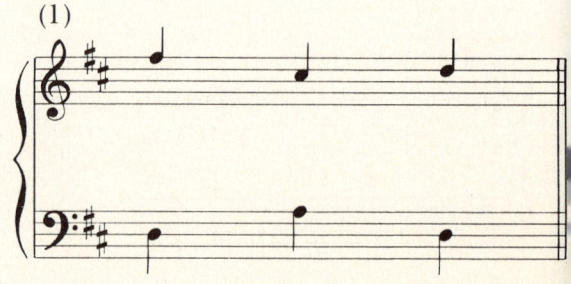

(2)

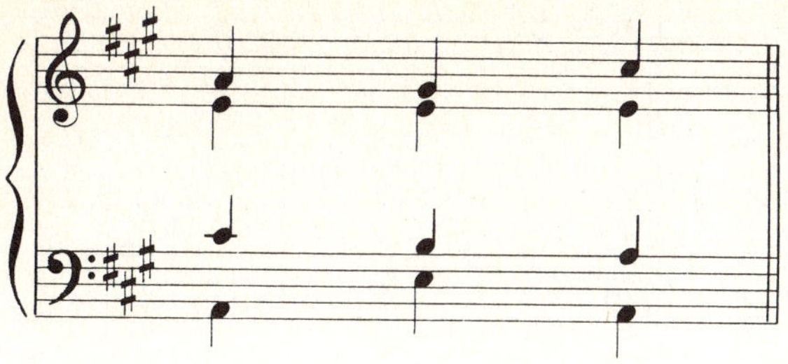

(3)

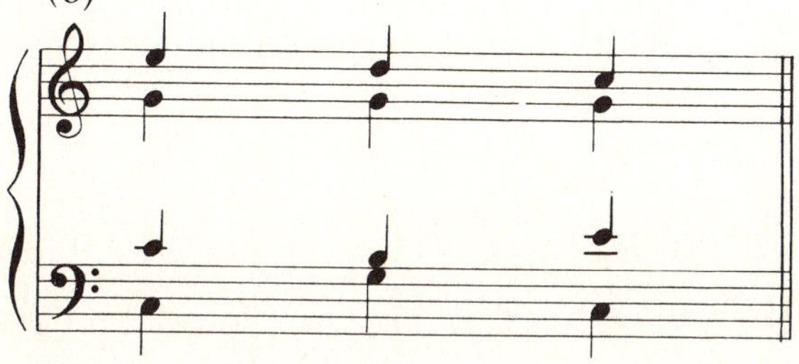

(4)

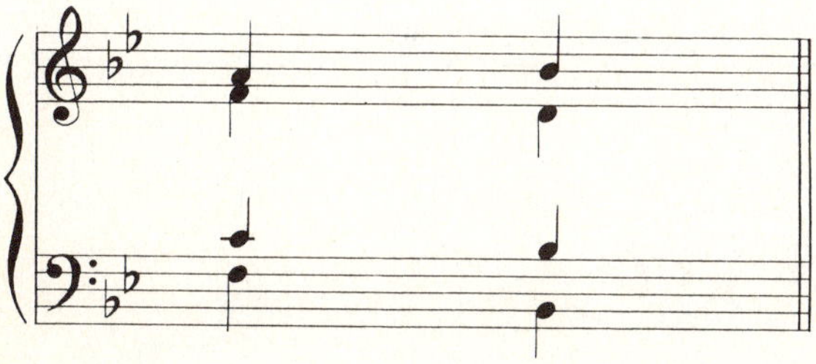

(5)

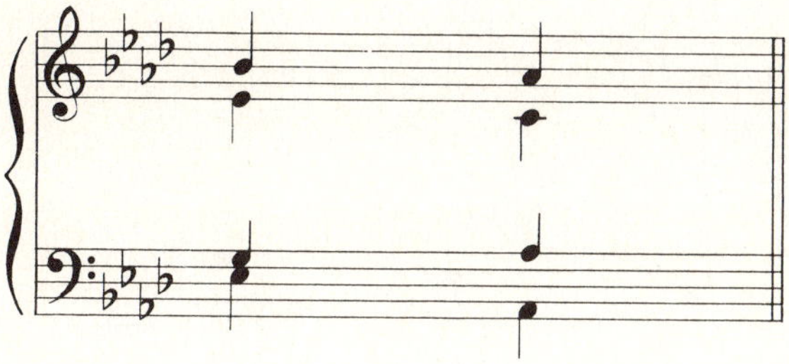

(2)

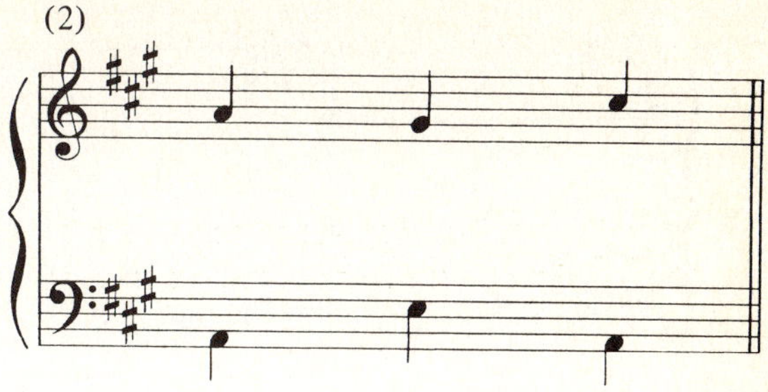

(3)

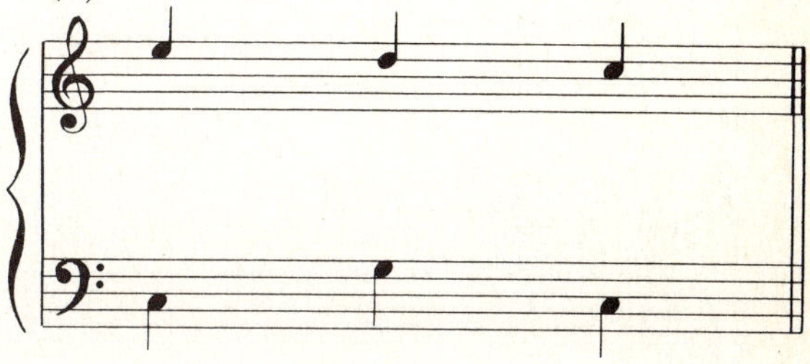

(4)

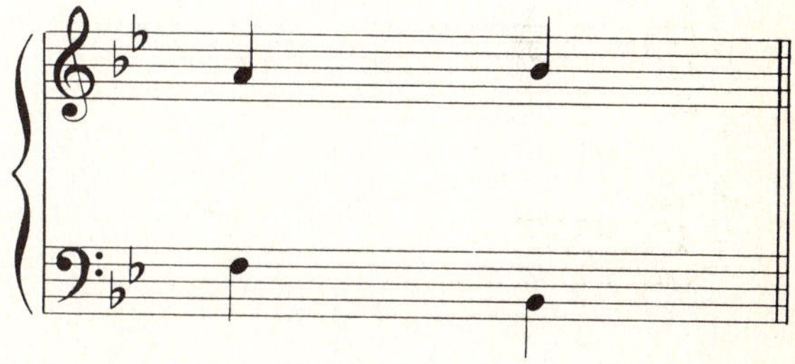

(5)

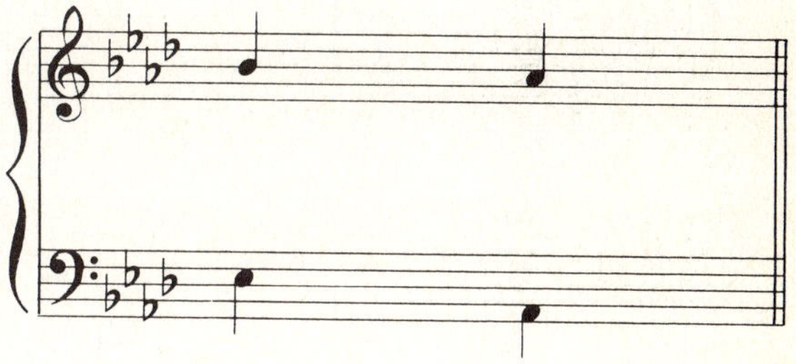

Assignment 5.7. (*EH*, p. 101). *a*) Part-write cadences when bass line only is given. Supply any correct soprano line. Place the chord number below each bass note.

(1) (2) (3) (4) (5)

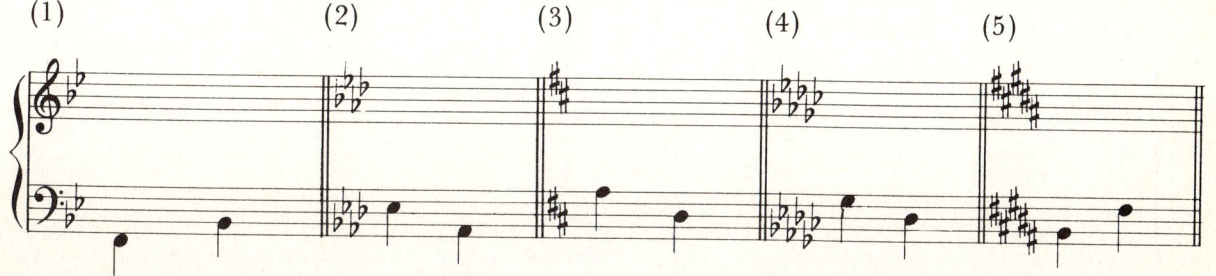

(6) (7) (8) (9) (10)

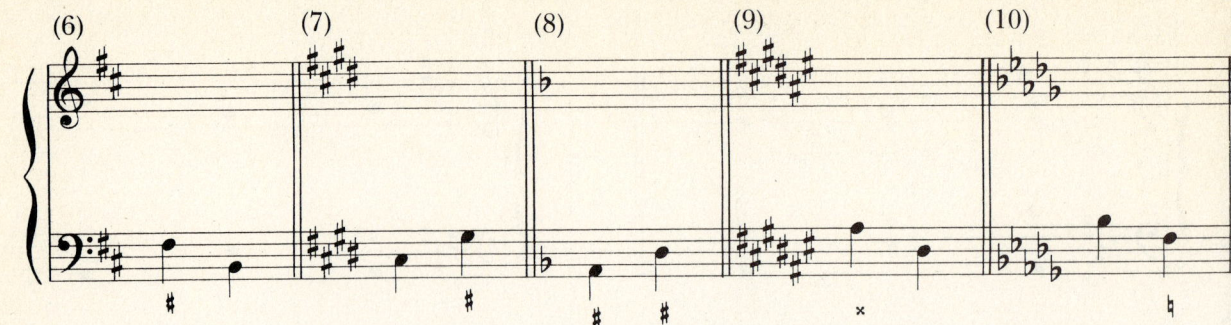

Assignment 5.8. (*EH*, p. 102). Write extended exercises, using all procedures for writing triads with roots in the bass a fifth apart. Include harmonic analysis.

a) Major Keys

(1)

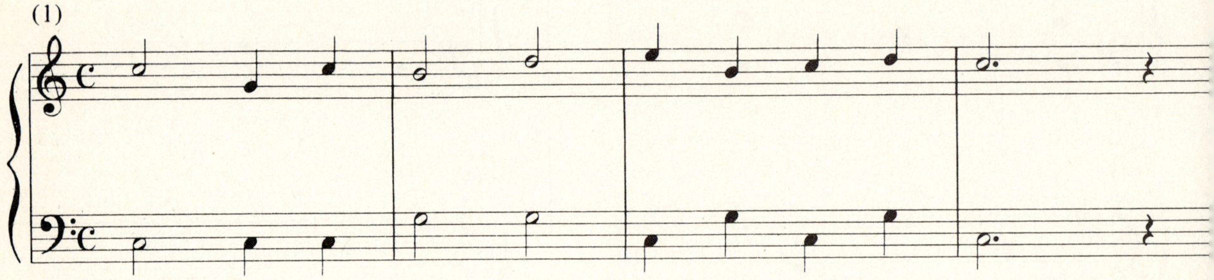

(2)

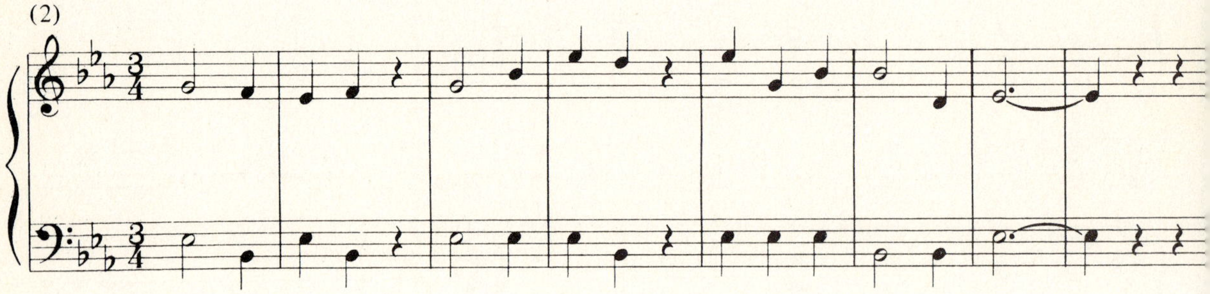

(3)

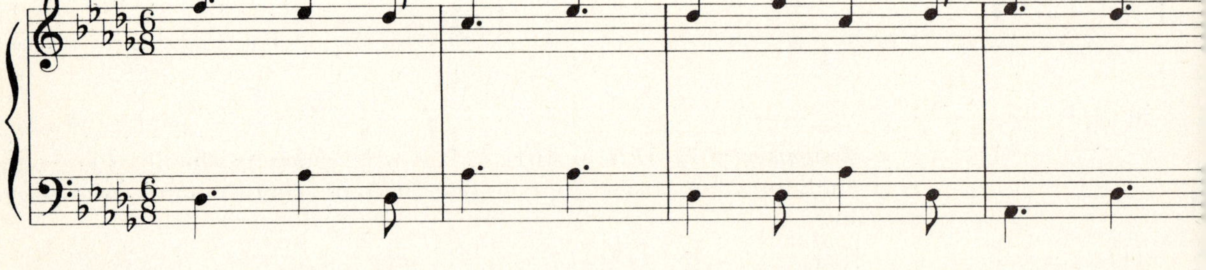

(4)

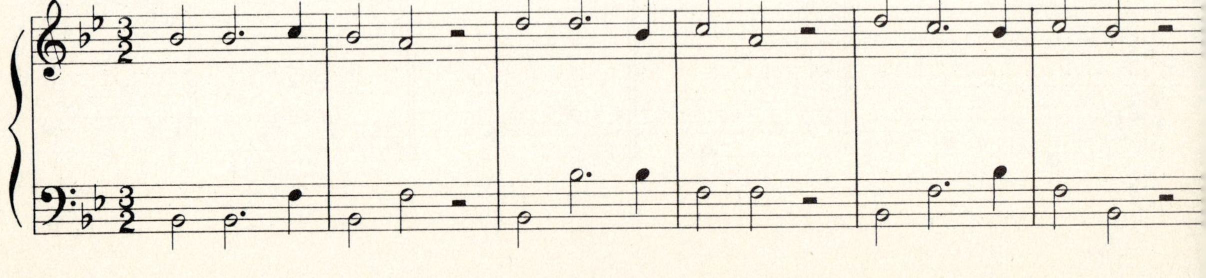

b) Minor Keys

(5)

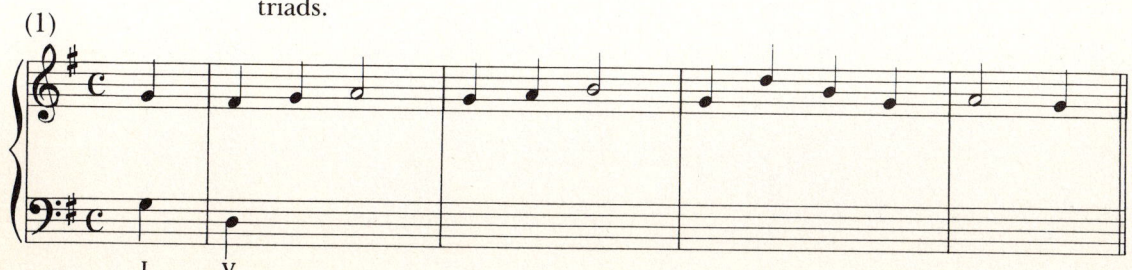

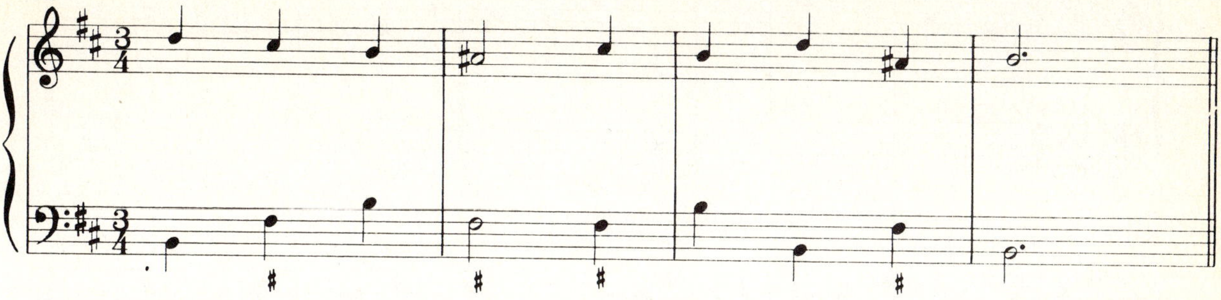

(6)

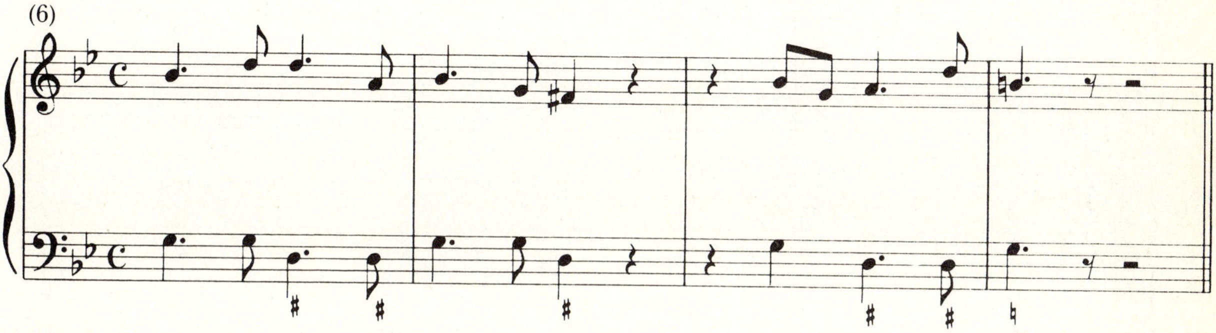

(7)

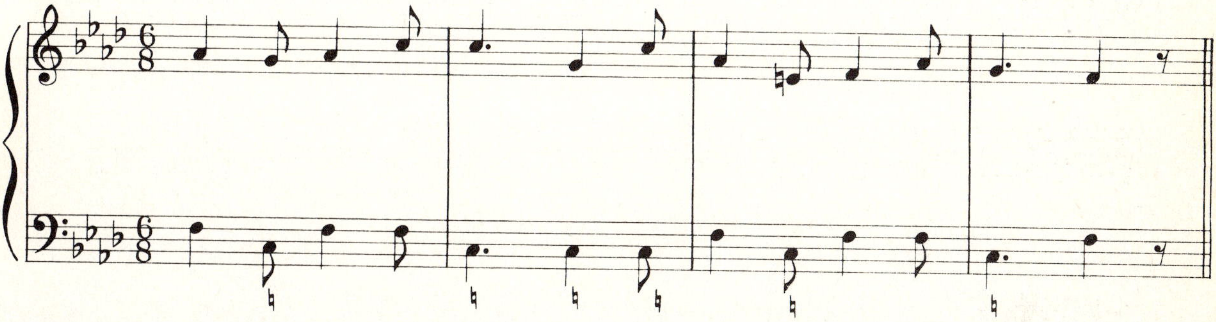

(8)

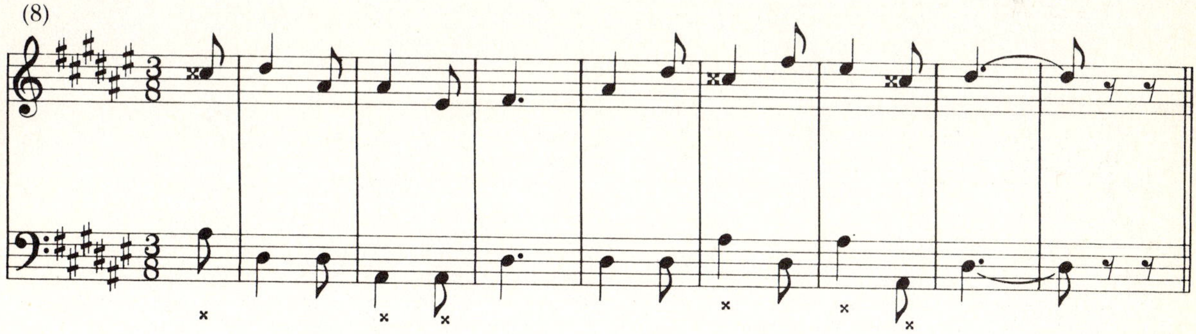

Assignment 5.9. (*EH*, p. 104). Melody harmonization. Following the four steps outlined in *EH*, p. 103, harmonize each melody using I (or i) and V triads.

(1)

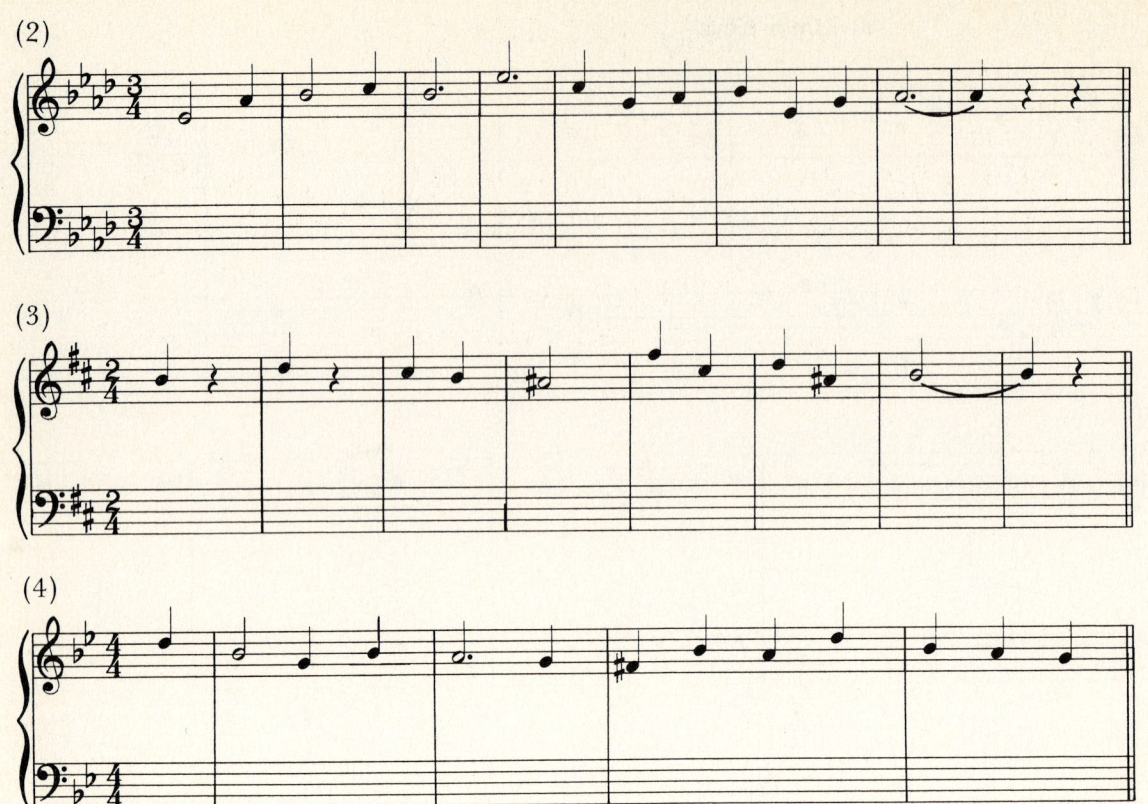

CHAPTER 6

THE SUBDOMINANT TRIAD

	Elementary Harmony	Workbook
Assignment 6.1	113	55
Assignment 6.2	113	56
Assignment 6.3	116	57
Assignment 6.4	117	57
Assignment 6.5	120	—
Assignment 6.6	122	59
Assignment 6.7	123	60
Assignment 6.8	128	—
Assignment 6.9	128	60
Assignment 6.10	129	61
Assignment 6.11	130	62

Assignment 6.1. (*EH*, p. 113). Spell the subdominant (IV) triad in each major key.

Key	Subdominant	Key	Subdominant
C	F A C	C	F A C
G	C E G	G	_ _ _
D	G B D	D	_ _ _
A	D F♯ A	A	_ _ _
E	A C♯ E	E	_ _ _

Key	Subdominant			Key	Subdominant		
B	E	G#	B	B	—	—	—
F#	B	D#	F#	F#	—	—	—
C#	F#	A#	C#	C#	—	—	—
F	B♭	D	F	F	—	—	—
B♭	E♭	G	B♭	B♭	—	—	—
E♭	A♭	C	E♭	E♭	—	—	—
A♭	D♭	F	A♭	A♭	—	—	—
D♭	G♭	B♭	D♭	D♭	—	—	—
G♭	C♭	E♭	G♭	G♭	—	—	—
C♭	F♭	A♭	C♭	C♭	—	—	—

Assignment 6.2. (*EH*, p. 113). Spell the subdominant triads (iv and IV) in each minor key.

Key	iv			IV			Key	iv			IV		
A	D	F	A	D	F#	A	A	<u>D</u>	<u>F</u>	<u>A</u>	<u>D</u>	<u>F#</u>	<u>A</u>
E	A	C	E	A	C#	E	E	—	—	—	—	—	—
B	E	G	B	E	G#	B	B	—	—	—	—	—	—
F#	B	D	F#	B	D#	F#	F#	—	—	—	—	—	—
C#	F#	A	C#	F#	A#	C#	C#	—	—	—	—	—	—
G#	C#	E	G#	C#	E#	G#	G#	—	—	—	—	—	—
D#	G#	B	D#	G#	B#	D#	D#	—	—	—	—	—	—
A#	D#	F#	A#	D#	F𝄪	A#	A#	—	—	—	—	—	—
D	G	B♭	D	G	B	D	D	—	—	—	—	—	—
G	C	E♭	G	C	E	G	G	—	—	—	—	—	—
C	F	A♭	C	F	A	C	C	—	—	—	—	—	—
F	B♭	D♭	F	B♭	D	F	F	—	—	—	—	—	—
B♭	E♭	G♭	B♭	E♭	G	B♭	B♭	—	—	—	—	—	—
E♭	A♭	C♭	E♭	A♭	C	E♭	E♭	—	—	—	—	—	—
A♭	D♭	F♭	A♭	D♭	F	A♭	A♭	—	—	—	—	—	—

Assignment 6.3. (*EH*, p. 116). Identify cadences. Most of these are plagal, a few are authentic. Place a chord number: I, i, IV, iv, or V below each triad. Name the cadence, PP, IP, PA, IA, or HC.

Assignment 6.4. (*EH*, p. 117). Harmonic analysis. Analyze these excerpts using the symbols I, i, IV, iv, V, or V^7. Circle all nonharmonic tones.

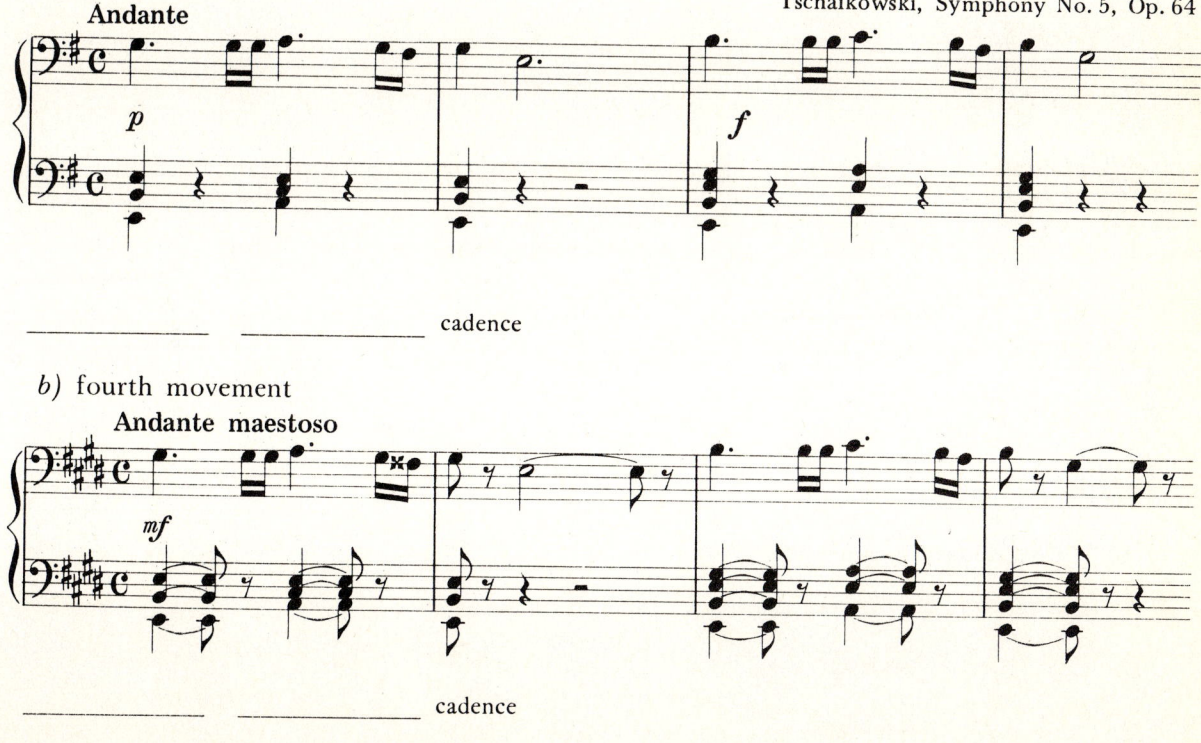

(2) **Nicht zu geschwind** Schubert, *Winterreise*, D. 911, "Rückblick"

vor ih - rem Hau - se stil - le - stehn.

_____ _____ cadence

(3) **Allegretto** Lotti, *Pur dicesti*

Pur di - ce - sti, o boc - ca, boc - ca

bel - la, o boc - ca, boc - ca bel - la

*Compare with measure 6.

(4) The infrequent use of V–IV (See *EH*, p. 116.)

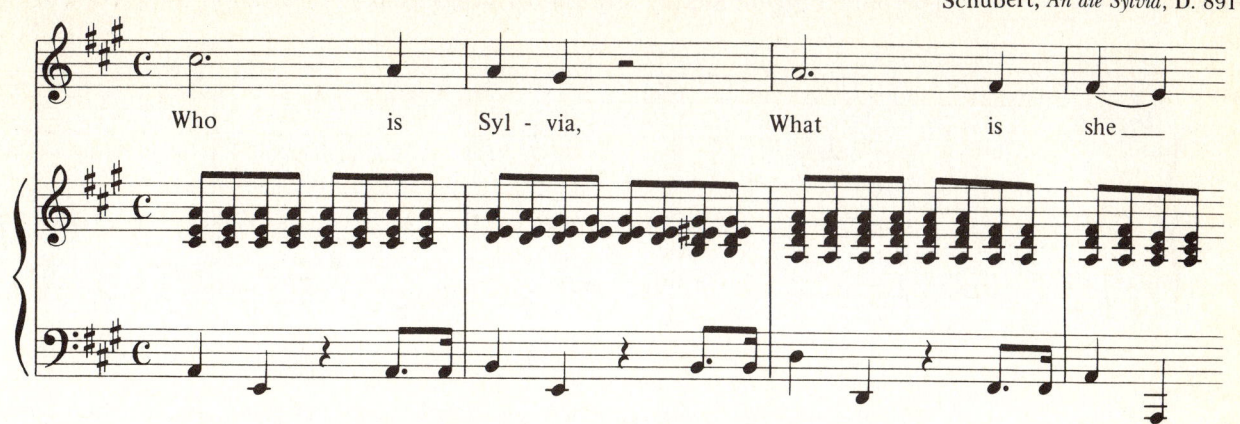

Schubert, *An die Sylvia*, D. 891

Who is Syl - via, What is she ___

Assignment 6.6. (*EH*, p. 122). Part-writing. Supply the name of the key and the chord symbols, and add inner voices. In numbers (1)–(5), also name the cadence. Each of (1)–(5) use a common tone, while the remainder require other procedures.

(1) Key ___ (2) Key ___ (3) Key ___ (4) Key ___ (5) Key ___

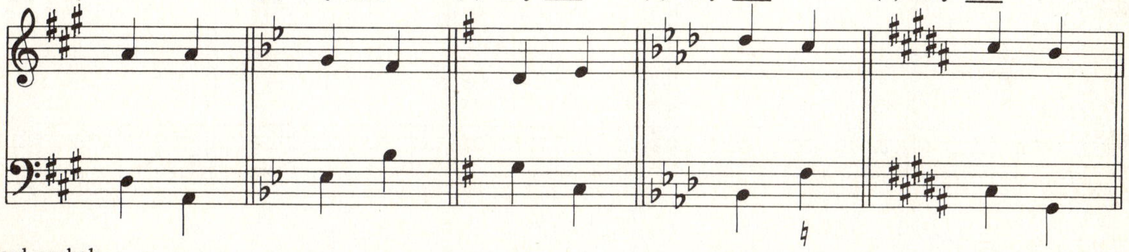

Chord symbol: ___ ___ ___ ___ ___ ___ ___ ___ ___ ___

Cadence: ______ ______ ______ ______ ______

(6) Key ___ (7) Key ___ (8) Key ___ (9) Key ___

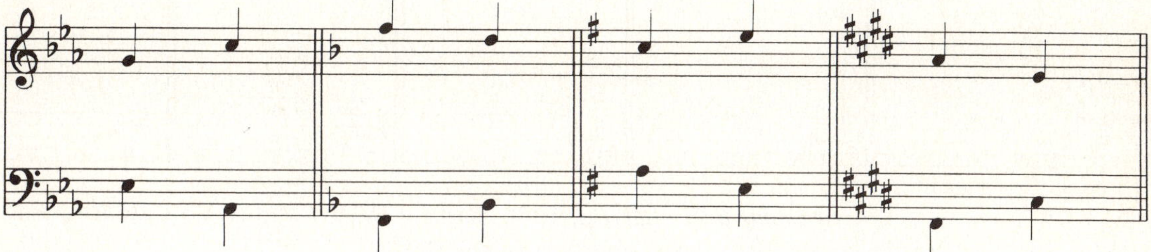

Chord symbol: ___ ___ ___ ___ ___ ___ ___ ___

(10) Key ___ (11) Key ___ (12) Key ___ (13) Key ___

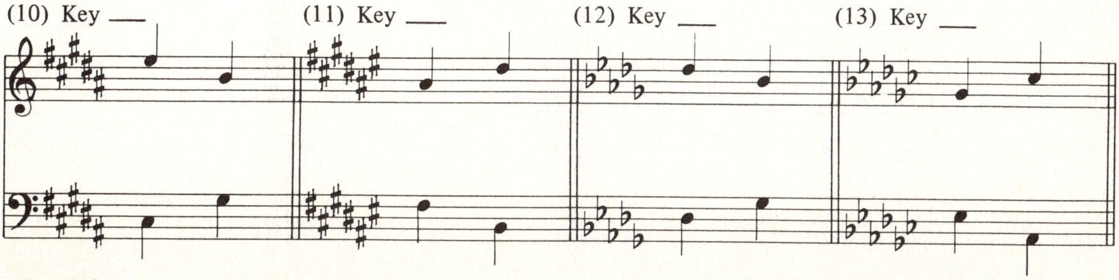

Chord symbol: ___ ___ ___ ___ ___ ___ ___ ___

Assignment 6.7. (*EH*, p. 123). *a*) Part-write plagal cadences when bass line only is given. Supply any correct soprano line.

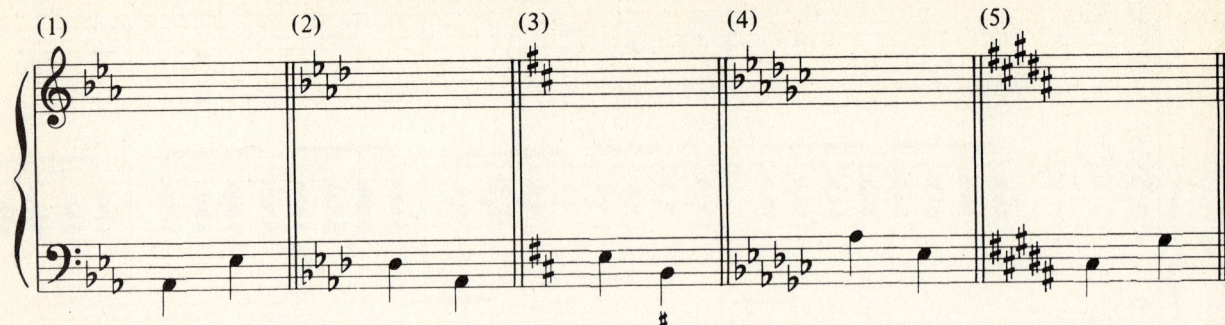

b) Part-write cadences when soprano line only is given. Be sure the bass note is always the root of the triad. Both authentic and plagal cadences are included.

Assignment 6.9. (*EH*, p. 128). Writing IV-V-I and iv-V-i cadences. Fill in inner voices. Place triad numbers below staff.

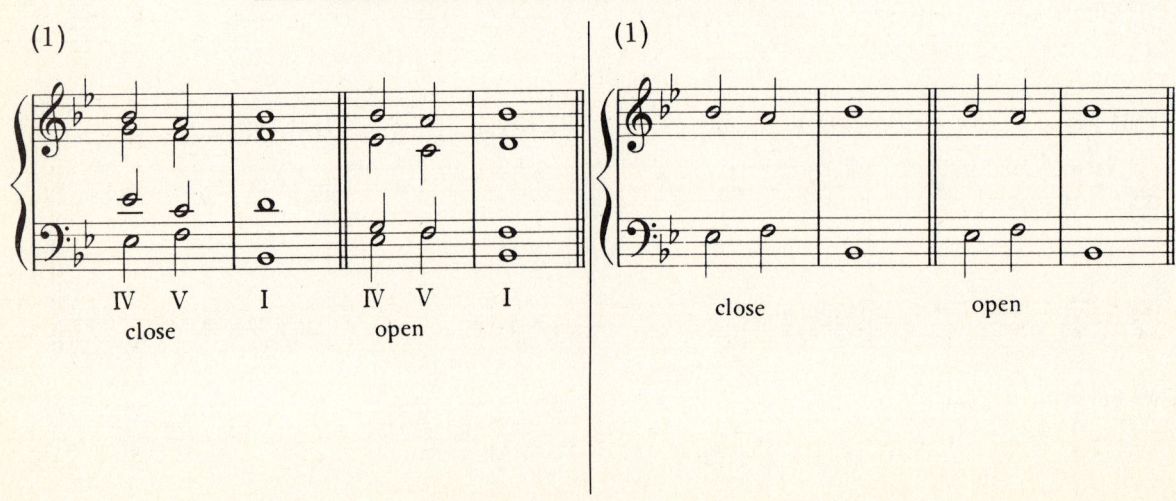

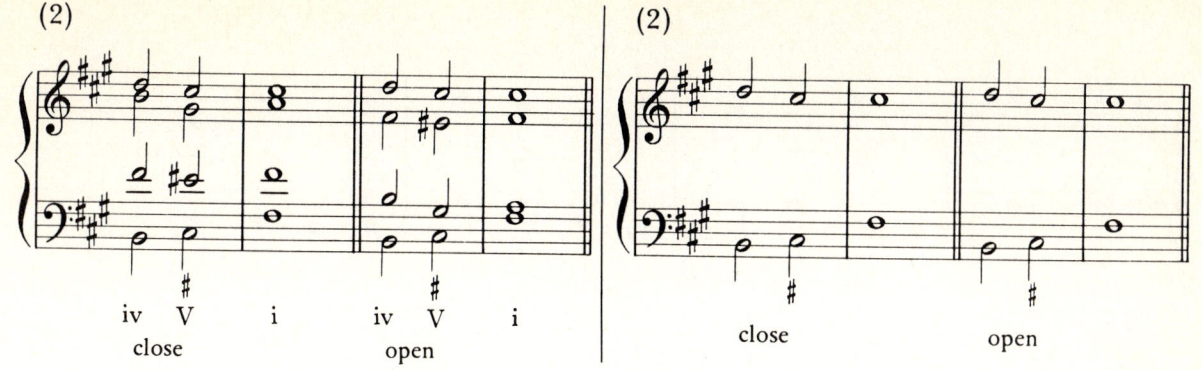

In (3) and (4), choose either open or close position, whichever is better.

Assignment 6.10. (*EH*, p. 129). Part-writing. Fill in alto and tenor voices. Place chord numbers below the bass line.

(3)

(4)

(5)

Assignment 6.11. (*EH*, p. 130). Melody harmonization. Follow the five-step procedure presented in *EH*, page 130.

(1)

(2)

(3)

(4)

CHAPTER 7
THE MELODIC LINE: I

	Elementary Harmony	Workbook
Assignment 7.1	143	64
Assignment 7.2	147	67
Assignment 7A	—	69
Assignment 7.3	150	—
Assignment 7.4	154	70
Assignment 7.5	158	71
Assignment 7.6	160	71
Assignment 7.7	161	72

Assignment 7.1. (*EH*, p. 143). Analyzing the form of a melody. Using the *Example* in *EH*, Assignment 7.1 as a guide, analyze each melody: *a*) locate and name each cadence, *b*) indicate phrase length by a bracket and identify phrase by name, *c*) name the type of the beginning and ending of each phrase, and *d*) name the form of the entire piece. The first two melodies of this assignment are repeated with correct analysis. Do your analysis first, then check the correct solution.

Germany

(1)

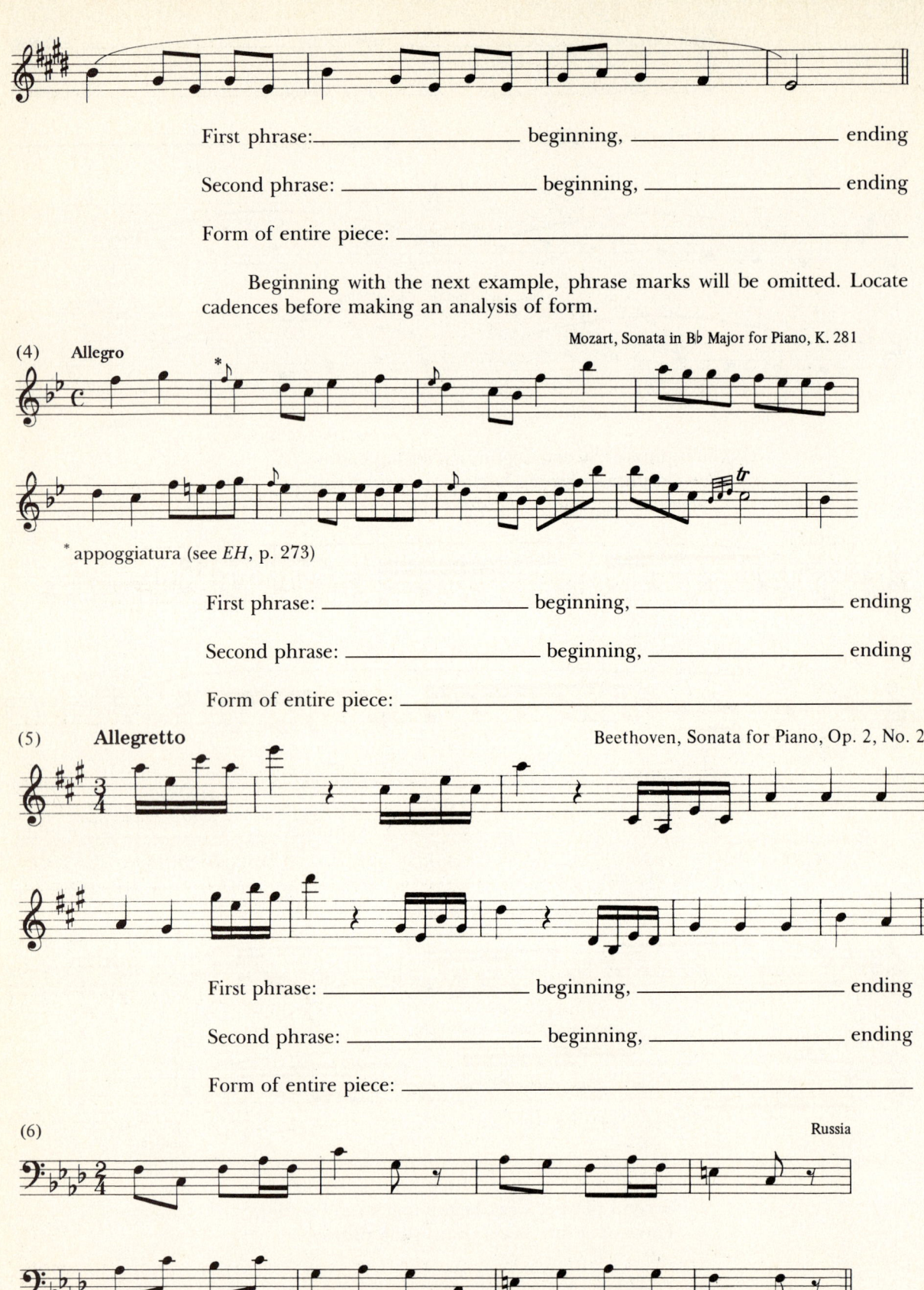

First phrase: _____ beginning, _____ ending

Second phrase: _____ beginning, _____ ending

Form of entire piece: _____

Beginning with the next example, phrase marks will be omitted. Locate cadences before making an analysis of form.

(4) Allegro — Mozart, Sonata in B♭ Major for Piano, K. 281

*appoggiatura (see *EH*, p. 273)

First phrase: _____ beginning, _____ ending

Second phrase: _____ beginning, _____ ending

Form of entire piece: _____

(5) Allegretto — Beethoven, Sonata for Piano, Op. 2, No. 2

First phrase: _____ beginning, _____ ending

Second phrase: _____ beginning, _____ ending

Form of entire piece: _____

(6) Russia

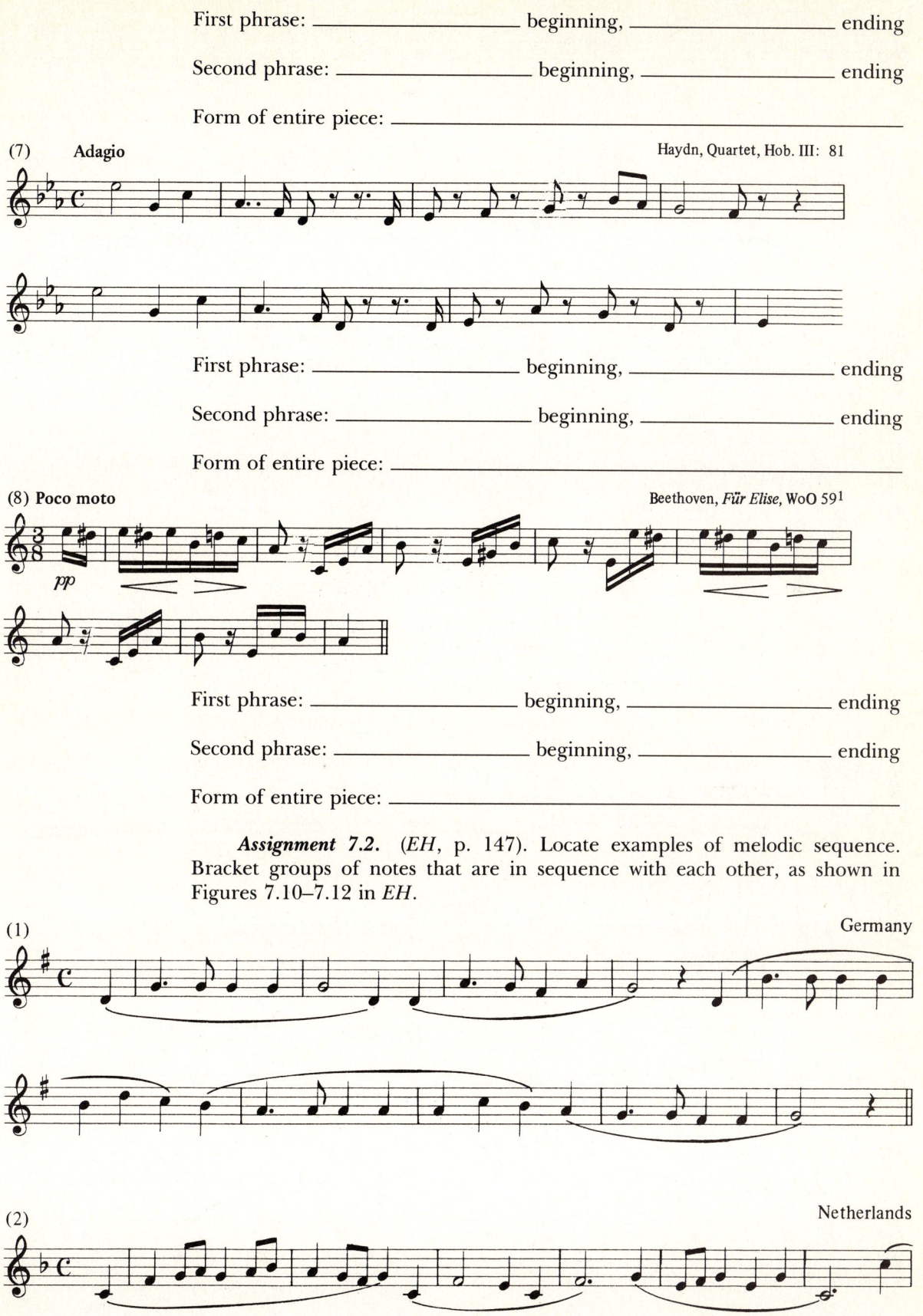

Assignment 7A. (*EH*, p. 152). Melodic analysis. In each of these melodies, locate and identify each $\hat{6}$ and $\hat{7}$. Where these are found in succession, bracket the group. Describe the use of each $\hat{6}$ and $\hat{7}$, or each group of $\hat{6}$'s and $\hat{7}$'s.

① $\sharp\hat{7}$ is used alone; it is raised and proceeds up.

② $\flat\hat{7}$ and $\flat\hat{6}$ descend between the tonic and dominant tones; they are lowered.

(1) Germany

Descriptions:

① _____

② _____

③ _____

④ _____

(2) Czechoslovakia

① _____

② _____

③ _____

(3) [music notation, bass clef, 3 flats, 6/4, France]

① _____

② _____

③ _____

④ _____

Assignment 7.4. (*EH*, p. 154). Write $\hat{6}$ or $\hat{7}$ above each such scale tone in these melodies. Add accidentals before notes where required.

(3)

Assignment 7.5. (*EH*, p. 158). Analyze the implied harmony in these melodies. Place the chord numers I, i, IV, iv, V, or V^7 and the chord spelling below the staff. Circle the nonharmonic tones.

(1) Sweden

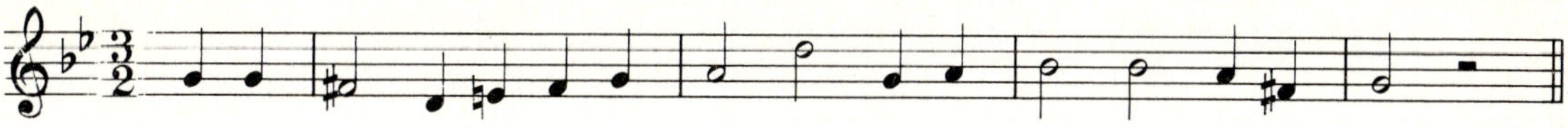

(2) Bohemia

(3) Netherlands

(4) Netherlands

Assignment 7.6. (*EH*, p. 160). Melody writing. Write original four-measure phrases in simple time.

(1) End with a perfect cadence.

(2) Use sequence; end with a perfect cadence.

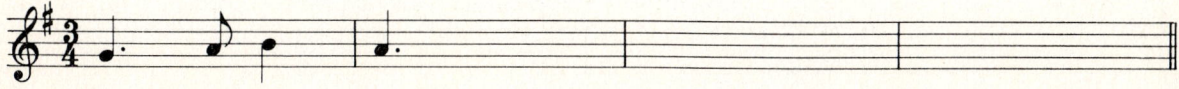

(3) End with a perfect cadence.

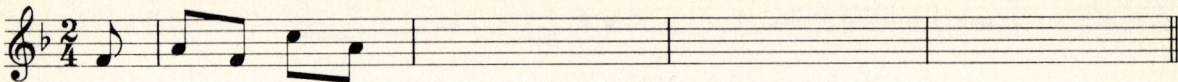

(4) Use sequence; end with a perfect cadence.

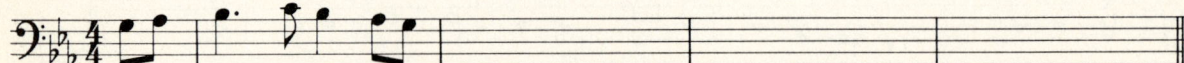

(5) Rewrite melody (1), but end with a half cadence or imperfect cadence.

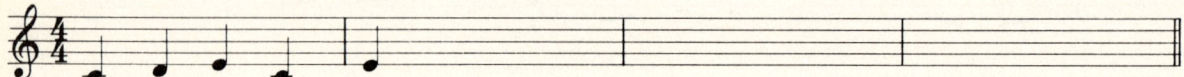

(6) Rewrite melody (2), but end with a half cadence or imperfect cadence.

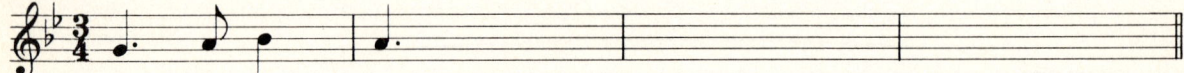

(7) Rewrite melody (3), but end with a half cadence or imperfect cadence.

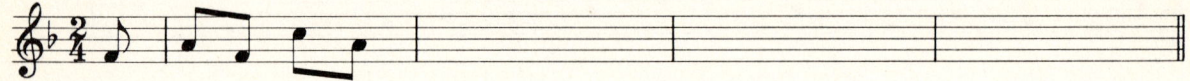

(8) Rewrite melody (4), but end with a half cadence or imperfect cadence.

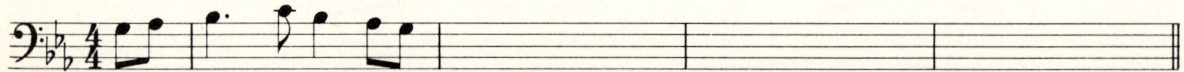

Assignment 7.7. (*EH*, p. 161). Melody writing. *a*) Using melodies 5–8 from Assignment 7.6 as antecedent phrases, add a consequent phrase to each to form a period. Of these four melodies, two should be parallel periods and two should be contrasting periods. Identify the period at the beginning of each melody as indicated. Include tempo and dynamic markings, and indicate motives and phrases by phrase marks.

(1) ——————— period.

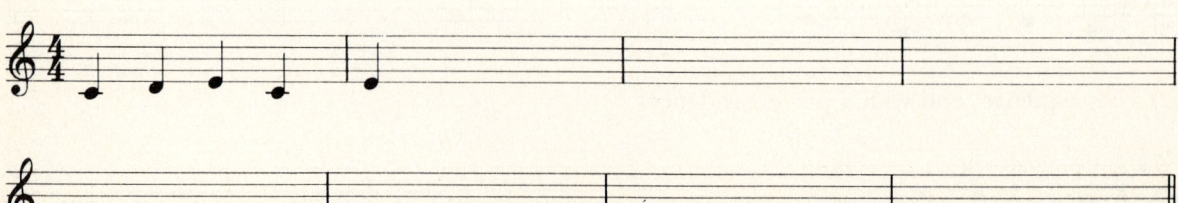

(4) _____ period.

CHAPTER 8

C CLEFS; TRANSPOSING INSTRUMENTS

	Elementary Harmony	*Workbook*
Assignment 8.1	167	75
Assignment 8.2	167	76
Assignment 8A	—	76
Assignment 8.3	168	77
Assignment 8.4	168	78
Assignment 8.5	168	79
Assignment 8B	—	80
Assignment 8C	—	82
Assignment 8.6	169	—
Assignment 8.7	172	82
Assignment 8.8	172	83

Assignment 8.1. (*EH*, p. 167). Alto clef. *a*) Identify each pitch by letter name and octave register.

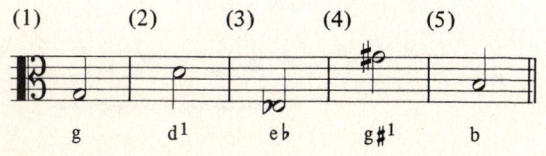
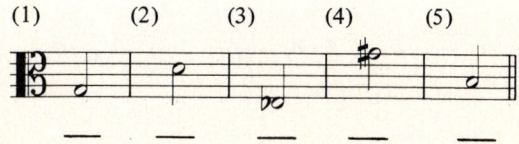

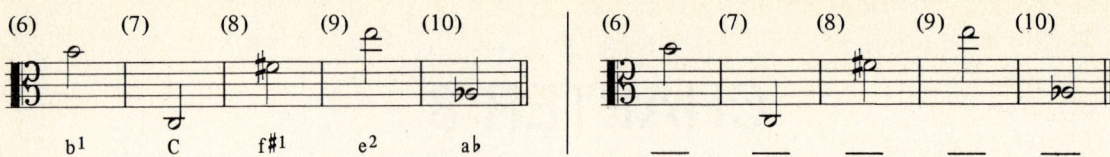

b) Place a note on the staff for each pitch name given. Observe octave register designations.

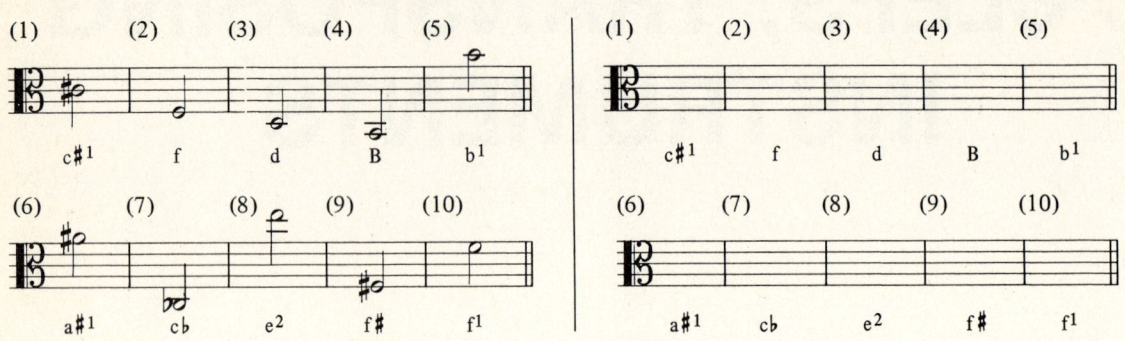

Assignment 8.2. (*EH*, p. 167). Tenor clef. *a*) Identify each pitch by letter name and octave register (review *EH*, p. 5).

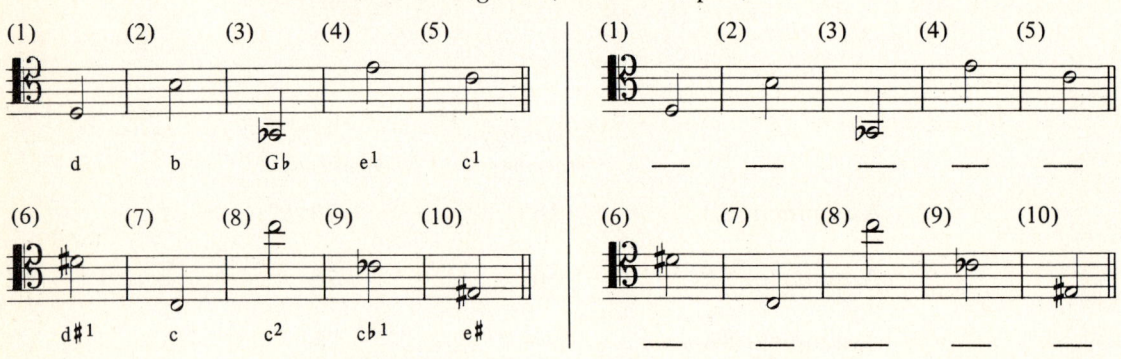

b) Place a note on the staff for each pitch name given. Observe the octave register indications.

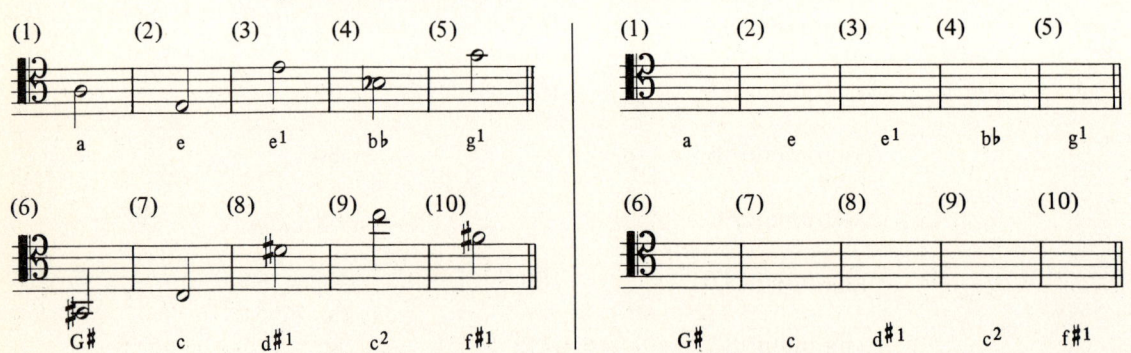

Assignment 8A. Identifying pitch names in alto and tenor clefs. Below each note of these music excerpts, place the correct pitch name, using octave register symbols.

(1) Beethoven, Quartet, Op. 59, No. 3

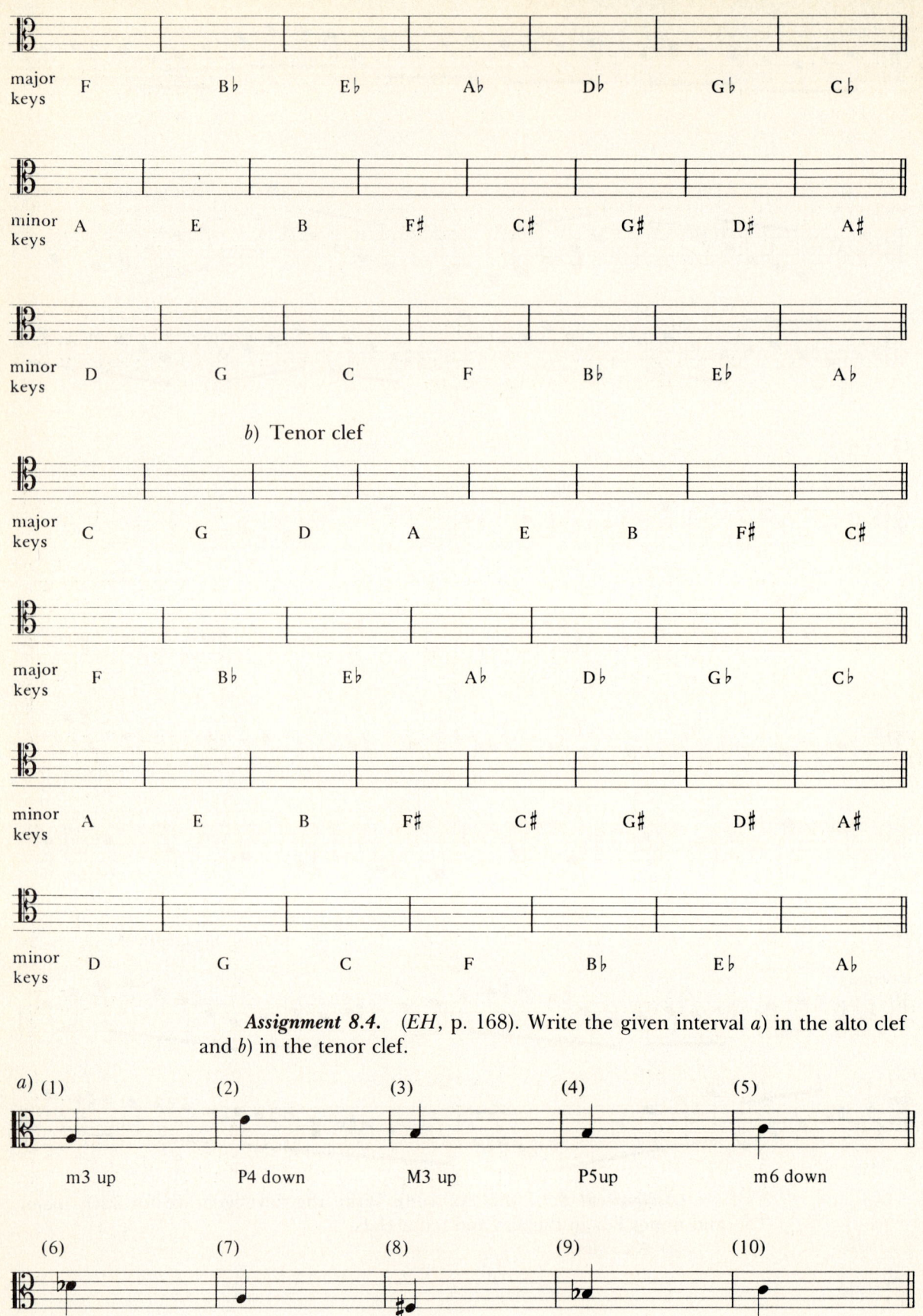

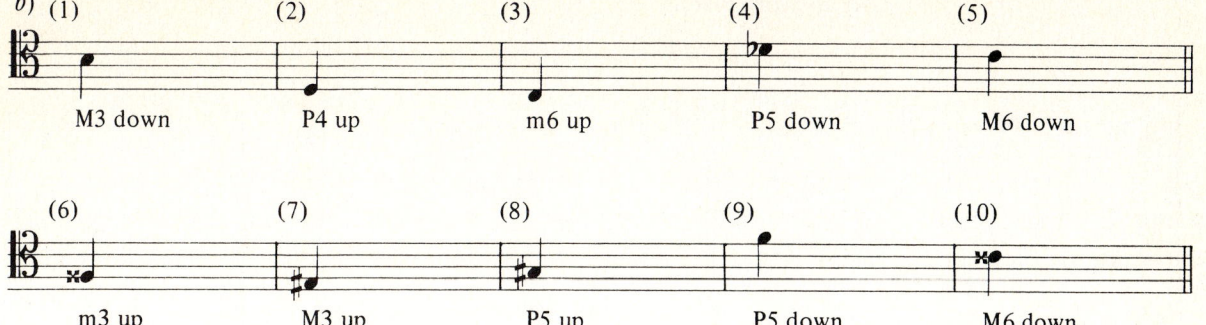

Assignment 8.5. (*EH*, p. 168). Writing cadences in open score. Fill in alto and tenor voices, using close or open position, as indicated. Place key signatures in alto and tenor clefs. Observe correct procedures for stem directions when a single melodic line is found in a staff (review *EH*, p. 34).

No answers given.

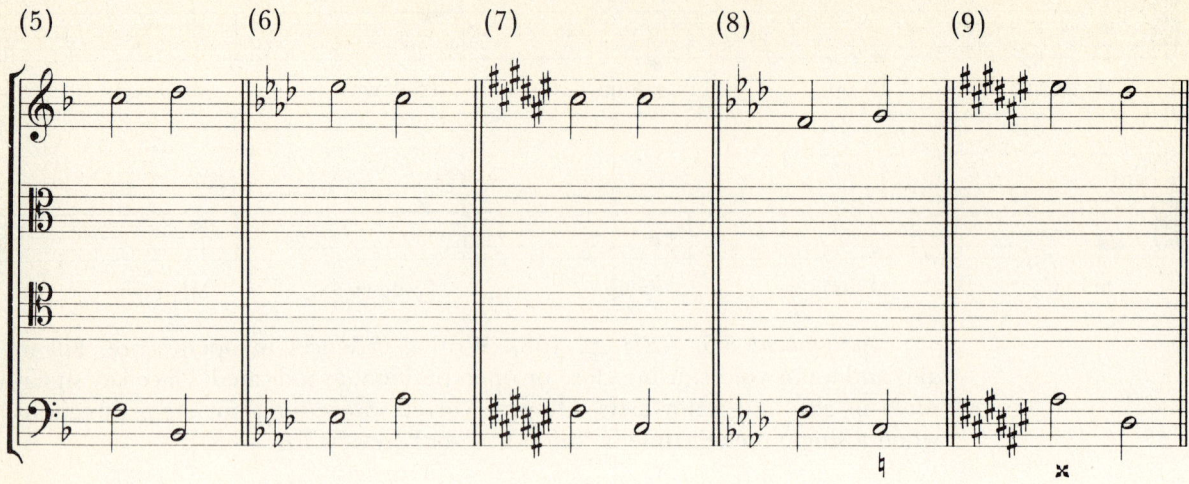

Assignment 8B. Part-writing in open score. Fill in alto and tenor voices. Remember that the C clef indicates *middle c*. Include harmonic analysis.

Assignment 8C. (*EH*, p. 170). Writing cadences in open score using the treble clefs, the vocal tenor clef, and the bass clef.

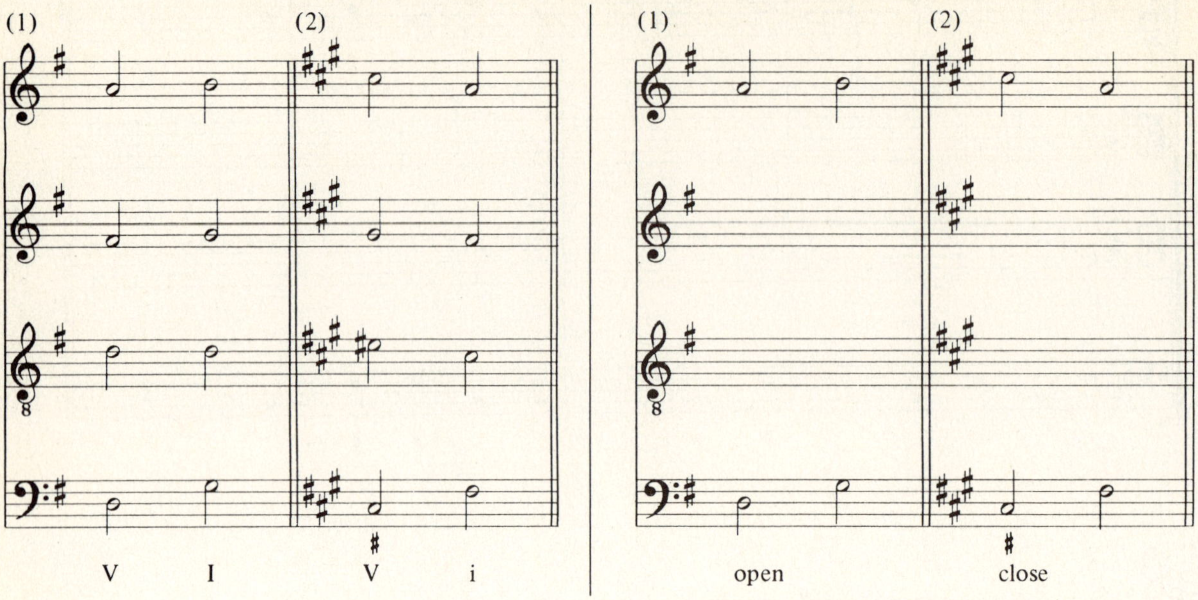

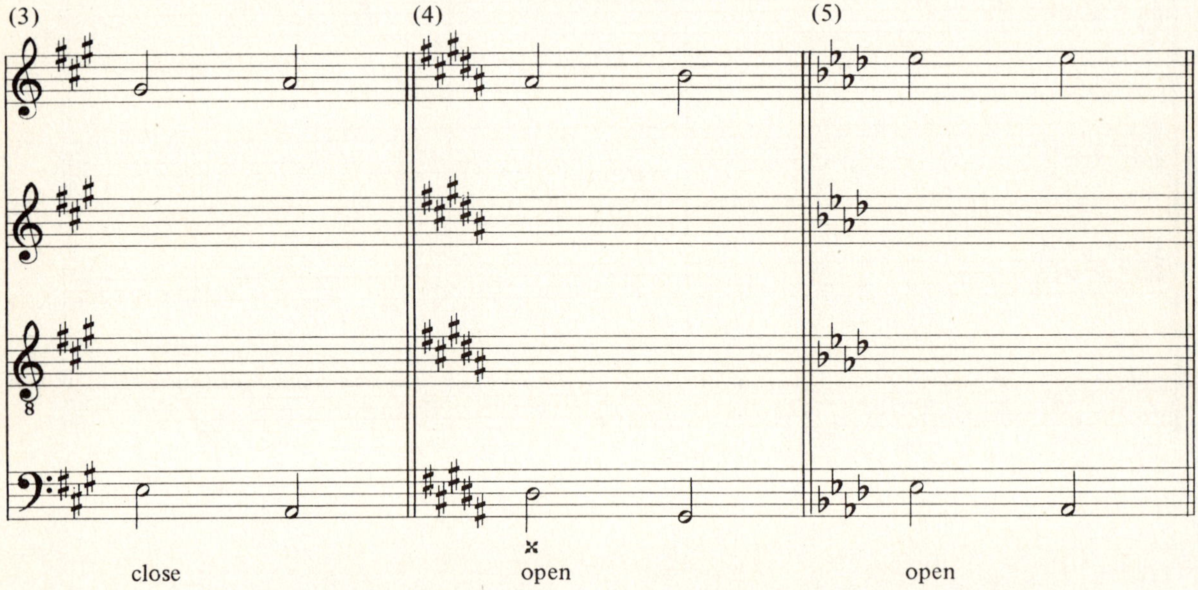

Assignment 8.7. (*EH*, p. 172). Writing for transposing instruments. Write the following melodic excerpt for each instrument designated. Consult *EH*, Appendix 2, for transposition and key signature requirements.

(1) Clarinet in B♭

(1) Clarinet in B♭

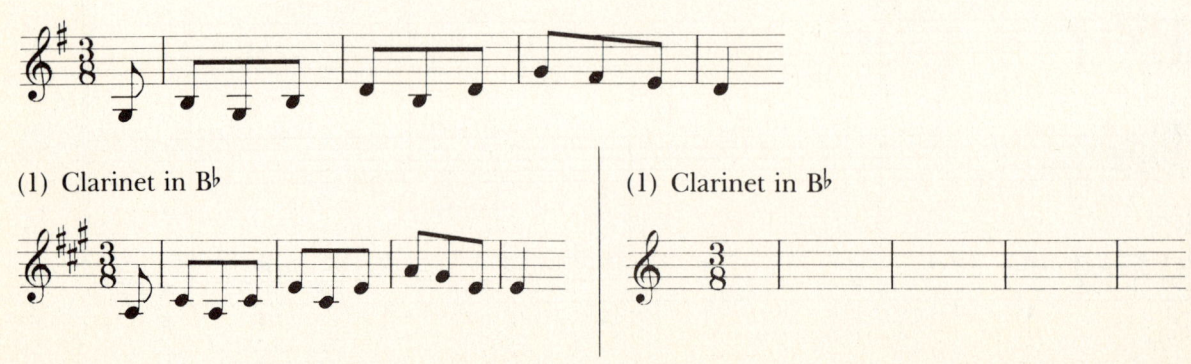

(2) Clarinet in A

(3) English Horn

(4) French Horn in F

(5) E♭ Alto Saxophone

(6) B♭ Tenor Saxophone

(2) Clarinet in A

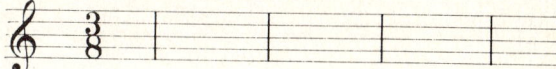

(3) English Horn

(4) French Horn in F

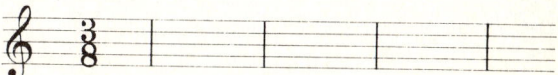

(5) E♭ Alto Saxophone

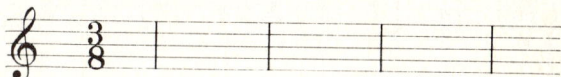

(6) B♭ Tenor Saxophone

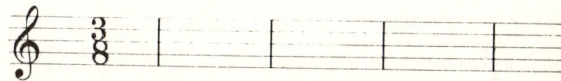

Assignment 8.8. (*EH*, p. 172). Writing for transposing instruments. A short except in four voices is given. Write it in open score.

a) Answers given

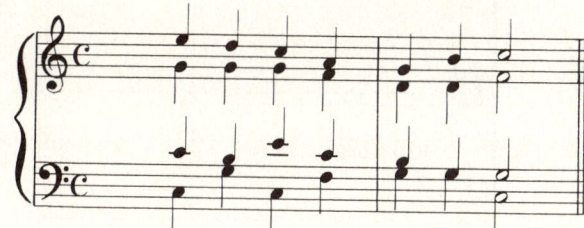

(1)

(2)

b) Answers not given

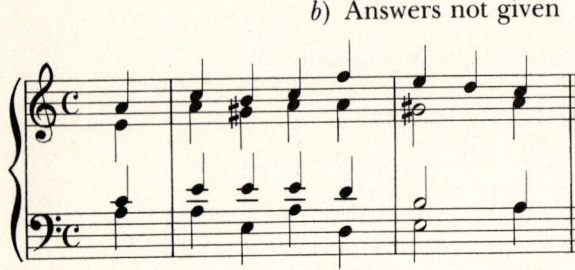

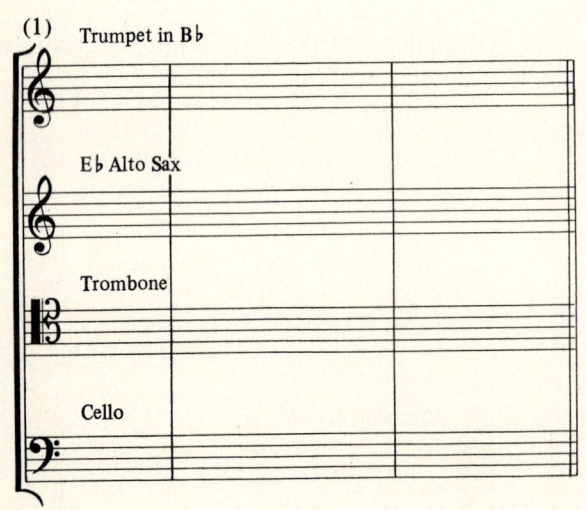

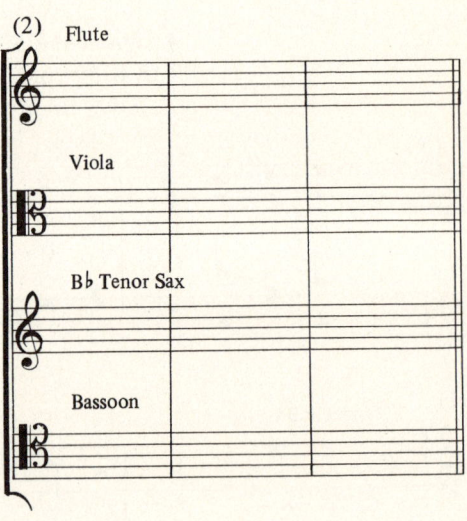

CHAPTER 9

THE TRIAD IN INVERSION

	Elementary Harmony	*Workbook*
Assignment 9.1	183	85
Assignment 9.2	186	88
Assignment 9.3	189	90
Assignment 9.4	190	91
Assignment 9.5	191	92
Assignment 9.6	195	94
Assignment 9.7	196	—
Assignment 9.8	198	—
Assignment 9.9	199	96

Assignment 9.1. (*EH*, p. 183).

a) First inversions. Each music excerpt includes a use of a triad in first inversion. Look for the example described and place its number, (1)–(5), where indicated.

Example No. _____. A triad, root in bass, is followed by its first inversion. Place a "6" under the triad in inversion.

Example No. _____. A triad in inversion allows the soprano and bass to move in tenths. Place a "6" under the first inversion and bracket the soprano and bass movement.

Example No. _____. A skip from "third to third" in the bass. Place a "6" under each of these triads.

Example No. _____. Two scale lines in the bass, (1) from G to g, and (2) from g to d^1. Bracket each of these scale passages, and place a "6" below each triad in first inversion.

Example No. ———. A series of first inversions. Place a "6" under each first inversion.

(1) Grazioso Beethoven, Sonata in A Major for Piano, Op. 2, No. 2

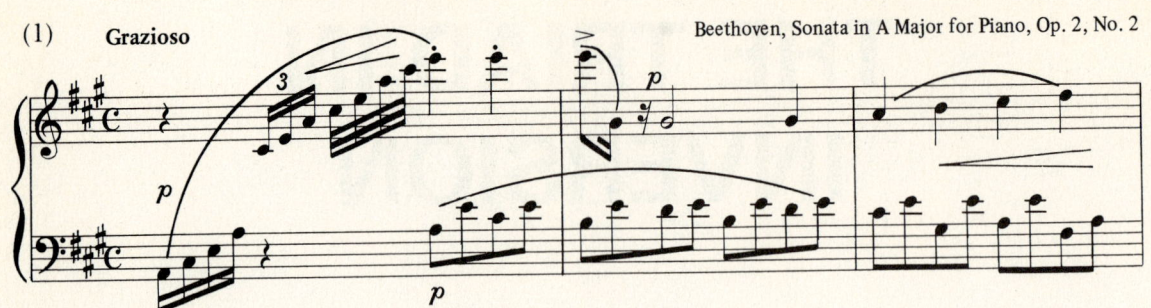

(2) Allegro vivace Mozart, Quartet in E♭ Major, K. 42

(3) Melchior Vulpius, *Jesu Leiden, Pain und Tod* (1603)

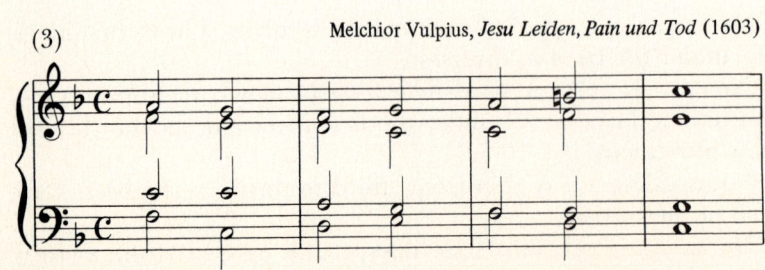

(4) Ziemlich langsam   Schubert, *Die Taubenpost*, D. 957, No. 14

(5)   Bach, *Für Freuden lasst uns springen* (#163)

Good Chris- tians all re- joice ye, With hearts and voic- es
For Christ, in heav'ns full glo- ry, Is now a- mong us

b) Second inversions.

Example No. _____. There are two pedal six–four chords and one passing six–four. Place the triad number, $^6_4$, under each, as well as its name, pedal, or passing.

Example No. _____. There is a single passing V^6_4 chord. Place its symbol below the chord. There are also two passing V^{4}_{3}'s (Chapter 13), spelled the same as the V^6_4, with a seventh added. Indicate each with its symbol. Also find two examples of the cadential six–four, and identify them.

Example No. _____. There are two cadential six–four chords, each with nonharmonic tones on the beat. Circle the nonharmonic tones and identify the six–four chords by their chord number.

(1) Moderato   Haydn, Sonata in E♭ Major, Hob. XVI: 25

B♭:

Assignment 9.2. (*EH*, p. 186). Writing single triads in first inversion. Write each example in two ways: 1) an octave or less between soprano and tenor, and 2) more than an octave between soprano and tenor.

a) Key signature given.

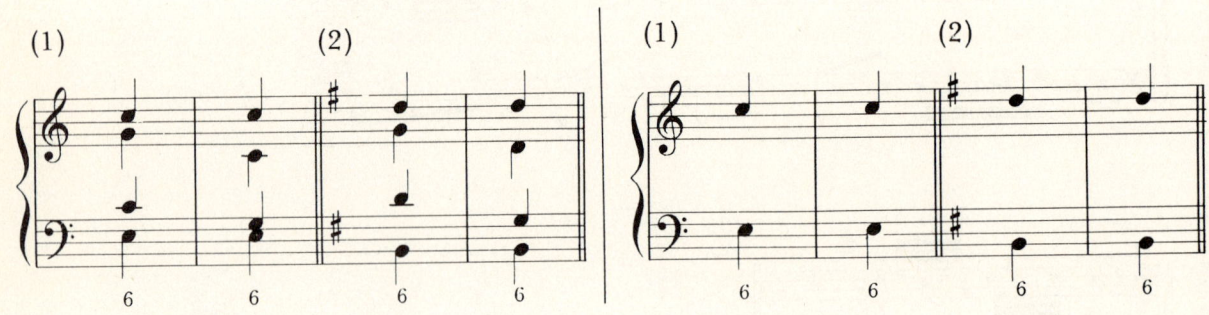

Key signature not given; quality of chord indicated by figured bass.

b) Write single triads in first inversion when bass note only is given. Write each example in each of the three possible soprano positions. Use any correct placement of inner voices.

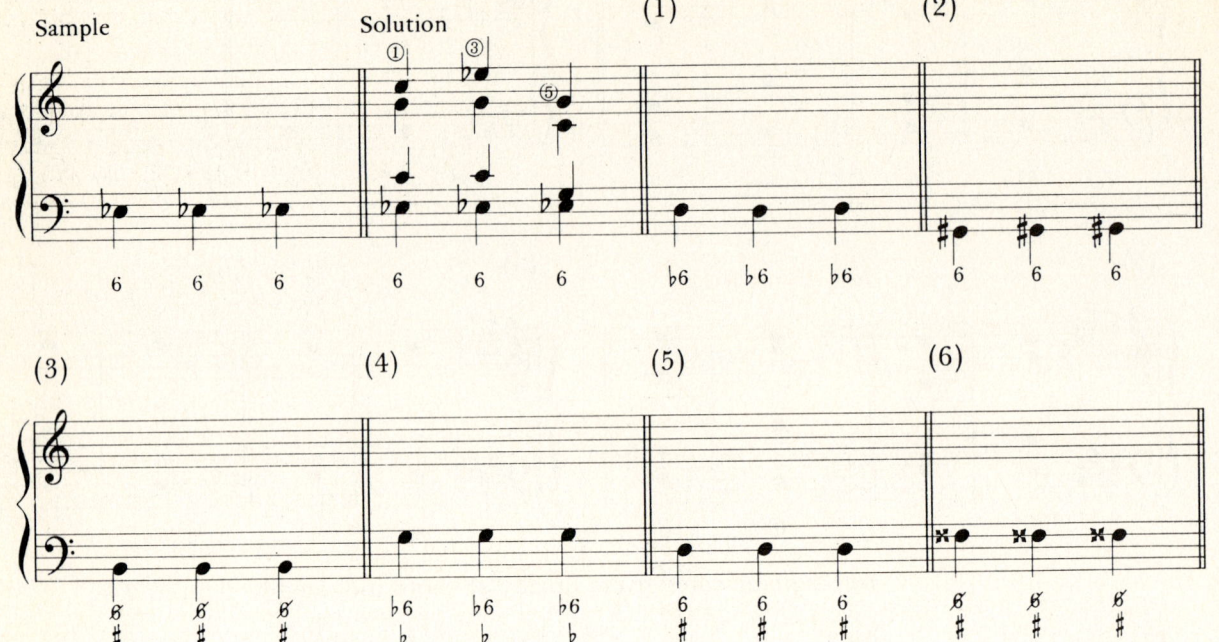

Assignment 9.3. (*EH*, p. 189). Writing triads in first inversion. Write each pair of triads, one triad of which is in first inversion. Place chord numbers below bass notes.

Assignment 9.4. (*EH*, p. 190). Writing successive first inversions. Place chord numbers below staff. The solutions shown use only contrary or oblique motion in approaching and leaving each doubled note, and use the least amount of movement in all voices. If your solution is different, check for 1) parallel octaves or fifths, 2) doubled leading tones, or 3) doubled altered notes.

(3)

(3)

(4)

(4)

(5)

(5)

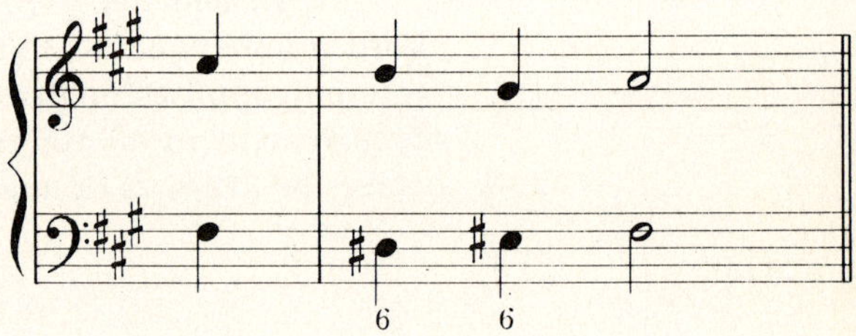

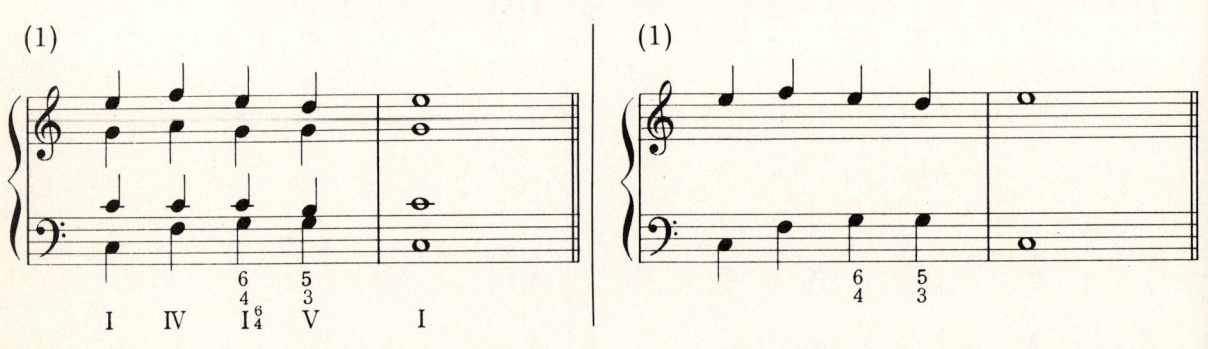

Assignment 9.5. (*EH*, p. 191). Part-writing six-four chords. Fill in inner voices. Make an harmonic analysis. Where space is provided, name the six–four chord illustrated in the musical example.

(1)

(1)

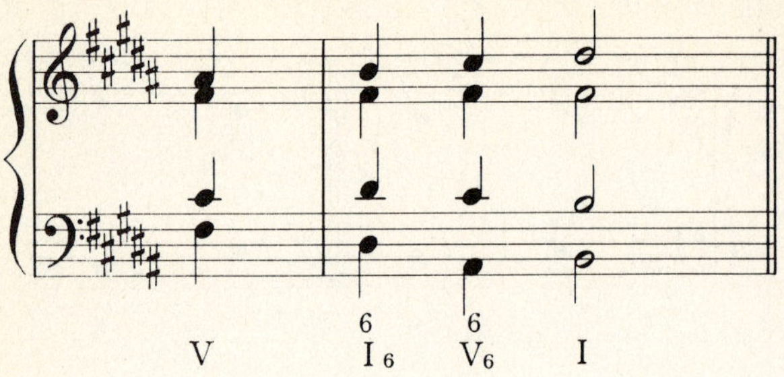

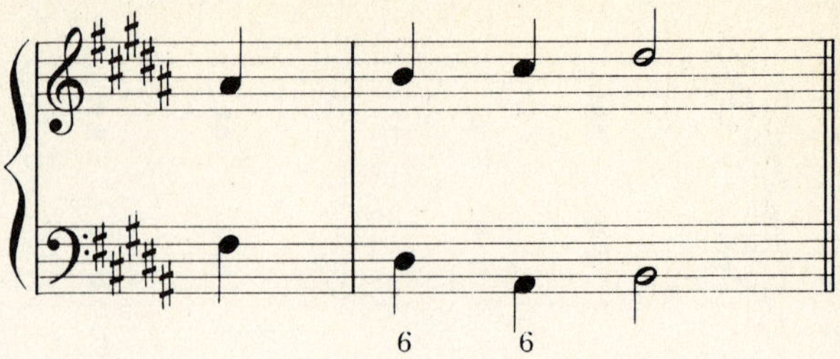

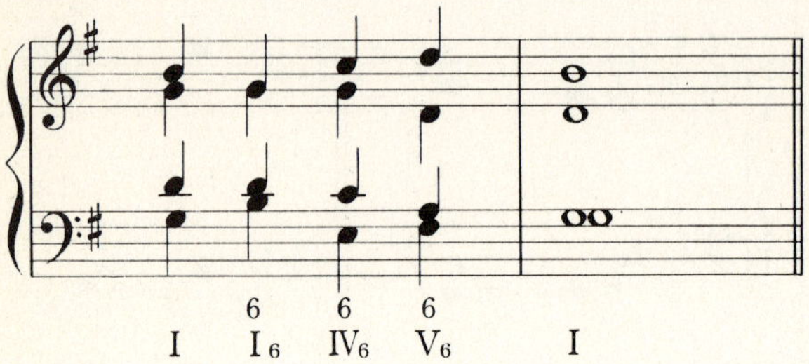

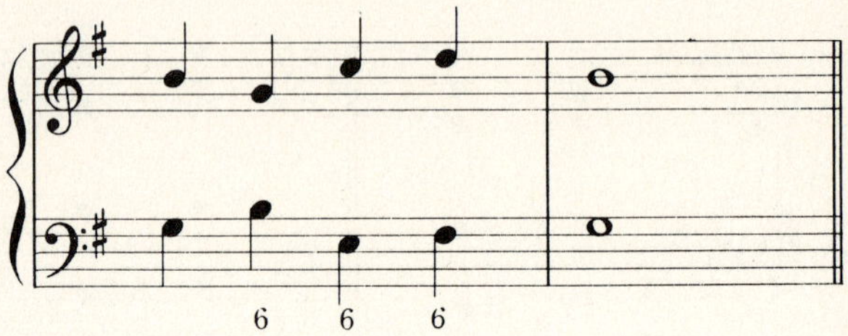

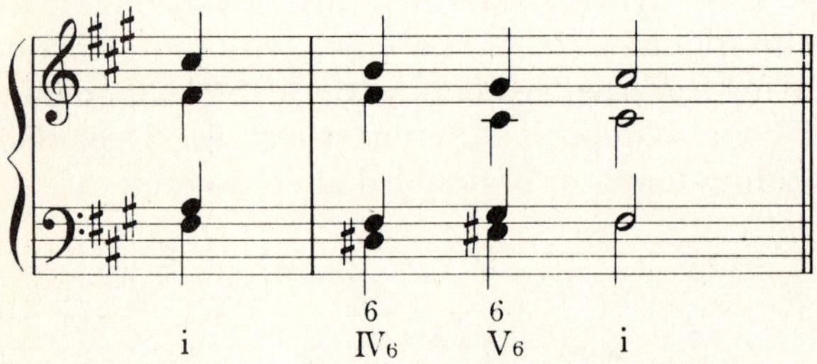

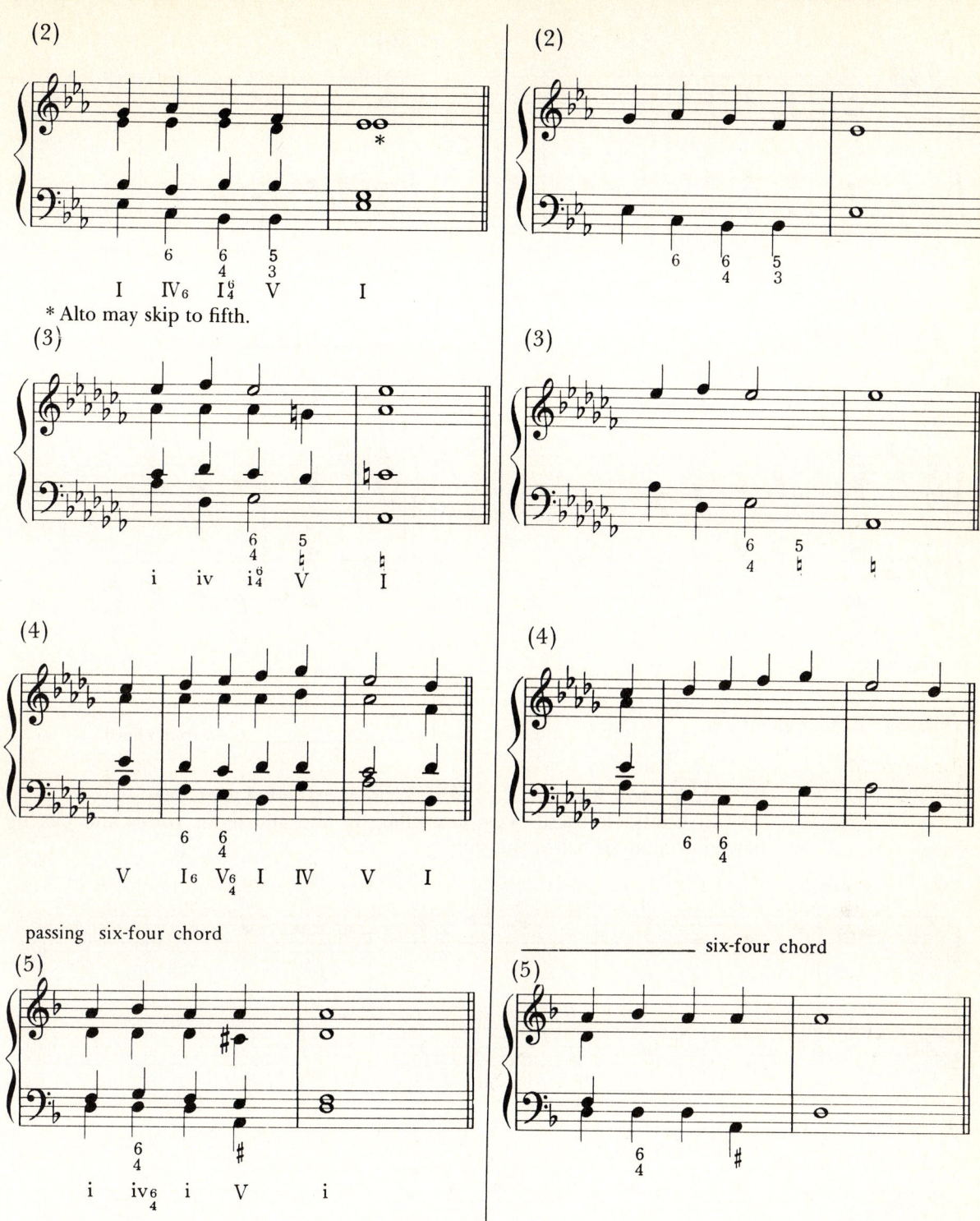

(6)

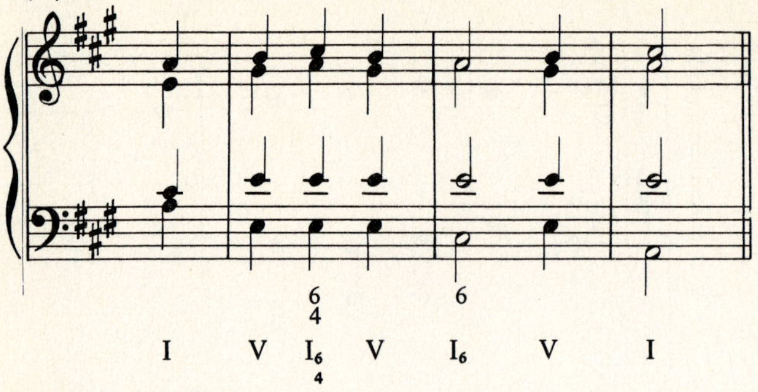

pedal six-four chord

(6)

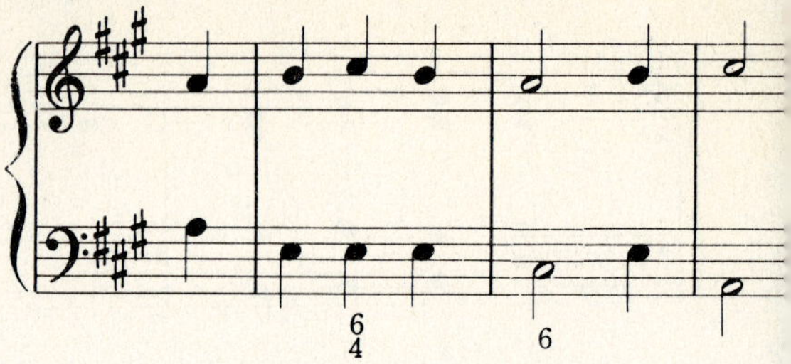

_______________ six-four chord

(7)

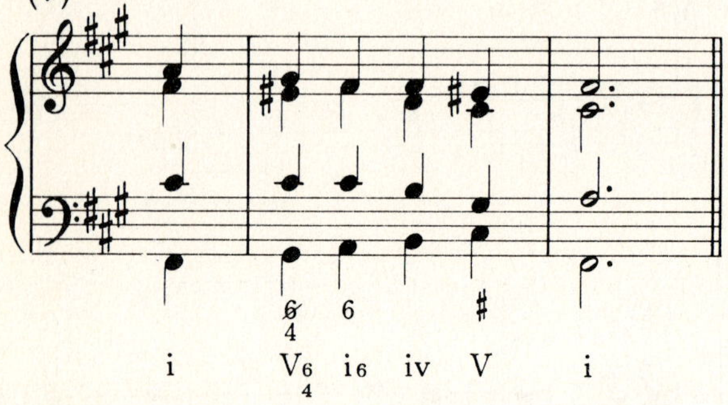

passing six-four chord

(7)

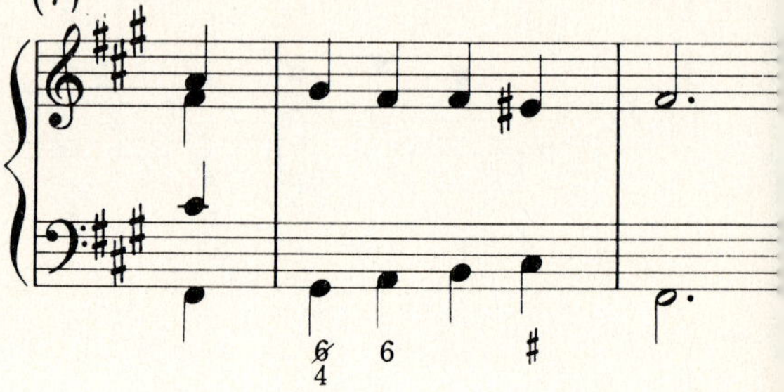

_______________ six-four chord

Assignment 9.6. (*EH*, p. 195). Writing extended exercises.

a) Complete these examples, filling in alto and tenor voices and placing harmonic analysis below the staff.

(1)

(2)

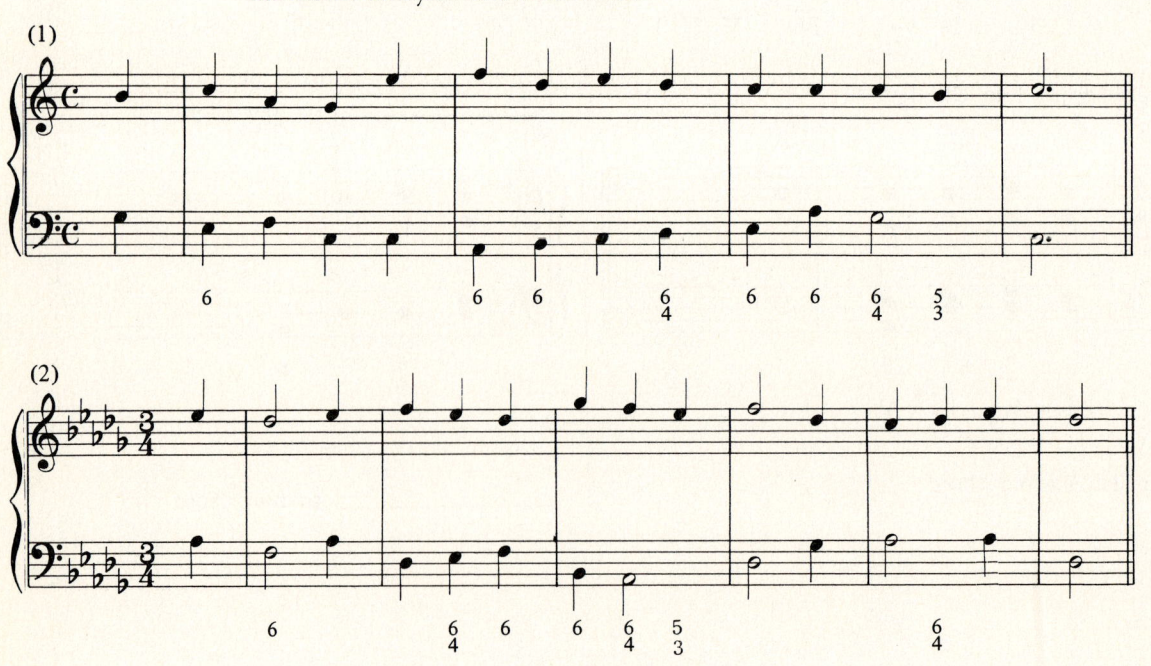

b) Bass only given. Write soprano line and fill in alto and tenor voices. Make an harmonic analysis.

Assignment 9.9. (*EH*, p. 199). Harmonize these melodies, using tonic, dominant, and subdominant triads only. There is ample opportunity to use all of the following. Strive to include at least one example of each.
    (1) first-inversion
    (2) second inversion; cadential, passing, pedal
    (3) IV$_6$—V$_6$ in *both* major and in minor

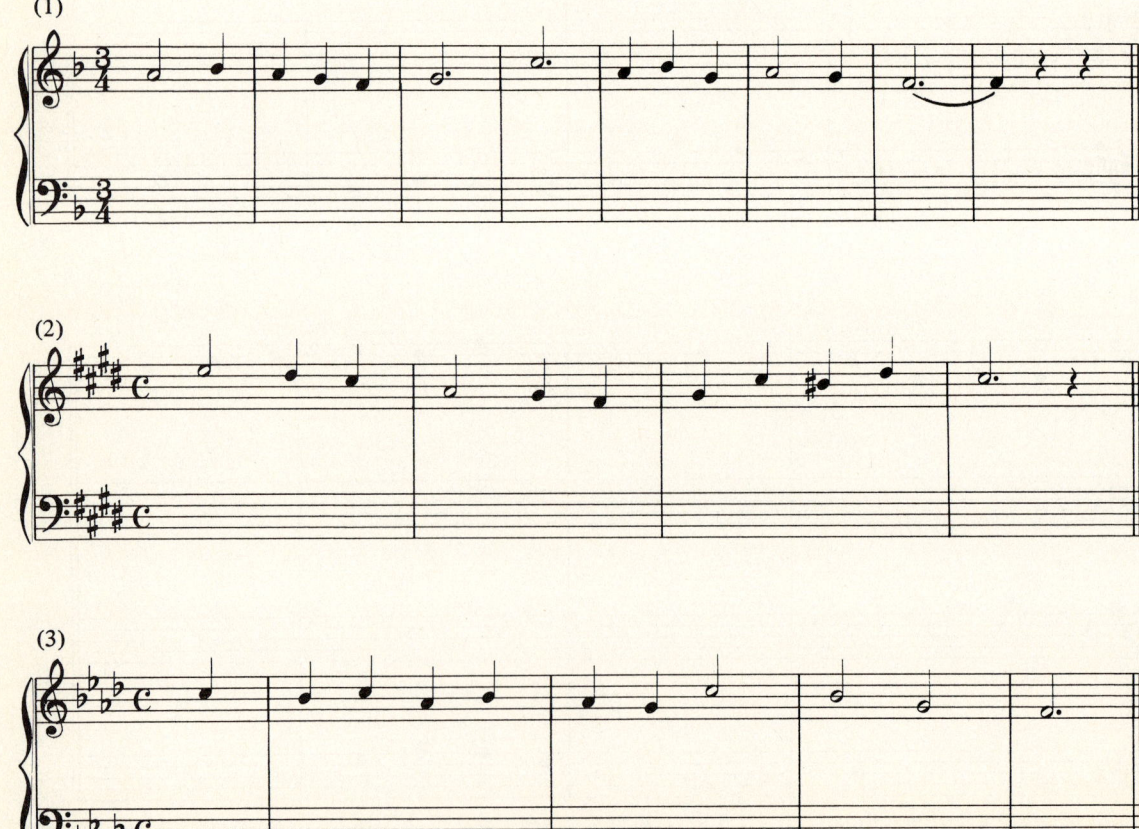

(4)
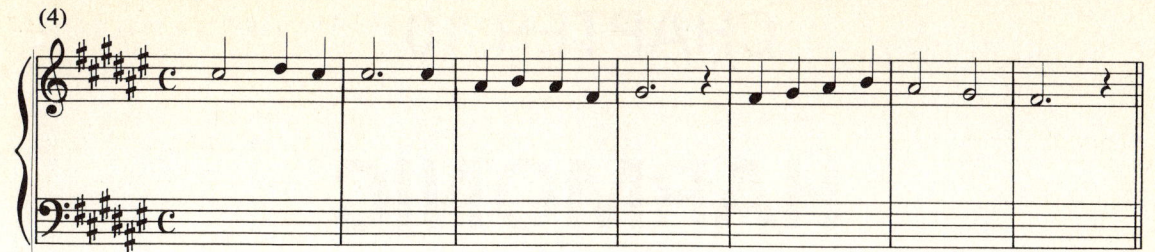

CHAPTER 10

HARMONIC PROGRESSION: Supertonic and Leading Tone Triads

	Elementary Harmony	*Workbook*
Assignment 10.1	216	—
Assignment 10A	—	99
Assignment 10.2	220	99
Assignment 10B	—	100
Assignment 10.3	222	101
Assignment 10.4	223	108
Assignment 10.5	226	—
Assignment 10.6	229	108
Assignment 10C	—	109
Assignment 10.7	232	110
Assignment 10.8	233	113
Assignment 10.9	233	115
Assignment 10.10	234	—
Assignment 10.11	234	115

Assignment 10A. Spelling the diminished triad. Complete the spelling of each of these diminished triads.

1. B D F	2. C♯ E G	1. B __ __	2. C♯ __ __
3. E♯ G♯ B	4. G B♭ D♭	3. E♯ __ __	4. G __ __
5. D♯ F♯ A	6. A C E♭	5. __ F♯ __	6. __ C __
7. E G B♭	8. B♭ D♭ F♭	7. __ G __	8. __ D♭ __
9. D F A♭	10. F𝄪 A♯ C♯	9. __ __ A♭	10. __ __ C♯
11. C E♭ G♭	12. A♯ C♯ E	11. __ __ G♭	12. __ __ E

Assignment 10.2. (*EH*, p. 220). Spelling the supertonic triad.

a) Spell the supertonic (ii) triad in each major key.

D F A	C: D F A
A C E	G: ____
E G B	D: ____
B D F♯	A: ____
F♯ A C♯	E: ____
C♯ E G♯	B: ____
G♯ B D♯	F♯: ____
D♯ F♯ A♯	C♯: ____
G B♭ D	F: ____
C E♭ G	B♭: ____
F A♭ C	E♭: ____
B♭ D♭ F	A♭: ____
E♭ G♭ B♭	D♭: ____
A♭ C♭ E♭	G♭: ____
D♭ F♭ A♭	C♭: ____

b) Spell the supertonic (ii⁰) triad in each minor key.

B D F	A: B D F
F♯ A C	E: ____
C♯ E G	B: ____
G♯ B D	F♯: ____
D♯ F♯ A	C♯: ____
A♯ C♯ E	G♯: ____
E♯ G♯ B	D♯: ____
B♯ D♯ F♯	A♯: ____
E G B♭	D: ____
A C E♭	G: ____
D F A♭	C: ____
G B♭ D♭	F: ____
C E♭ G♭	B♭: ____
F A♭ C♭	E♭: ____
B♭ D♭ F♭	A♭: ____

c) Spell the minor supertonic (ii) triad in each minor key.

B D F♯	A: B D F♯
F♯ A C♯	E: ____
C♯ E G♯	B: ____

G♯ B D♯	F♯: _____
D♯ F♯ A♯	C♯: _____
A♯ C♯ E♯	G♯: _____
E♯ G♯ B♯	D♯: _____
B♯ D♯ F𝄪	A♯: _____
E G B	D: _____
A C E	G: _____
D F A	C: _____
G B♭ D	F: _____
C E♭ G	B♭: _____
F A♭ C	E♭: _____
B♭ D♭ F	A♭: _____

Assignment 10B. Spell various supertonic triads in various keys.

1. ii triad in G major _____
2. ii⁰ triad in B minor _____
3. ii triad in E♭ major _____
4. ii triad in B minor _____
5. ii triad in E major _____
6. ii⁰ triad in E minor _____
7. ii⁰ triad in C♯ minor _____
8. ii triad in A♭ major _____
9. ii triad in F♯ major _____
10. ii⁰ triad in B♭ minor _____
11. ii triad in F♯ minor _____
12. ii⁰ triad in A♭ minor _____
13. ii⁰ triad in G♯ minor _____
14. ii triad in D♭ major _____
15. ii triad in D♯ minor _____

Assignment 10.3. (*EH*, p. 222). Harmonic analysis. Identify chords by Roman numeral and inversion. Circle nonharmonic tones.

(1) Allegro molto

Haydn, Sonata in C Major for Piano, Hob. XVI: 50

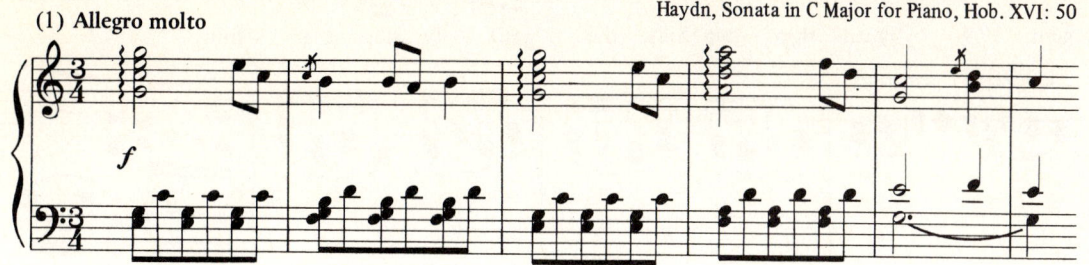

(2)

Chopin, Mazurka, Op.33, No.2

(3)

Haydn, *The Creation*, Hob. XXI:2

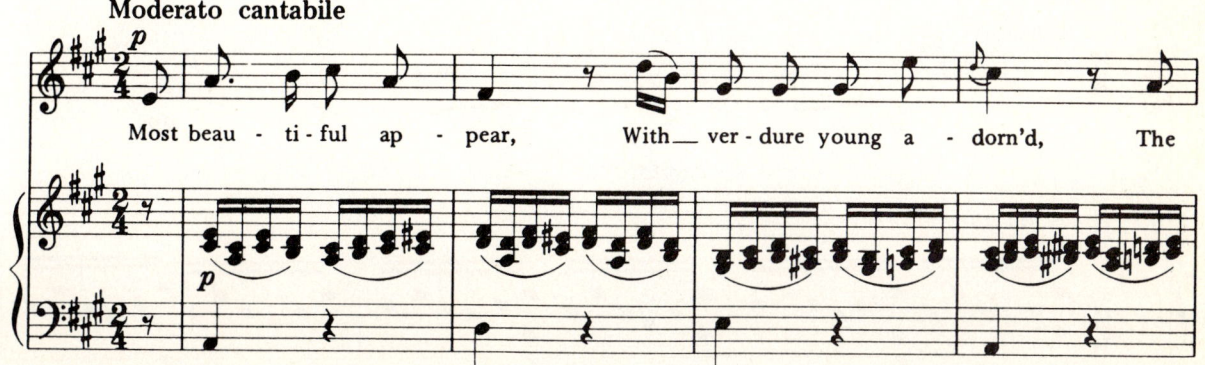

(4) Be sure to check the final cadence to determine the key of this excerpt.

Beethoven, Piano Concerto No. 4, Op. 58

(5) Observe that although the two halves of this excerpt appear different to the eye, actually there is repetition. How does Mozart achieve variety while repeating the same musical idea?

Mozart, Sonata in F Major for Violin and Piano, K.377

(6) In measures 3 and 4, does the note C create a new chord, or does it sound more like a nonharmonic tone to the E minor triad? Listen to the excerpt in tempo before deciding.

Verdi, *Il Trovatore*

Beethoven, Quartet, Op.18, No.2

Mozart, Symphony No.36, "Linz," K.425

(9) At the point in the score from which this excerpt is taken, only these two instruments are playing. From your work in part-writing, you should be able to deduce the implied harmonic structure.

Please do not read the paragraph following this example until you have completed your analysis.

Mozart, Concerto in D Major for Horn and Orchestra, K.412

You have presumably read this music by transposing the horn part and reading the viola part in its clef. But did you notice that the two voices can be read, as written, in the key of C major? Read the horn part as is, without transposing, and read the viola part as though it were in treble clef with no key signature.

Assignment 10.4. (*EH*, p. 223). Spell the vii⁰ triad in each major and minor key. Remember that in minor, vii⁰ is built on the *raised* seventh scale degree (leading tone).

Major keys		*Minor keys*	
C:	B __ __	A:	G♯ __ __
G:	F♯ __ __	E:	D♯ __ __
D:	__ __ __	B:	__ __ __
A:	__ __ __	F♯:	__ __ __
E:	__ __ __	C♯:	__ __ __
B:	__ __ __	G♯:	__ __ __
F♯:	__ __ __	D♯:	__ __ __
C♯:	__ __ __	A♯:	__ __ __
F:	__ __ __	D:	__ __ __
B♭:	__ __ __	G:	__ __ __
E♭:	__ __ __	C:	__ __ __
A♭:	__ __ __	F:	__ __ __
D♭:	__ __ __	B♭:	__ __ __
G♭:	__ __ __	E♭:	__ __ __
C♭:	__ __ __	A♭:	__ __ __

Assignment 10.6. (*EH*, p. 229). Writing the diminished triad. Write each triad in the given position when so indicated. Double the third when root or third is in the soprano; double the fifth an octave lower when the fifth is in the soprano.

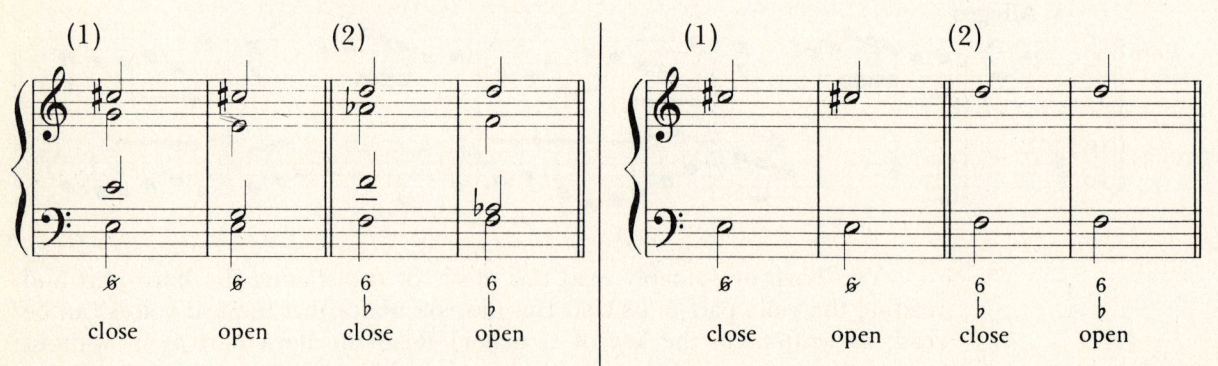

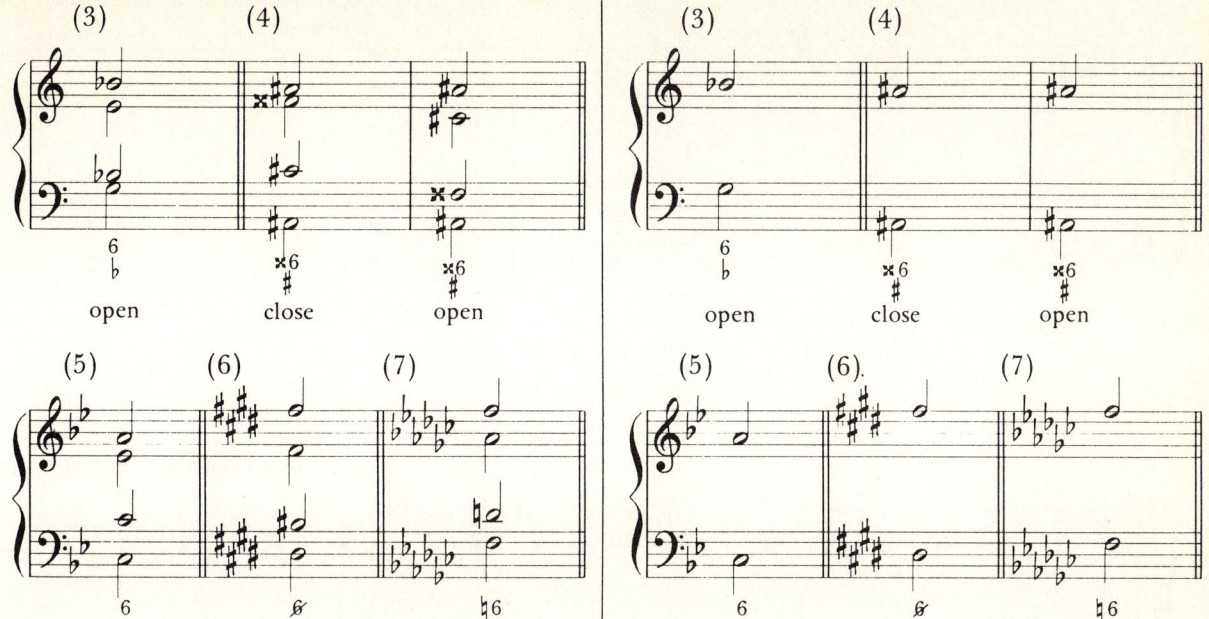

Assignment 10C. Harmonic analysis. Write harmonic analysis below the staff and circle nonharmonic tones. Each displays one of the following uses of vii^0; indicate which below each example.

  a) After the IV triad when the melody ascends (*EH*, Figure 10.17).

  b) The vii$^0_6$, third in the soprano, found between tonic and its first inversion, or reverse (*EH*, Figure 10.16).

  c) The vii$^0_6$, fifth in the soprano ascending, found between tonic and its first inversion (*EH*, Figure 10.25).

  d) The vii$^0_6$, fifth in the soprano descending, found between tonic and its first inversion (*EH*, Figure 10.22).

Bach, *Vater unser im Himmelreich* (#47)

Analysis: Use of vii$^0_6$; circle one: *a, b, c, d*.

Bach, *Herr Jesu Christ, wahr Mensch und Gott* (#284)

Analysis: Use of vii$^0_6$; circle one: *a, b, c, d*.

(3) Bach, *Jesu, Jesu, du bist mein* (#244)

Analysis: Use of vii$^0_6$; circle one: *a, b, c, d.*

(4) Bach, *Das neugeborne Kindelein* (#53)

Analysis: Use of vii$^0_6$; circle one: *a, b, c, d.*

Assignment 10.7. (*EH*, p. 232). Writing supertonic and leading tone triads. Add alto and tenor voices; supply harmonic analysis.

a) ii and ii^0

b) vii⁰–I (i)

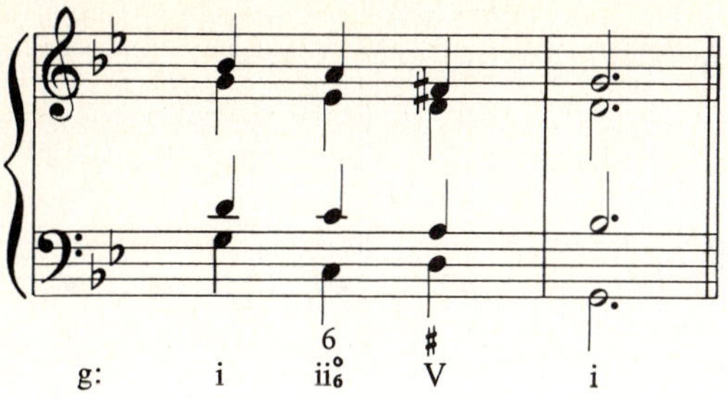

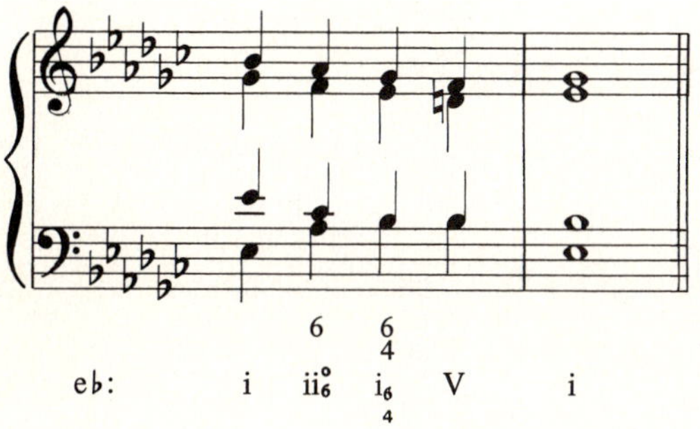

d) ii–vii⁰ (Review *EH*, Figure 10.20, applicable to major and minor keys.)

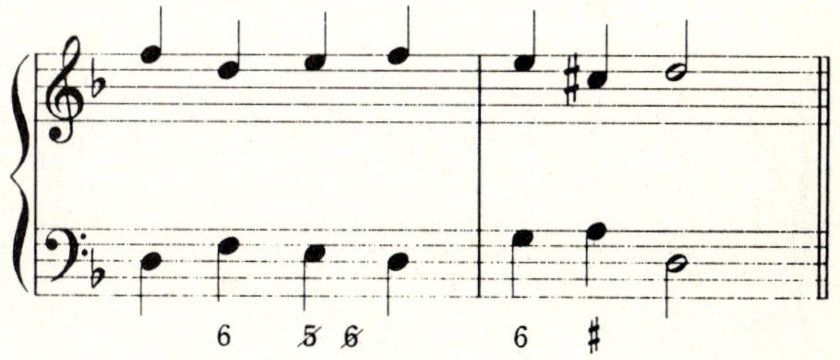

Assignment 10.8. (*EH*, p. 233). Part-writing supertonic and leading tone triads. Fill in inner voices and make an harmonic analysis.

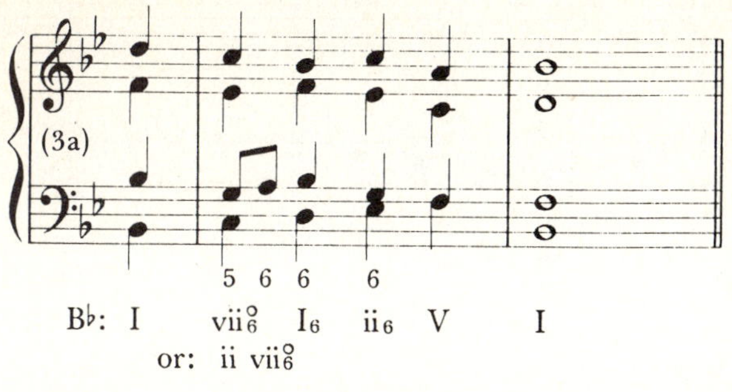

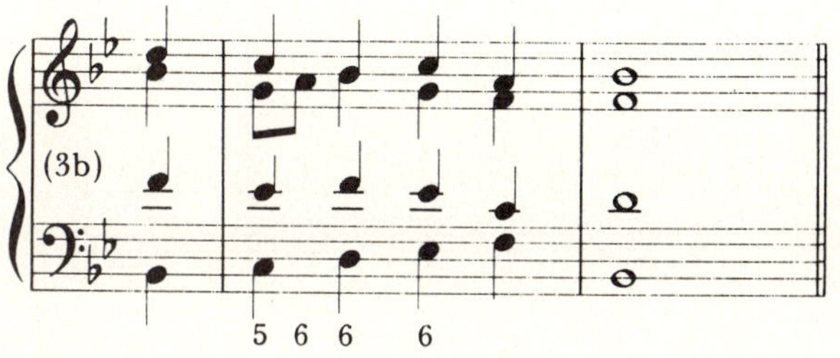

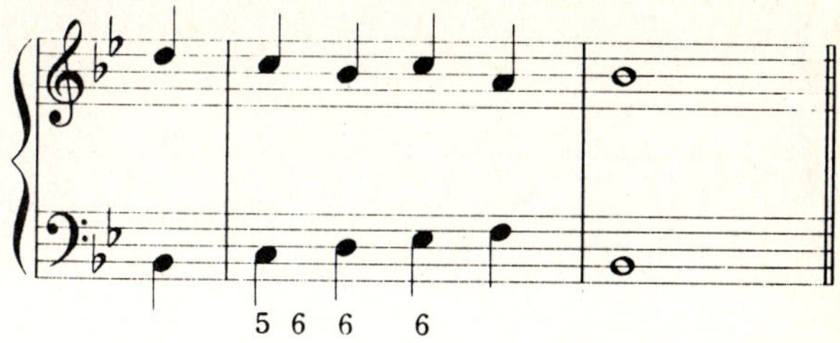

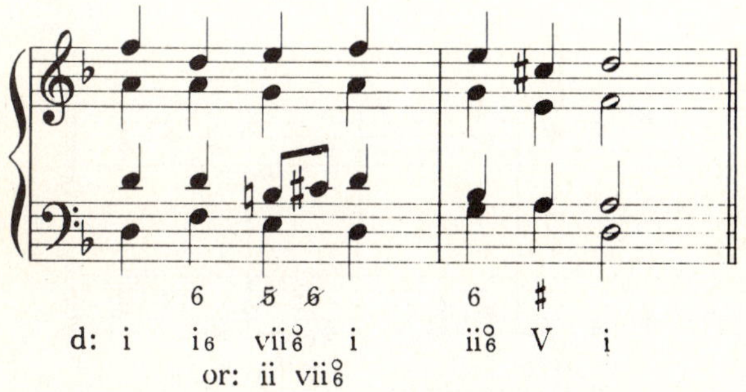

Assignment 10.9. (*EH*, p. 233). Add soprano, alto, and tenor voices when bass line only is given. Make harmonic analysis.

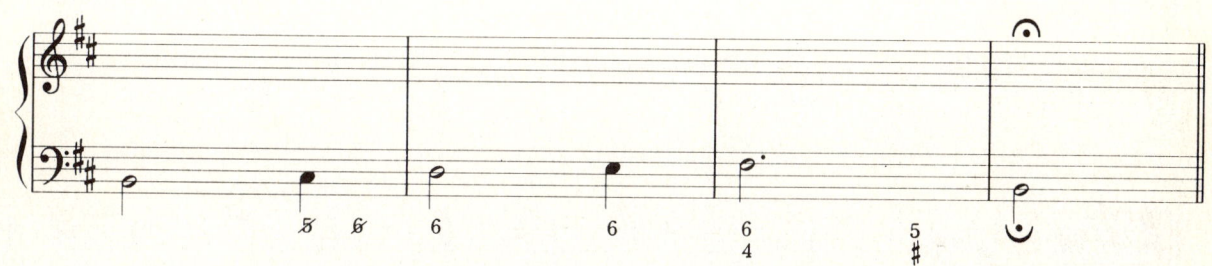

Assignment 10.11. (*EH*, p. 234). Melody harmonization. Harmonize these melodies, using the supertonic and leading tone triads where appropriate. Complete either the *a* version or the *b* version, as assigned. Review procedures for melody harmonization in *EH*, page 130.

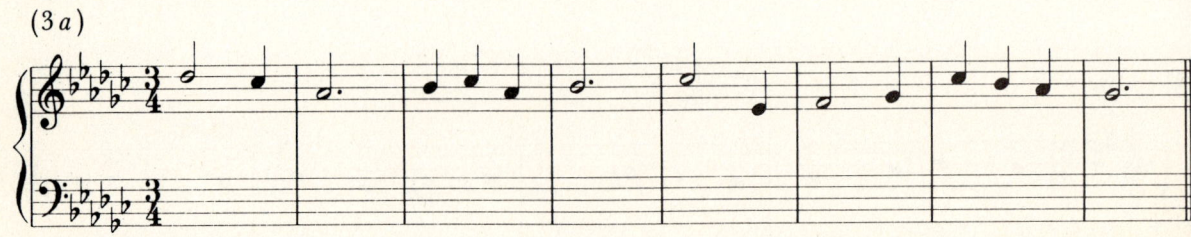

CHAPTER 11

NONHARMONIC TONES I: Passing Tones and Neighbor Tones

	Elementary Harmony	*Workbook*
Assignment 11.1	247	118
Assignment 11.2	250	119
Assignment 11A	—	120
Assignment 11.3	251	121
Assignment 11.4	253	—

Assignment 11.1. (*EH*, p. 247). Analysis. From *Workbook*, Assignment 10.3 (page 101), find various examples of passing and neighbor tones. The example number and measure are given: "(1)–2" means example 1, measure 2. Find the passing or neighbor tone, locate its description in the list of abbreviations, and place its number in the blank space.

	Example and Measure	Answer	*Abbreviations*
1.	(1)–2	_____	1. UPT
2.	(2)–3	_____	2. APT
3.	(2)–5	_____	3. UN
4.	(3)–1	_____	4. LN
5.	(3)–2	_____	5. UPT, chromatic
6.	(3)–4	_____	6. APT, chromatic

	Example and Measure	Answer	Abbreviations
7.	(8)–2	_____	7. UN, chromatic
8.	(8)–9	_____	8. LN, chromatic
9.	(8)–10	_____	9. LN, double, chromatic

Answers:

```
9. 6. 7. 8. 2. 7. 6. 9. 5. 4. 1. 3. 3. 2. 1.
```

Assignment 11.2. (*EH*, p. 250). Writing passing and neighbor tones. These excerpts are phrases from Bach chorales with the nonharmonic tones omitted. Add passing and neighbor tones where effective. An harmonic tone may be moved to the second half of the beat to accommodate an accented nonharmonic tone. Compare your versions with those of Bach, page 120.

Bach, *Lobt Gott ihr Christen allzugleich* (#342)

Bach, *Herr Jesu Christ, du höchstes Gut* (#294)

Bach, *O Welt, ich muss dich lassen* (#117)

Assignment 11A. (*EH*, p. 248). Writing passing and neighbor tones from a figured bass. These short examples provide practice in interpreting a few of the many varieties of figured bass symbols needed in working with nonharmonic tones. Review *EH* at the page number above for specific instructions.

(5)

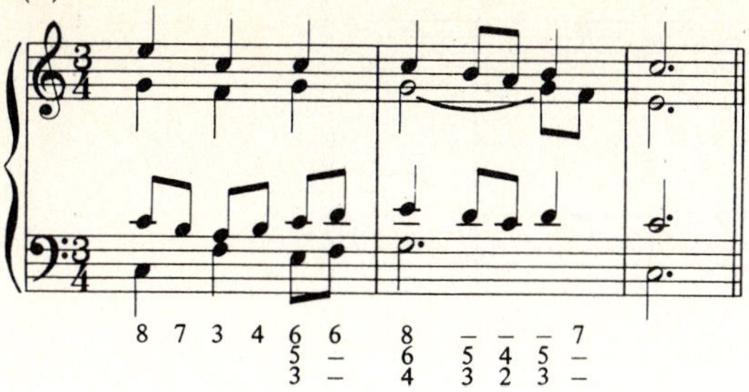

(6)

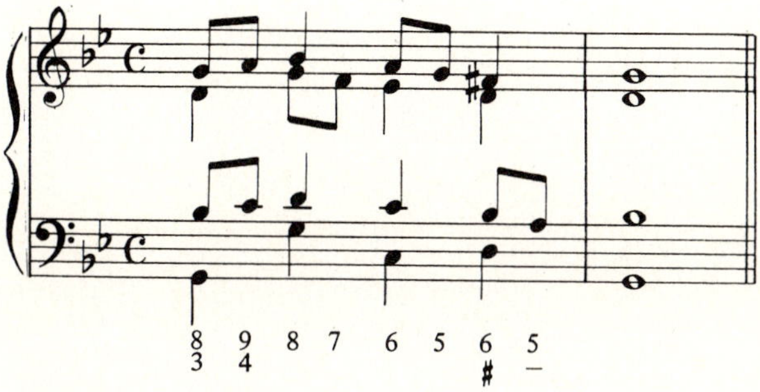

(7)

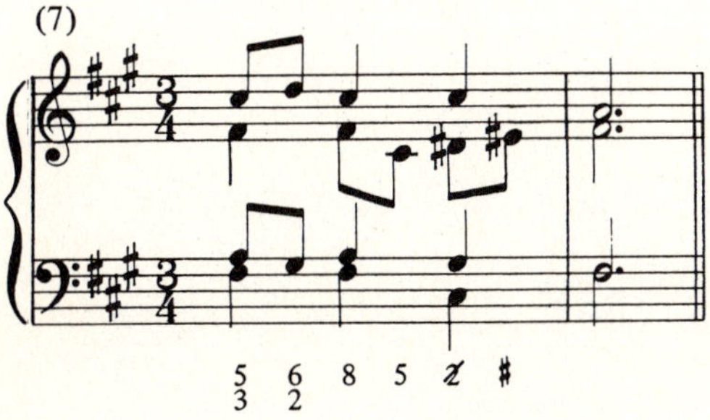

(5)

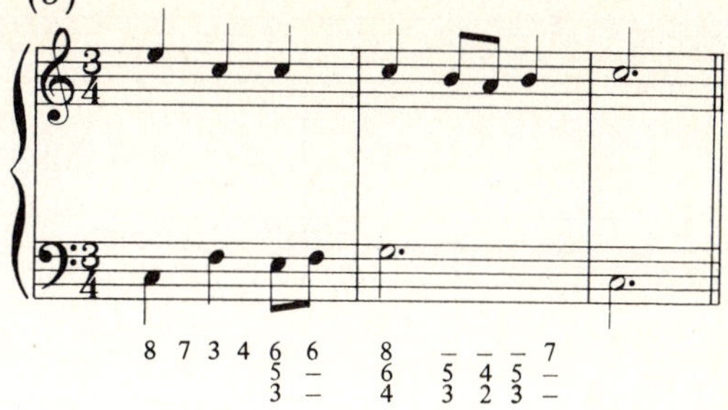

(6)

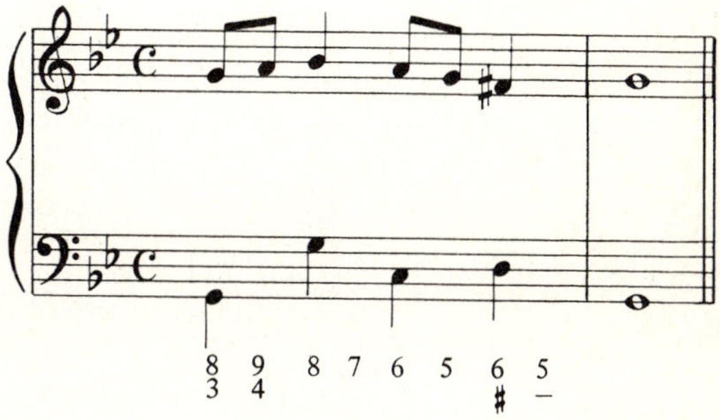

(7)

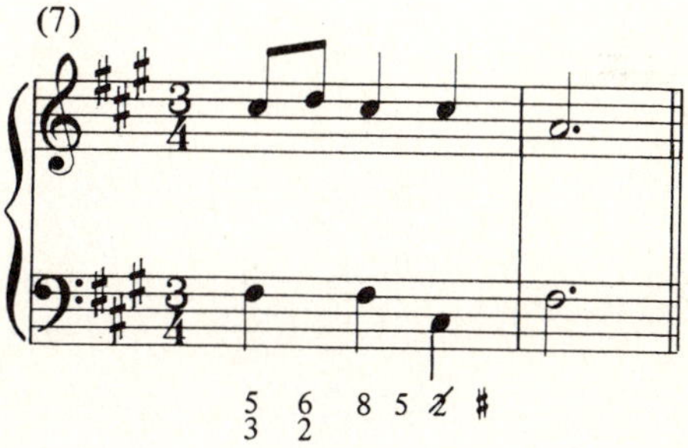

Assignment 11.3. (*EH*, p. 251). Part-writing. Fill in inner voices and make an harmonic analysis.

(1)

(2)

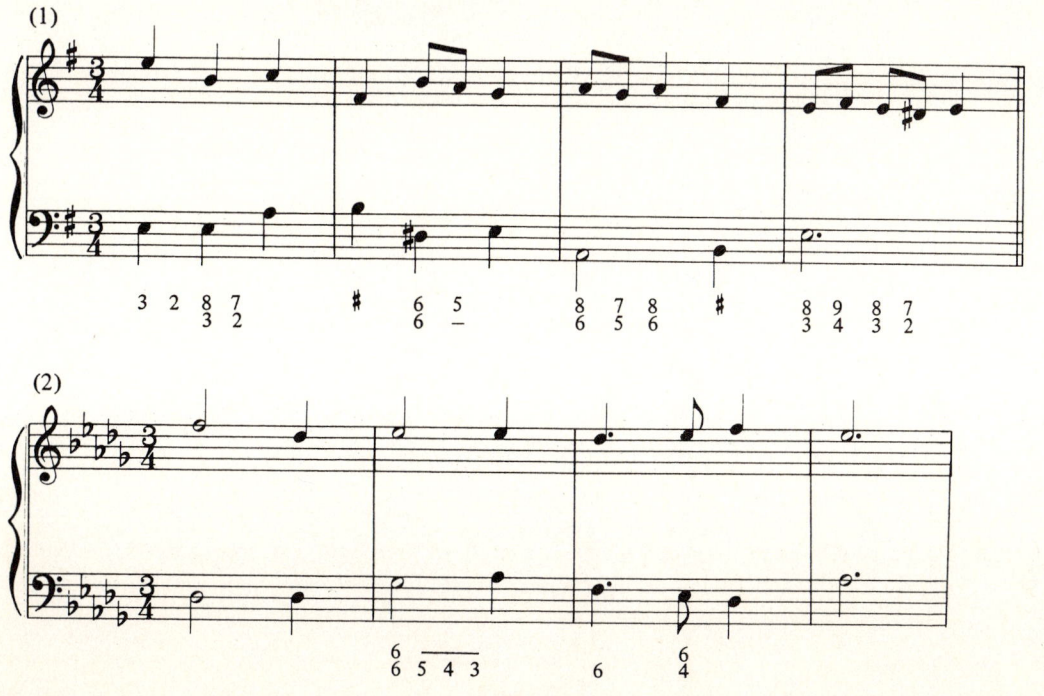

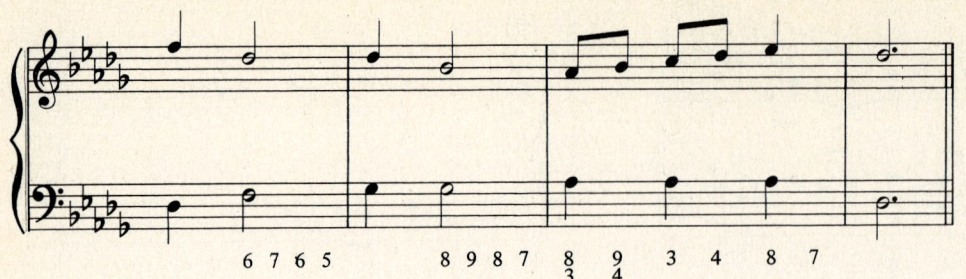

CHAPTER 12

NONHARMONIC TONES II: Suspensions and Other Dissonances

	Elementary Harmony	*Workbook*
Assignment 12A	—	123
Assignment 12.1	262	125
Assignment 12.2	263	125
Assignment 12.3	264	126
Assignment 12.4	264	127
Assignment 12B	—	128
Assignment 12C	—	129
Assignment 12D	—	135
Assignment 12E	—	136

Assignment 12A. Analysis of nonharmonic tones. In each example, one note is nonharmonic. Analyze the three–note figure—note of approach, dissonance, and note of resolution—and compare this melodic figure with those in *EH*, Figure 12.1 (page 258). Circle the NH tone and identify it by name. (Passing and neighbor tones are included.)

1. G in the bass is an unaccented passing tone.
2. F in the soprano is an escaped tone.

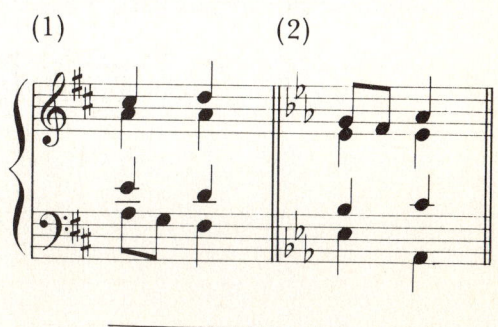

3. F♯ in the alto is a suspension.

4. D in the soprano is an appoggiatura.

(3)   (4)

5. B♭ in the bass is a suspension.

6. C in the soprano is an accented passing tone.

(5)   (6)

7. C♯ in the tenor is an anticipation.

8. A♭ in the soprano is an upper neighboring tone.

(7)   (8)

9. G♯ in the soprano is a retardation.

10. G-E in the alto are changing tones.

(9)   (10)

11. D in the bass is a lower neighboring tone.

12. B in the bass is a pedal point.

Assignment 12.1. (*EH*, p. 262). Analysis. These two excerpts include a total of nine suspensions: 9 8 (3), 7 6 (1), 4 3 (4), and 2 3 (1). Locate each and place its correct figured bass symbol below the bass note (use $^5_2$ for the 2 3 suspension).

Assignment 12.2. (*EH*, p. 263). Writing suspensions. In each example, one voice is missing. Supply that voice so it includes the S indicated by the figured bass.

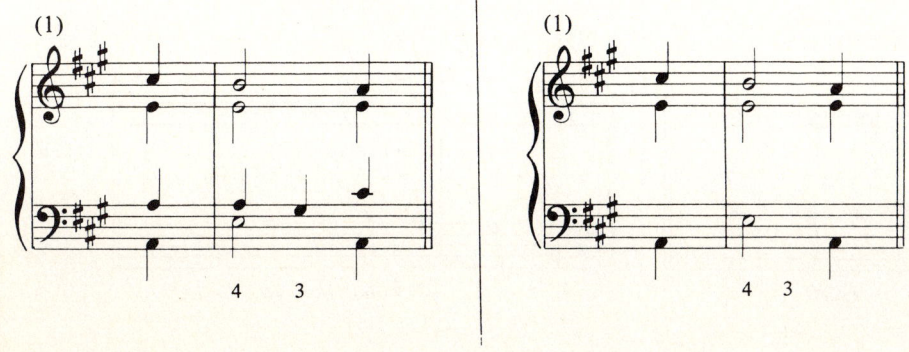

(2)

(2)

(3)

(3)

(4)

(4)

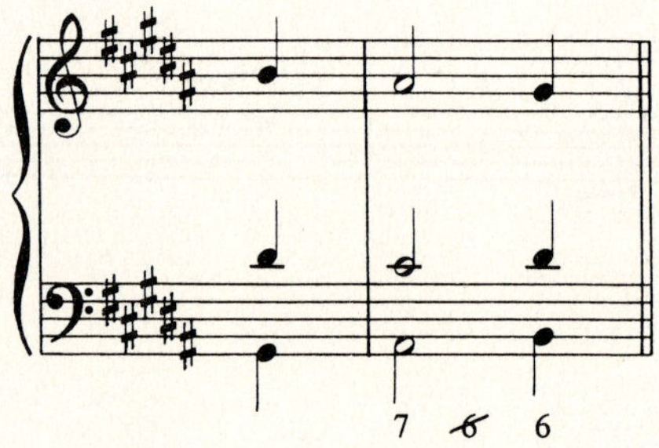

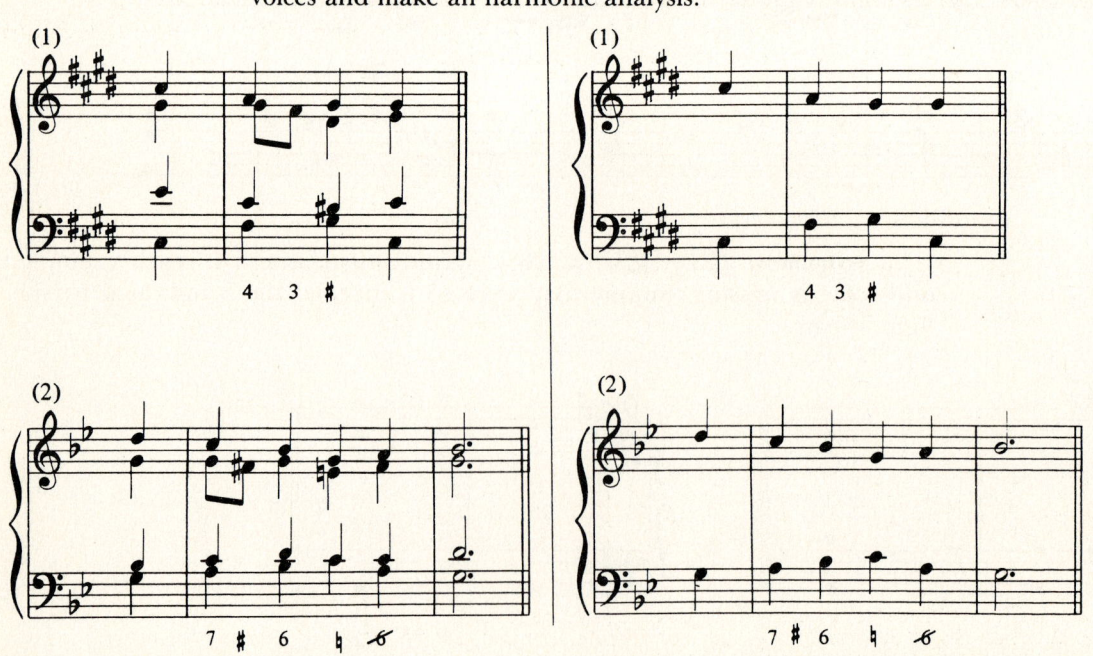

Assignment 12.3. (*EH*, p. 264). Writing suspensions. Fill in alto and tenor voices and make an harmonic analysis.

(1)

(1)

(2)

(2)

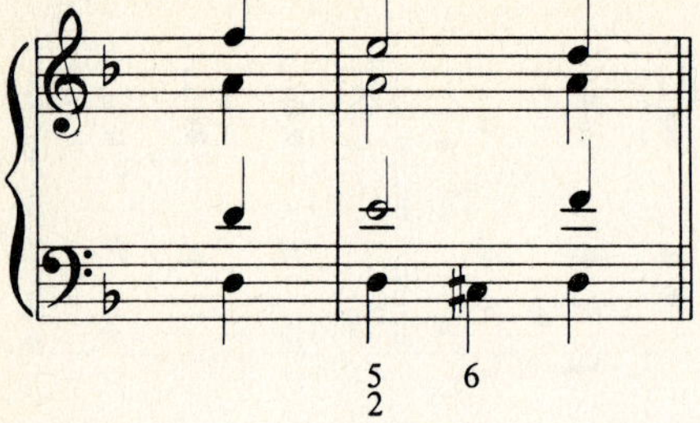

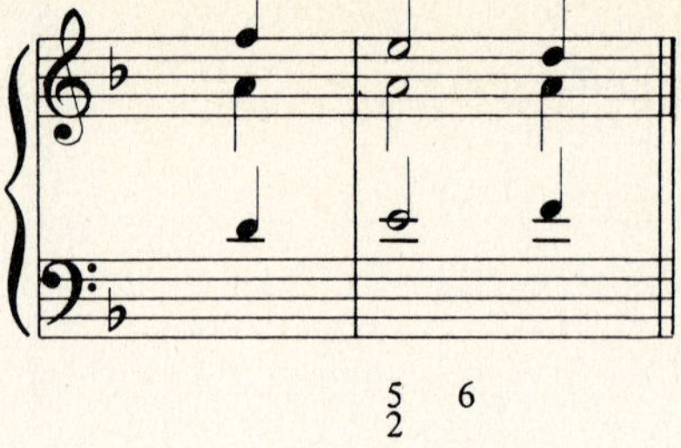

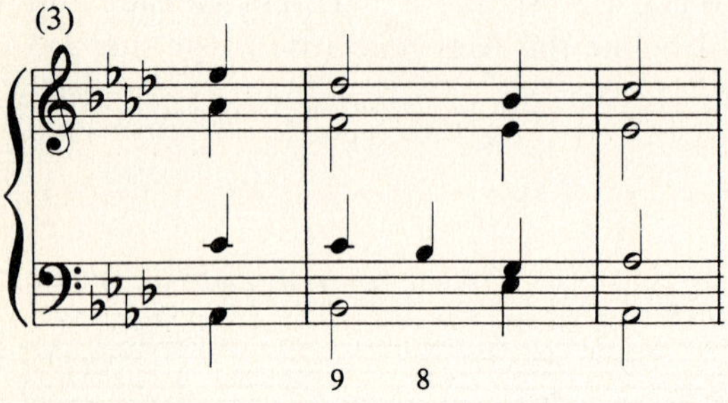

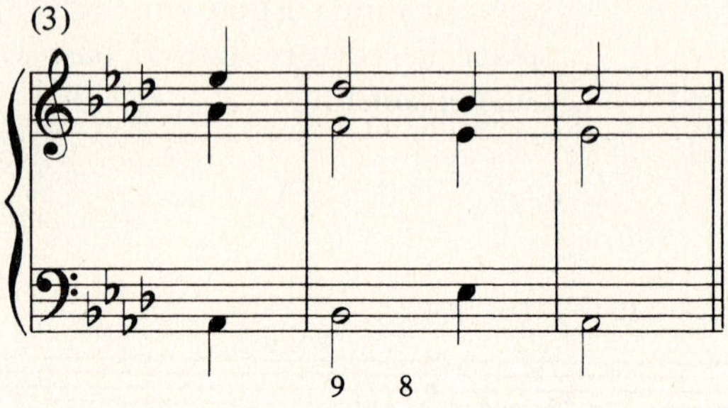

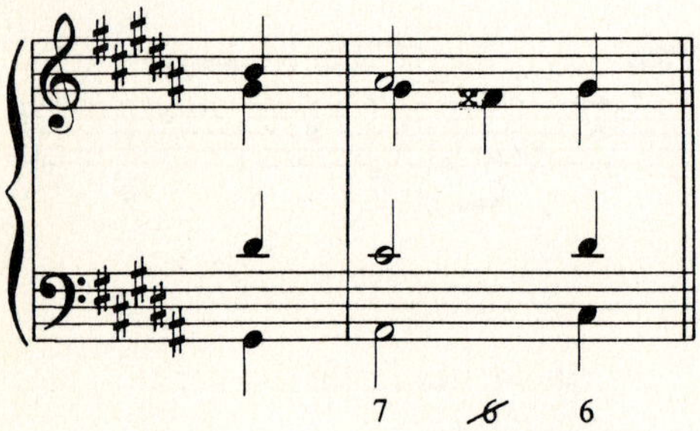

(3)

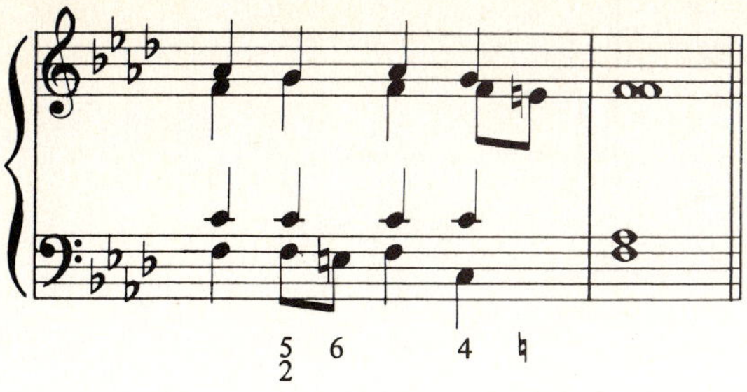

(4)

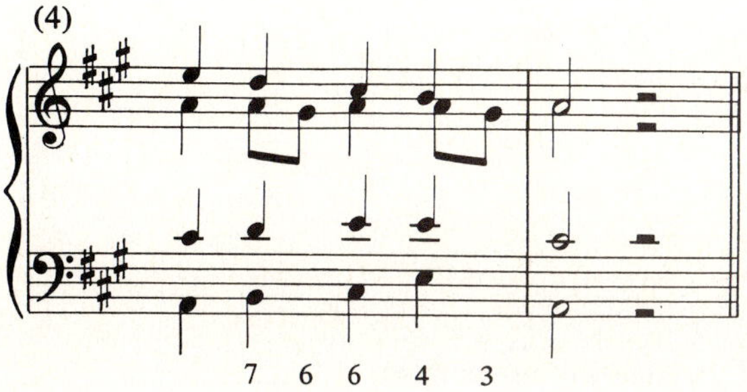

(5)

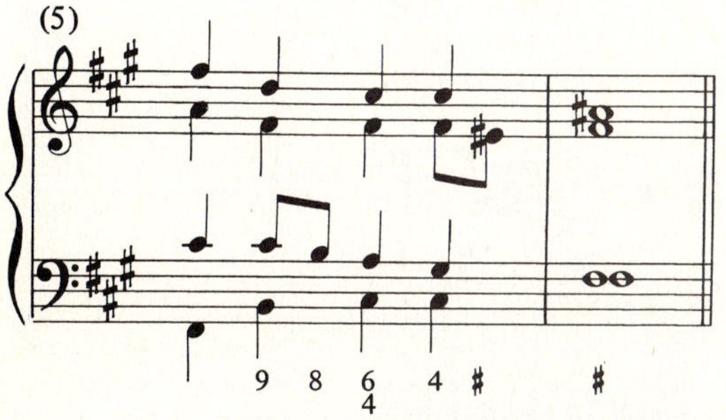

(3)

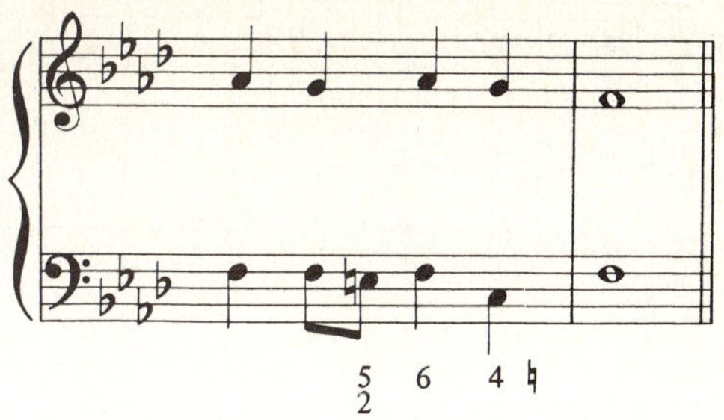

(4)

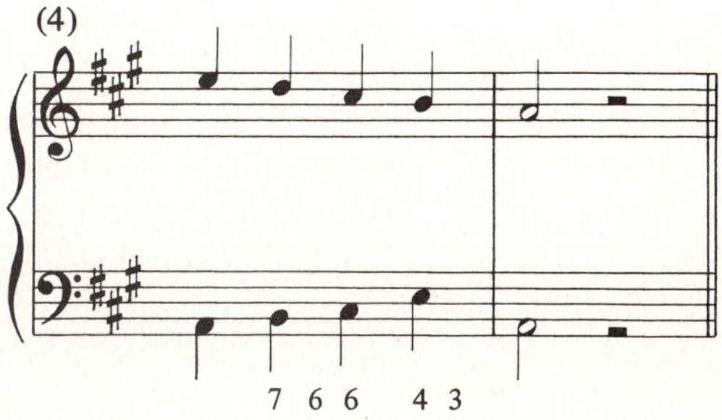

(5)

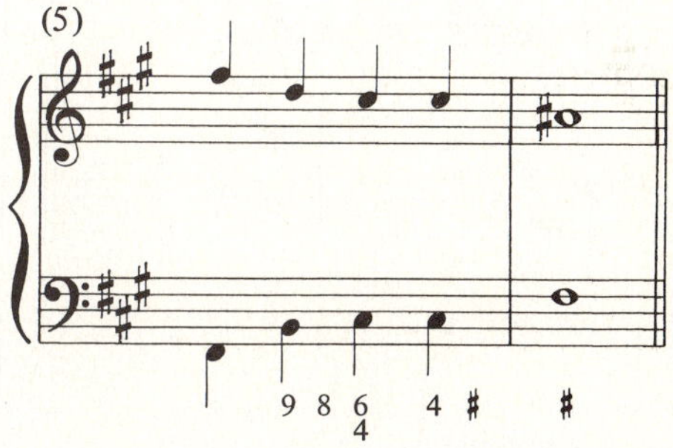

Assignment 12.4. (*EH*, p. 264). Music in four voices is provided. Locate places to add suspensions. In any voice, any tone may be moved to the next weak beat or weak part of the beat to provide a place for the suspended note. Passing and neighbor tones also may be added.

(1)

(2)

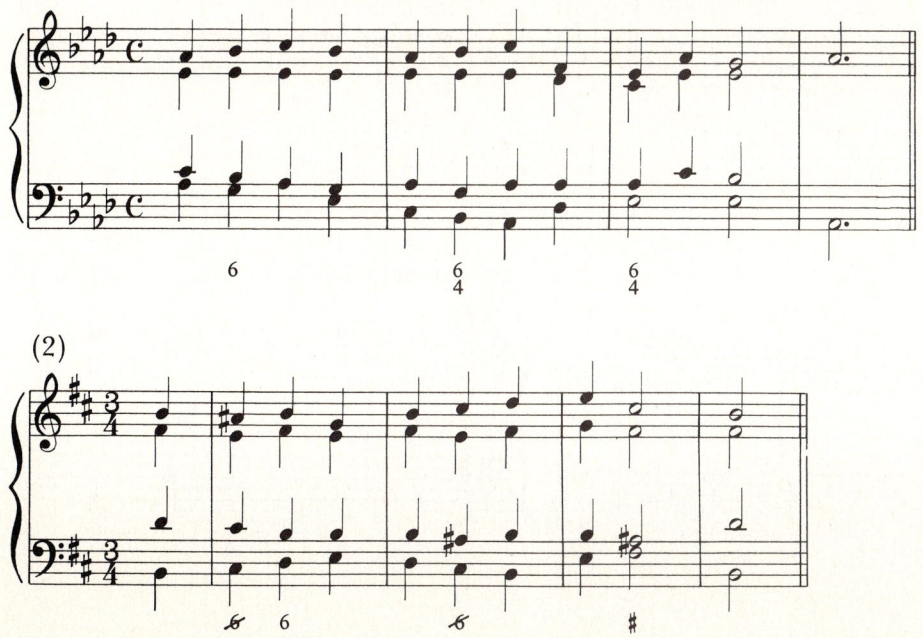

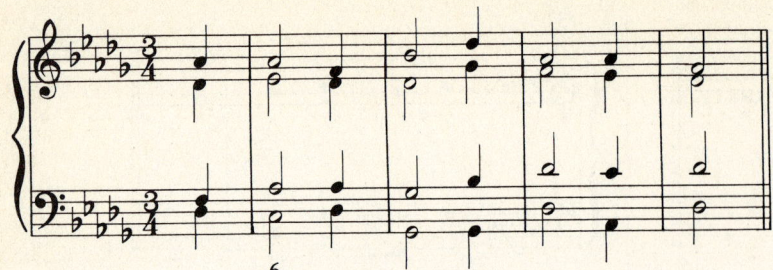

Assignment 12B. Part-writing. Each example features one of the "special uses" of the S (see *EH*, p. 265–269). Fill in inner voices and indicate the special use by its number from this list. Add harmonic analysis.
  (1) Change of bass note as S resolves
  (2) Ornamental resolution of S
  (3) S in the six-four chord
  (4) Double suspension
  (5) Chain suspension

(1) Example of use number 1.

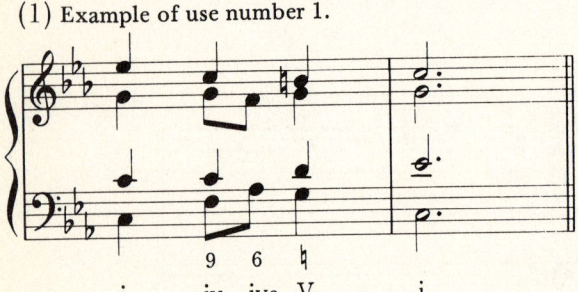

(1) Example of use number _____

(2) Example of use number 3.

(2) Example of use number _____

(3) Example of use number 5.

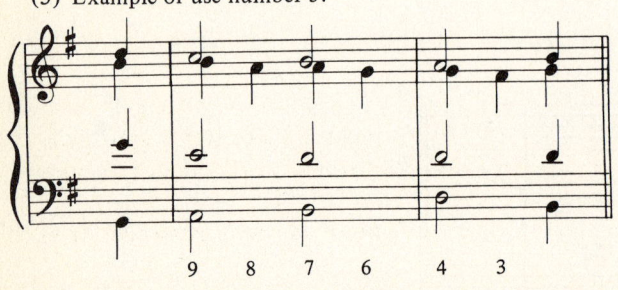

(3) Example of use number _____.

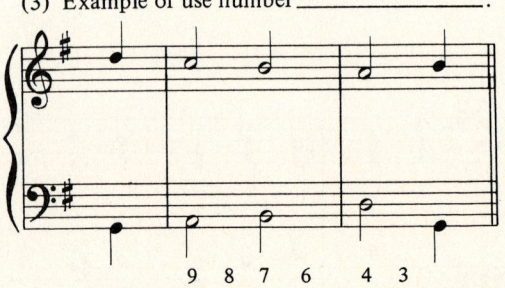

Assignment 12C. Analysis. These excerpts include examples of nonharmonic tones other than the passing and neighbor tones, and the suspension. Each features a specific nonharmonic device.

(1) This excerpt includes five examples of one of the nonharmonic tones other than a passing tone.

Schubert, Ländler, No. 14, Op. 18

(2) The nonharmonic tone featured here appears twice as the high point of a repeated melodic line. Bracket each of the occurrences of this melody, and circle and identify the nonharmonic tone of each.

Schumann, *Kinderszenen*, Op. 15, "Glückes genug"

(3) The opening four-note figure appears four times in this excerpt. Three of them can be accounted for by the same nonharmonic device, while the other requires a different analysis. Can you explain why?

Bach, *Orgelbüchlein*, "Christ lag in Todesbanden," BWV 636

(4) The cadence is the most common location of this nonharmonic tone, as at *a*. Example *b* shows a different location. Circle each of these, and spell the chord with which each is found. Also, locate an APP in one of the excerpts.

a) Bach, *Keinen hat Gott verlassen* (#129)

b) Bach, *Herzliebster Jesu* (#59)

(5) Analyze the harmony and nonharmonic tones beginning at the i_6 given in the example.

Bach, Prelude and Fugue in E Minor, BWV 533

e: i_6

(6) The long-held *pedal* in this example is obvious (in the symphony it continues for another seven measures). Many different chord spellings are found above it. You are asked to spell some of these: the *first chord* in each measure listed below. Be sure to take into consideration the C clef and the transpositions.

Measure 225 _____

Measure 226 _____

Measure 229 _____

Measure 230 _____

Measure 232 _____

Measure 236 _____

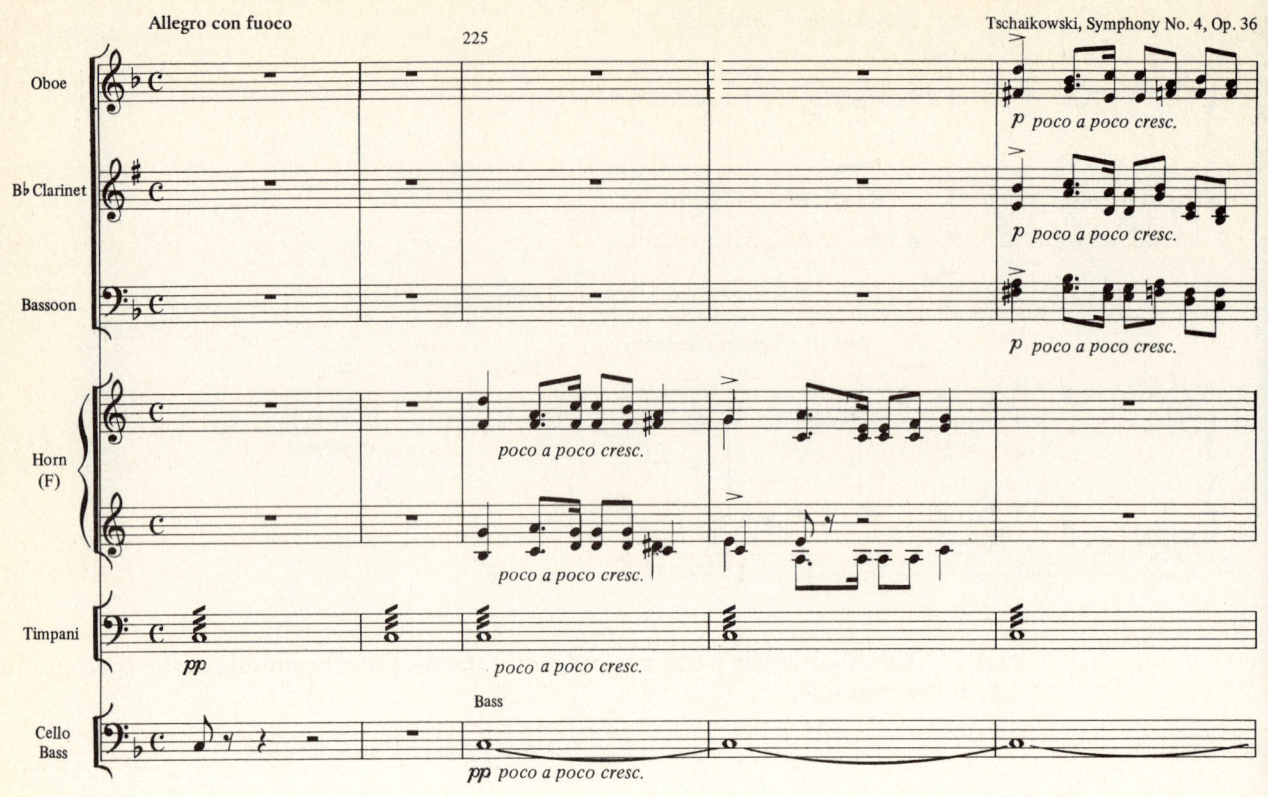

(7) The *pedal* is found here in two upper voices. One is interrupted by rests, the other occurs in arpeggiation. Spell each chord, noting that the pedal tone may or may not be a part of that chord.

Schumann, *Dichterliebe,* Op. 48, "Ein Jüngling liebt ein Mädchen"

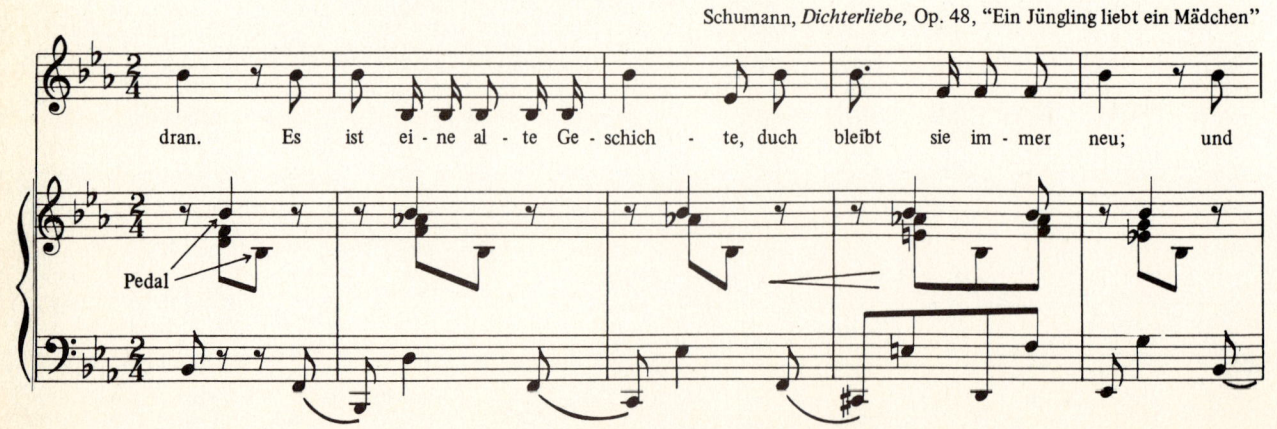

Assignment 12D. Writing anticipations, escaped tones, and appoggiaturas. Fill in inner voices. Make an harmonic analysis. Circle and identify each nonharmonic tone.

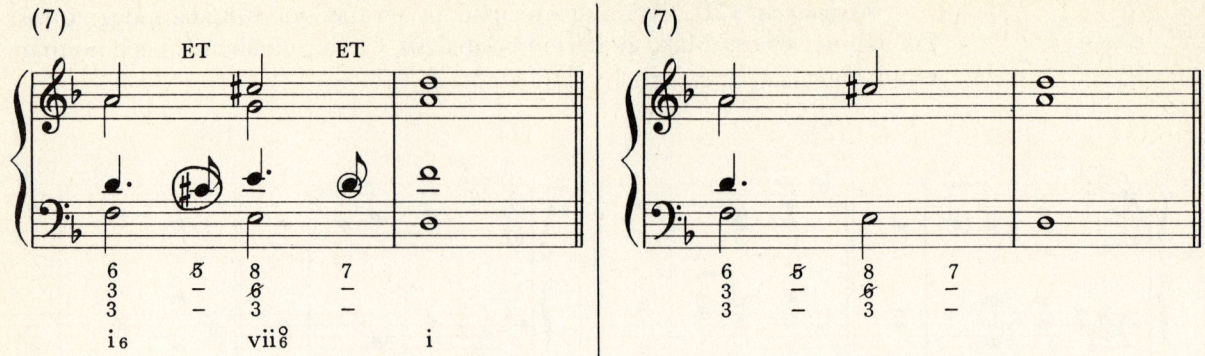

Assignment 12E. Analysis of harmonic tones. These four excerpts illustrate those uses of nonharmonic tones described in *EH*, pages 278–283. Analyze the harmony and all the nonharmonic tones. In the following list, place in each blank the number of the example illustrating that usage.

    a. Successive nonharmonic tones _____
    b. Simultaneous different nonharmonic tones _____
    c. Unprepared nonharmonic tone _____
    d. "Consonant" nonharmonic tone _____

Schubert, Waltz, D. 365, No. 12

(3) Larghetto   Chopin, Nocturne, Op. 15, No. 2

(4) Allegro   Haydn, Sonata in E♭ Major for Piano, Hob. XVI: 20

CHAPTER 13

THE DOMINANT SEVENTH AND SUPERTONIC SEVENTH CHORDS

	Elementary Harmony	*Workbook*
Assignment 13A	—	138
Assignment 13.1	293	139
Assignment 13.2	293	140
Assignment 13.3	295	144
Assignment 13.4	296	145
Assignment 13.5	297	146
Assignment 13.6	298	148
Assignment 13B	—	149
Assignment 13.7	299	149
Assignment 13C	—	150
Assignment 13D	—	150
Assignment 13.8	300	—
Assignment 13.9	301	151

Assignment 13A. Analysis of V^7 chords. You have already analyzed many V^7 chords, recognizing them by their spellings. In this assignment, you are asked to look at some previous assignments from this *Workbook*, and identify the **V⁷** chords by their nonharmonic tone derivations, as shown in *EH*, Figure 13.1.

Check the **V⁷**'s note of approach and note of resolution in the examples listed below, placing in the blank space one of these abbreviations to represent the three-note nonharmonic tone figure:

App—appoggiatura
UN—neighbor tone
PT—passing tone
S—suspension

Page 25 Assignment 4.8(3)   measure 5 _____

Page 27 Assignment 4.9(1)   measure 3 _____

Page 28 Assignment 4.9(5)   measure 3 _____

Page 58 Assignment 6.4(3)   measure 6 _____

Page 59 Assignment 6.4(4)   measure 1 _____

Page 101 Assignment 10.3(1)   measure 2 _____

Page 105 Assignment 10.3(8)   measure 2 _____

Page 136 Assignment 12E(1)   measure 2 _____

Assignment 13.1. (*EH*, p. 293). Spell the supertonic seventh chord in each major and minor key in the circle of fifths.
  a) Answers given.

	Major (ii⁷)	Minor (ii⌀⁷)		Major (ii⁷)	Minor (ii⌀⁷)
C	D F A C	D F A♭ C	C	__ __ __ __	__ __ __ __
G	A C E G	A C E♭ G	G	__ __ __ __	__ __ __ __
D	E G B D	E G B♭ D	D	__ __ __ __	__ __ __ __
A	B D F♯ A	B D F A	A	__ __ __ __	__ __ __ __
E	F♯ A C♯ E	F♯ A C E	E	__ __ __ __	__ __ __ __
B	C♯ E G♯ B	C♯ E G B	B	__ __ __ __	__ __ __ __
F♯	G♯ B D♯ F♯	G♯ B D F♯	F♯	__ __ __ __	__ __ __ __
C♯	D♯ F♯ A♯ C♯	D♯ F♯ A C♯	C♯	__ __ __ __	__ __ __ __
G♯	---------	A♯ C♯ E G♯	G♯		__ __ __ __
D♯	---------	E♯ G♯ B D♯	D♯		__ __ __ __
A♯	---------	B♯ D♯ F♯ A♯	A♯		__ __ __ __
F	G B♭ D F	G B♭ D♭ F	F	__ __ __ __	__ __ __ __
B♭	C E♭ G B♭	C E♭ G♭ B♭	B♭	__ __ __ __	__ __ __ __

	Major (ii^7)	Minor (ii^{ø7})		Major (ii^7)	Minor (ii^{ø7})
E♭	F A♭ C E♭	F A♭ C♭ E♭	E♭	— — — —	— — — —
A♭	B♭ D♭ F A♭	B♭ D♭ F♭ A♭	A♭	— — — —	— — — —
D♭	E♭ G♭ B♭ D♭	----------	D♭	— — — —	----------
G♭	A♭ C♭ E♭ G♭	----------	G♭	— — — —	----------
C♭	D♭ F♭ A♭ C♭	----------	C♭	— — — —	----------

b) No answers given.

D major — — — —	G minor — — — —	
F♯ minor — — — —	B♭ major — — — —	
B♭ minor — — — —	C♭ major — — — —	
G major — — — —	C minor — — — —	
B major — — — —	G♯ minor — — — —	
D♭ major — — — —	A major — — — —	
E minor — — — —	A♯ minor — — — —	
C♯ minor — — — —	A♭ minor — — — —	
A♭ major — — — —	F major — — — —	
D minor — — — —	E♭ major — — — —	
E♭ minor — — — —	B minor — — — —	
C♯ major — — — —	F♯ major — — — —	
G♭ major — — — —	C major — — — —	
F minor — — — —	A minor — — — —	
D♯ minor — — — —	E major — — — —	

Assignment 13.2. (*EH*, p. 293). Analysis of supertonic seventh chords. Analyze all chords and nonharmonic tones in these examples. Describe the three–note nonharmonic tone figure for each supertonic seventh cord.

(1) The ii^7 in the first phrase is unadorned and obvious. But what about the same sonority in the second phrase? Is the progression I$_6$–ii^7–I, or might it be I$_6$–V$^4_3$–I, or even both, one chord for each eighth note? There is no "correct" answer—only what seems best to you!

(1) Bach, *Du grosser Schmerzensmann* (#167)

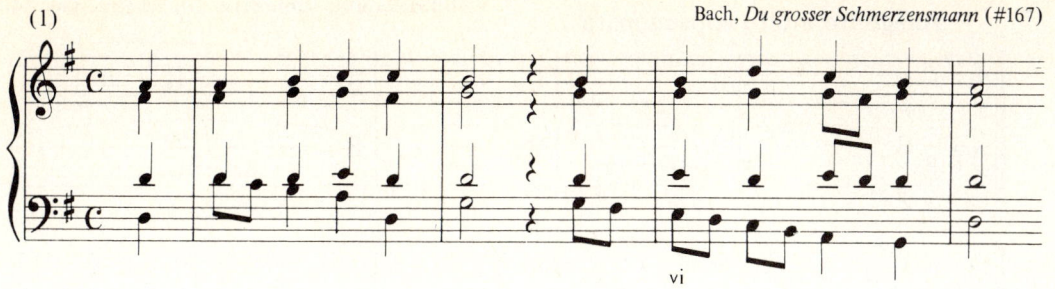

vi

(2) Bach, *Auf meinen lieben Gott* (#281)

(3) Bach, *Komm, Gott Schöpfer* (#188)

B♭:

(4) **Andante sostenuto** (♩ = 58)   Verdi, *Don Carlo*

Per me giun - to è il di su - pre - mo,

(5) Allegretto molto appassionata — Mendelssohn, Concerto for Violin, Op. 64

Assignment 13.3. (*EH*, p. 295). Writing dominant seventh chords with root in bass. Below each example, name the pitches of the three-note nonharmonic figure and state the name of this figure (PT = passing tone, S = suspension, UN = upper neighboring tone, App = appoggiatura).

(7) (8)

D♭ — E♭ — D♭ UN B — C♯ — B UN

(7) (8)

___ ___ ___ ___ ___ ___ ___ ___

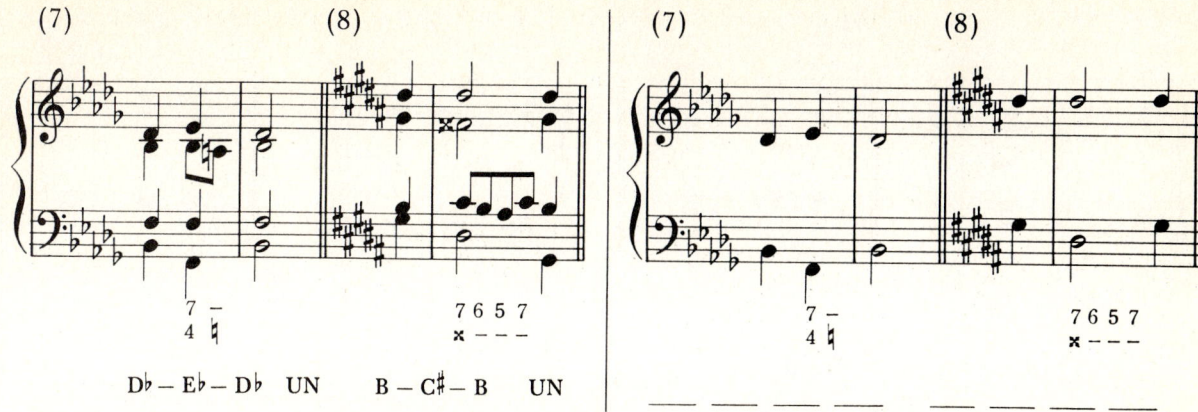

Assignment 13.4. (*EH*, p. 296). Writing dominant seventh chords in inversion. Follow the directions for the previous assignment.

(1) (2)

A — B♭ — A UN G — A♭ — G UN

(1) (2)

___ ___ ___ ___ ___ ___ ___ ___

(3) (4)

B — E — D App B♭ — B♭ — A♭ S

(3) (4)

___ ___ ___ ___ ___ ___ ___ ___

(5) (6)

G♯ — A — B PT D — G — F App

(5) (6)

___ ___ ___ ___ ___ ___ ___ ___

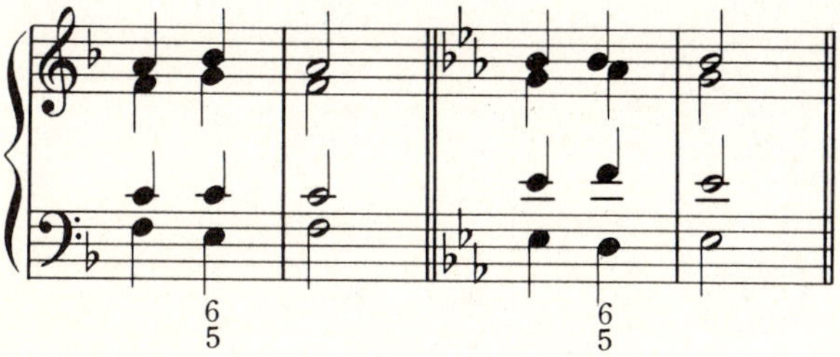

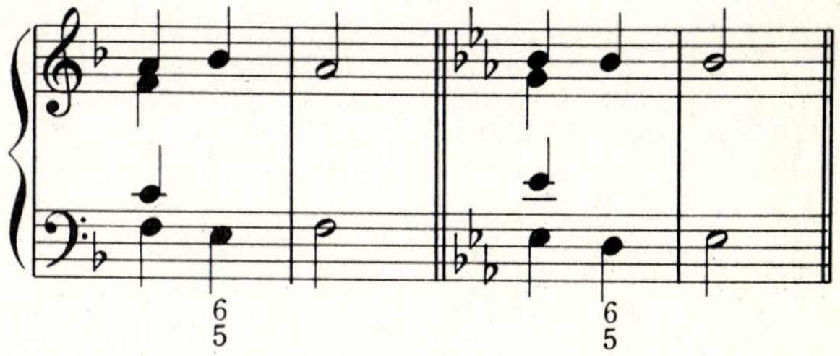

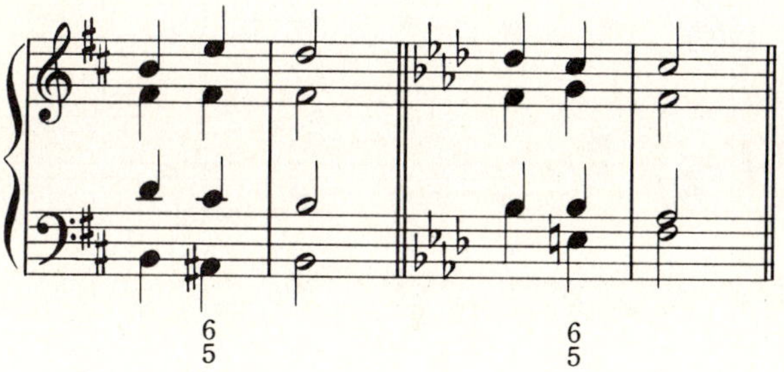

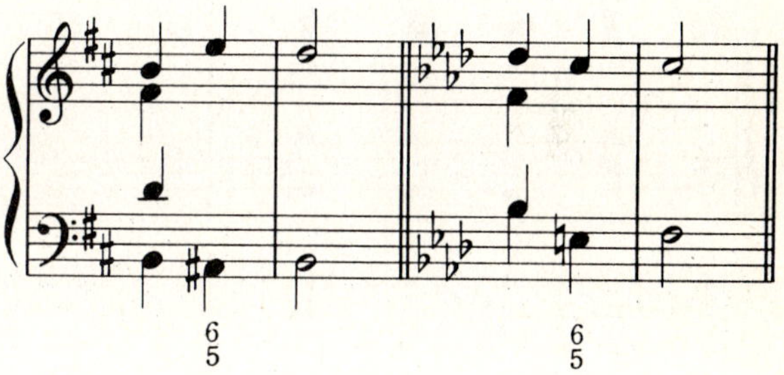

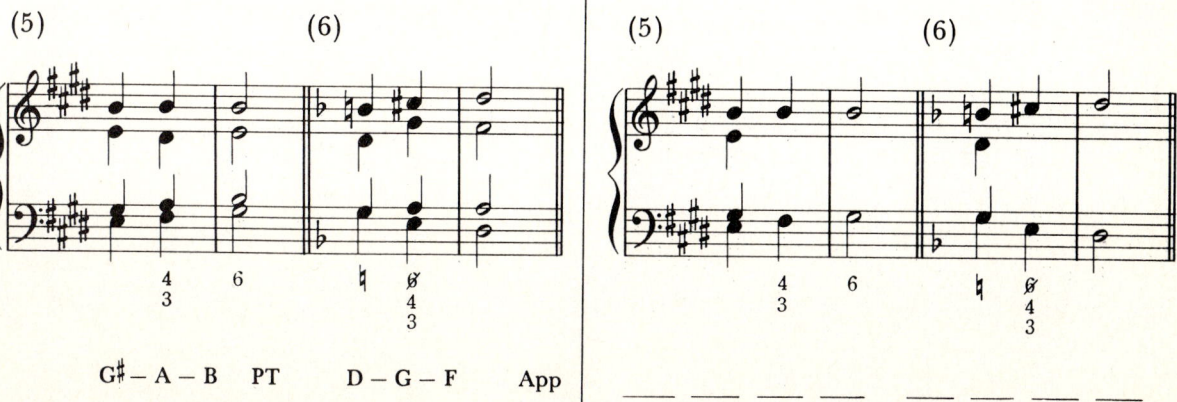

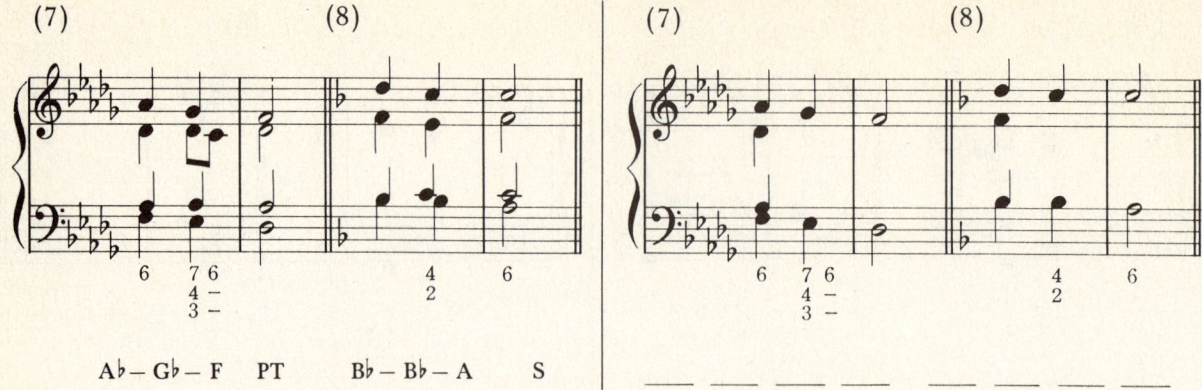

(7) (8)

A♭ – G♭ – F PT B♭ – B♭ – A S

(7) (8)

___ ___ ___ ___ ___ ___ ___ ___

Assignment 13.5. (*EH*, p. 297). Writing supertonic seventh chords. The approach and resolution of the seventh in the supertonic seventh chord is invariably a suspension figure. Check each supertonic seventh you write for this feature. Make an harmonic analysis.

(1)

(1)

(2)

(2)

(3)

(3)

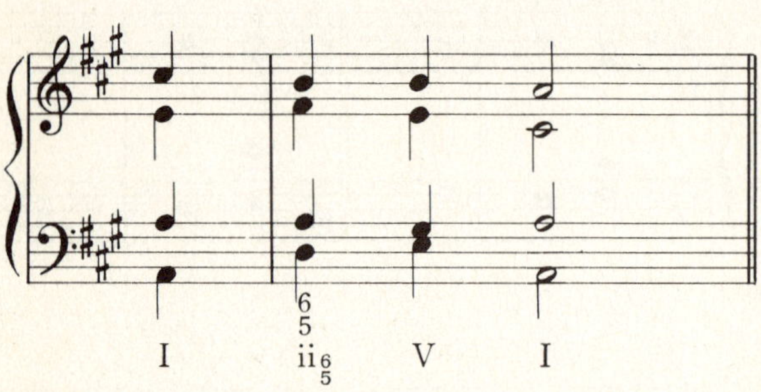

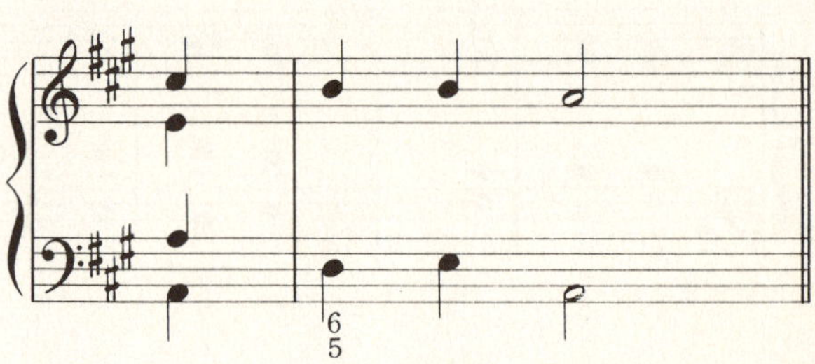

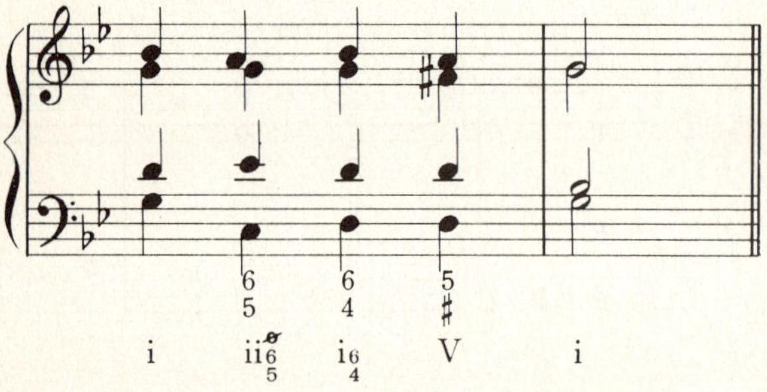

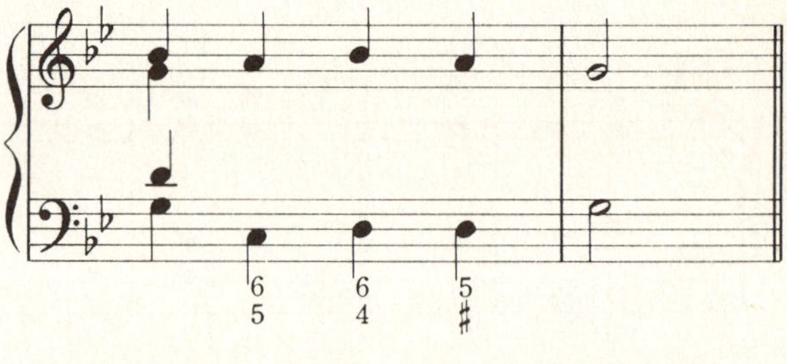

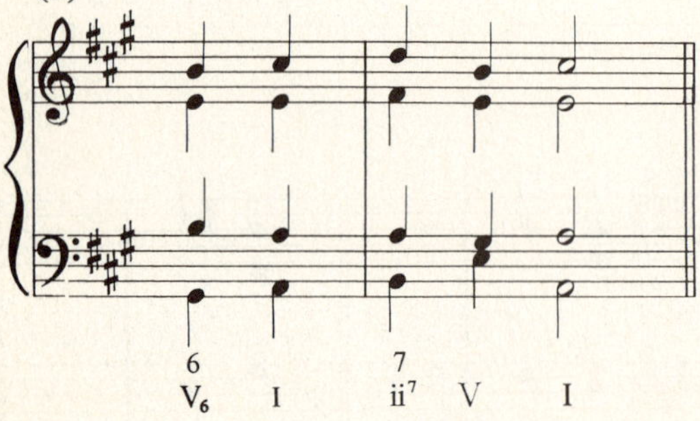

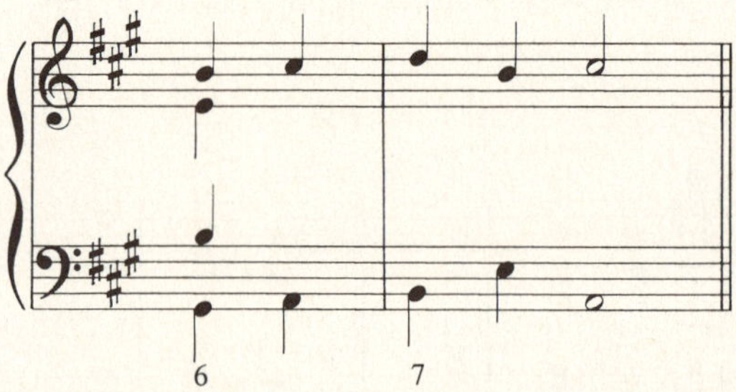

(4)

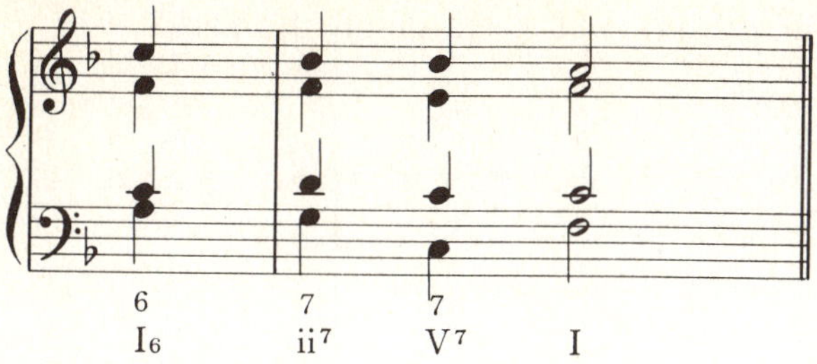
6 7 7
I6 ii7 V7 I

(4)

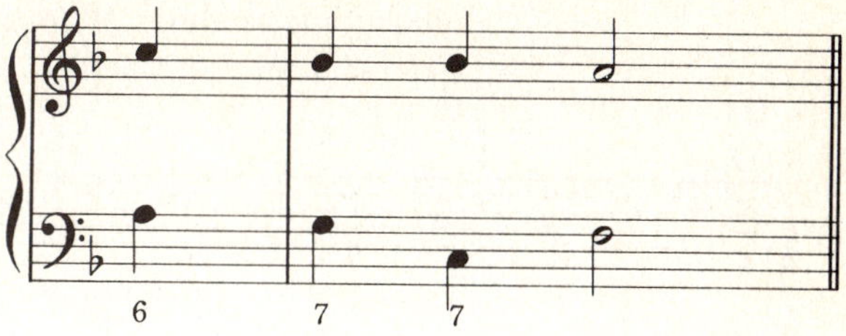
6 7 7

(5)

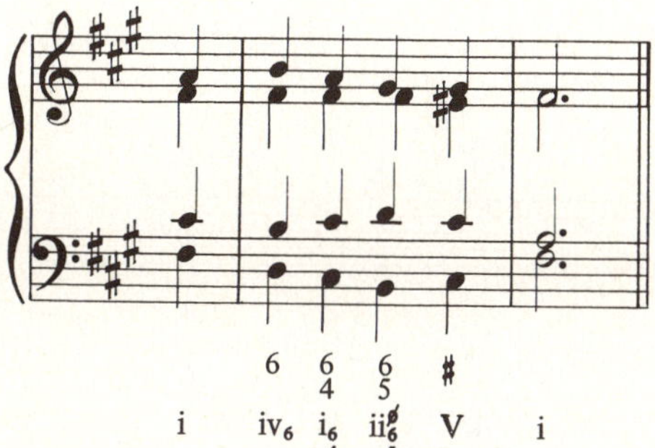
6 6/4 6/5 ♯
i iv6 i6/4 iiø6/5 V i

(5)

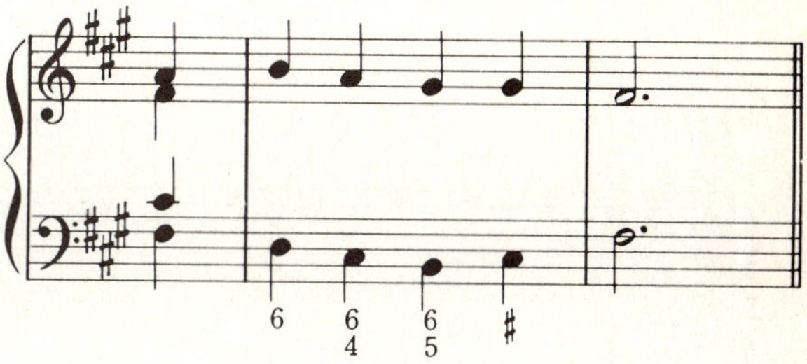
6 6/4 6/5 ♯

(6)

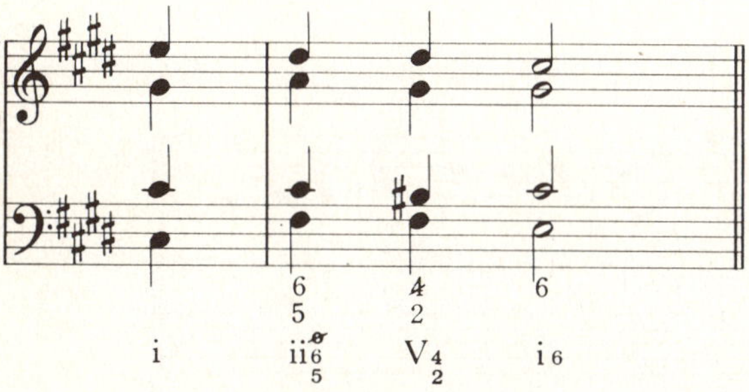
6/5 4/2 6
i iiø6/5 V4/2 i6

(6)

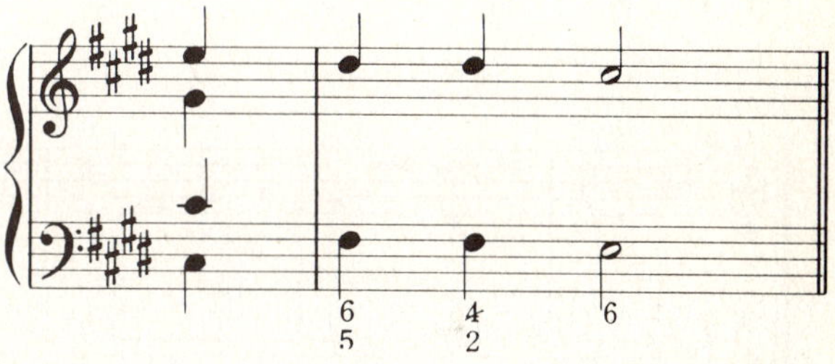
6/5 4/2 6

(7)

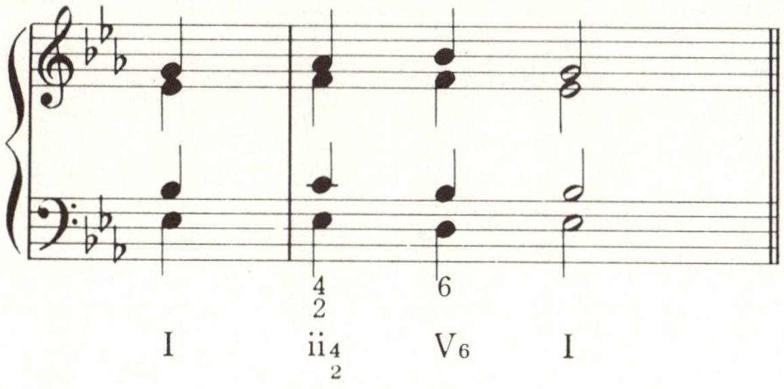
4/2 6
I ii4/2 V6 I

(7)

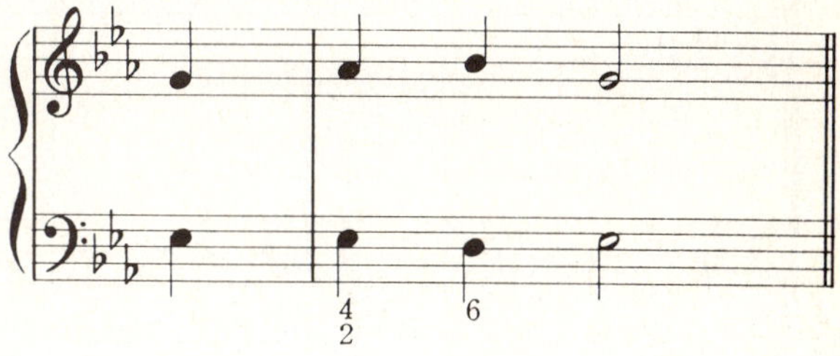
4/2 6

(8)

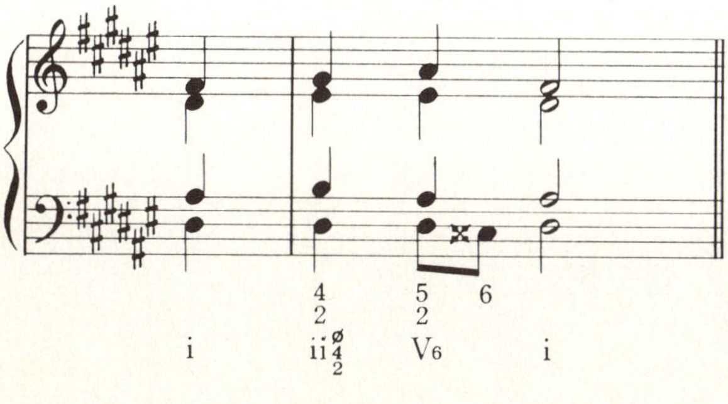
4/2 5/2 6
i iiø4/2 V6 i

(8)

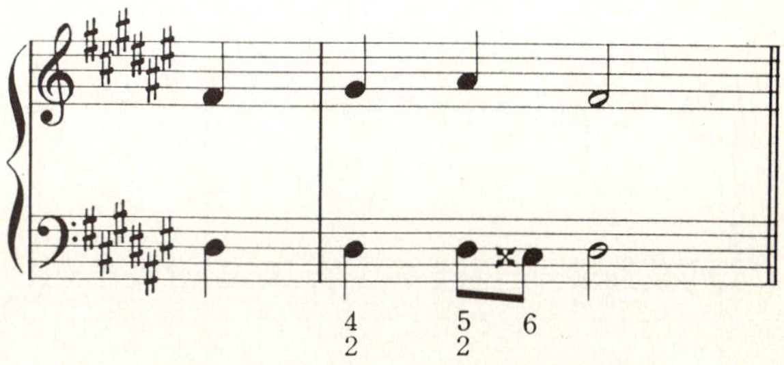
4/2 5/2 6

Assignment 13.6. (*EH*, p. 298). Part-writing extended exercises using dominant seventh and supertonic seventh chords. Add inner voices and make an harmonic analysis. Where figured bass is not given, supply this first.

Assignment 13B. Harmonizing the cadence with the supertonic seventh chord. This chord is particularly valuable in harmonizing the melodic line $\hat{2}-\hat{1}$ at the cadence, as shown in the illustrations of Assignment 13.11. (*EH*, p. 302). Harmonize these cadences using the supertonic seventh chord. Use these cadential progressions when harmonizing melodies from Assignment 13.9 in *EH*.

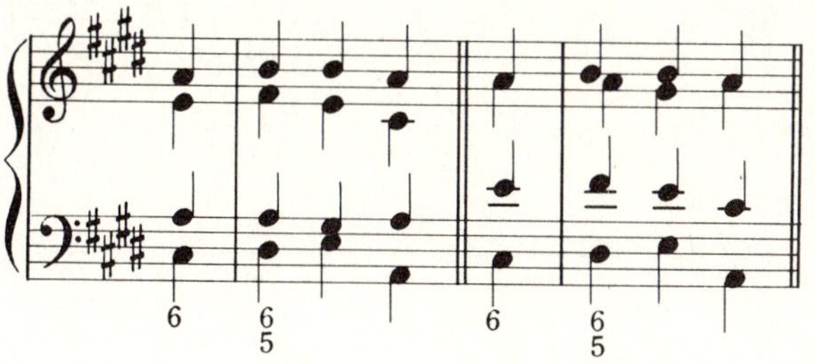

Assignment 13.7. (*EH*, p. 299). Spell intervals from the V^7 chord. In the key indicated, spell the given intervals from the V^7 chord of that key.

G: m7   D up to C | G   m7   ___ up to ___

     d5   F♯ up to C | d5   ___ up to ___

     A4   C up to F♯ | A5   ___ up to ___

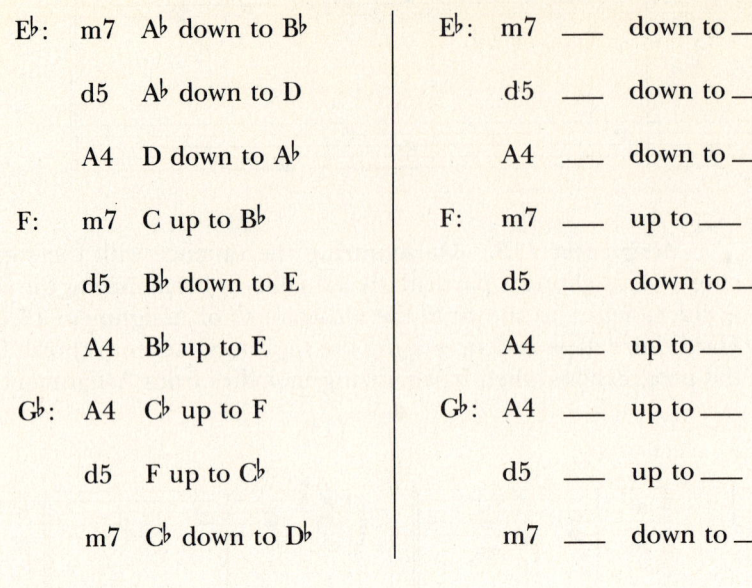

Answers not given.

Assignment 13C. Identify intervals from the V⁷ chord. Write the name of each interval below the staff.

Assignment 13D. Write intervals from the V⁷ chord in the keys indicated.

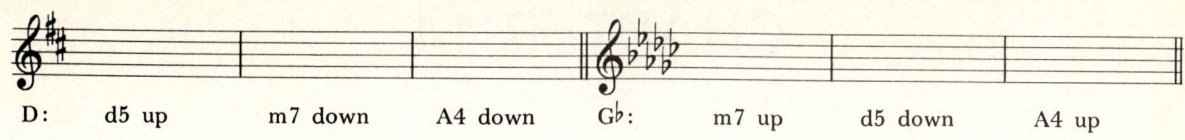

D: d5 up   m7 down   A4 down   G♭:   m7 up   d5 down   A4 up

B♭: A4 down   m7 down   d5 up   c♯:   d5 down   A4 up   m7 up

Assignment 13.9. (*EH*, p. 301). Melody harmonization. Harmonize these melodies in four voices, using dominant and supertonic seventh chords. You are encouraged to use various inversions of these chords. Since there are many opportunities for placing these chords, use of nonharmonic tones may be minimal.

As usual in harmonizing a melody, choose an harmonic progression and a bass line *before* adding inner voices.

(1)

(2)

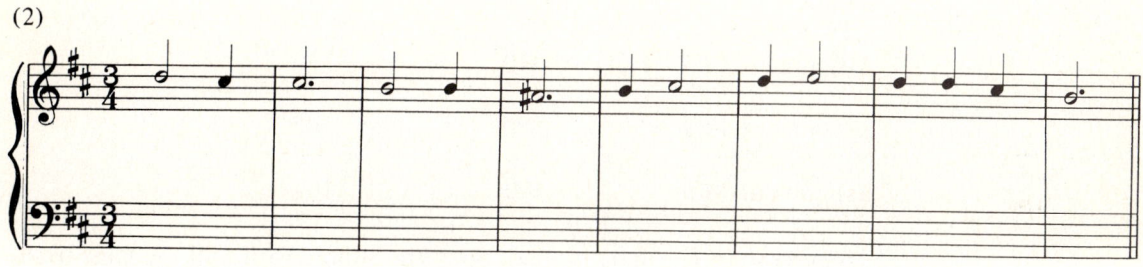

151

CHAPTER 14

THE SUBMEDIANT AND MEDIANT TRIADS

	Elementary Harmony	Workbook
Assignment 14.1	304	152
Assignment 14.2	313	154
Assignment 14.3	319	160
Assignment 14.4	320	163
Assignment 14.5	321	164

Assignment 14.1. (*EH*, p. 304). Spell the submediant and mediant triads in each major and minor key.

Major key	vi	iii	Major key	vi	iii
C	A C E	E G B	C	___ ___ ___	___ ___ ___
G	E G B	B D F♯	G	___ ___ ___	___ ___ ___
D	B D F♯	F♯ A C♯	D	___ ___ ___	___ ___ ___
A	F♯ A C♯	C♯ E G♯	A	___ ___ ___	___ ___ ___
E	C♯ E G♯	G♯ B D♯	E	___ ___ ___	___ ___ ___
B	G♯ B D♯	D♯ F♯ A♯	B	___ ___ ___	___ ___ ___
F♯	D♯ F♯ A♯	A♯ C♯ E♯	F♯	___ ___ ___	___ ___ ___
C♯	A♯ C♯ E♯	E♯ G♯ B♯	C♯	___ ___ ___	___ ___ ___

Major key	vi	iii	Major key	vi	iii
F	D F A	A C E	F		
B♭	G B♭ D	D F A	B♭		
E♭	C E♭ G	G B♭ D	E♭		
A♭	F A♭ C	C E♭ G	A♭		
D♭	B♭ D♭ F	F A♭ C	D♭		
G♭	E♭ G♭ B♭	B♭ D♭ F	G♭		
C♭	A♭ C♭ E♭	E♭ G♭ B♭	C♭		

Minor key	VI	III	Minor key	VI	III
A	F A C	C E G	A		
E	C E G	G B D	E		
B	G B D	D F♯ A	B		
F♯	D F♯ A	A C♯ E	F♯		
C♯	A C♯ E	E G♯ B	C♯		
G♯	E G♯ B	B D♯ F♯	G♯		
D♯	B D♯ F♯	F♯ A♯ C♯	D♯		
A♯	F♯ A♯ C♯	C♯ E♯ G♯	A♯		
D	B♭ D F	F A C	D		
G	E♭ G B♭	B♭ D F	G		
C	A♭ C E♭	E♭ G B♭	C		
F	D♭ F A♭	A♭ C E♭	F		
B♭	G♭ B♭ D♭	D♭ F A♭	B♭		
E♭	C♭ E♭ G♭	G♭ B♭ D♭	E♭		
A♭	F♭ A♭ C♭	C♭ E♭ G♭	A♭		

b) Answers not given. X's indicate keys not found in the circle of fifths.

	Major key		Minor key	
Tonic	vi	iii	VI	III
A				
B				

	Major key		Minor key	
	vi	iii	vi	iii
E♭	— — —	— — —	— — —	— — —
C♯	— — —	— — —	— — —	— — —
G	— — —	— — —	— — —	— — —
D♯	X X X	X X X	— — —	— — —
D♭	— — —	— — —	X X X	X X X
F	— — —	— — —	— — —	— — —
B♭	— — —	— — —	— — —	— — —
G♯	X X X	X X X	— — —	— — —

Assignment 14.2. (*EH*, p. 313). Harmonic analysis. Analyze the harmony and the nonharmonic tones in these excerpts.

(1)

Berlioz, *Romeo and Juliet*, Op. 17

(2)

Schumann, *Dichterliebe*, Op. 48, "Hör' ich das Liedchen klingen"

(3)

Mozart, Sonata for Violin and Piano, K. 378

(4) Mozart, *The Magic Flute*, K. 620

Allegro

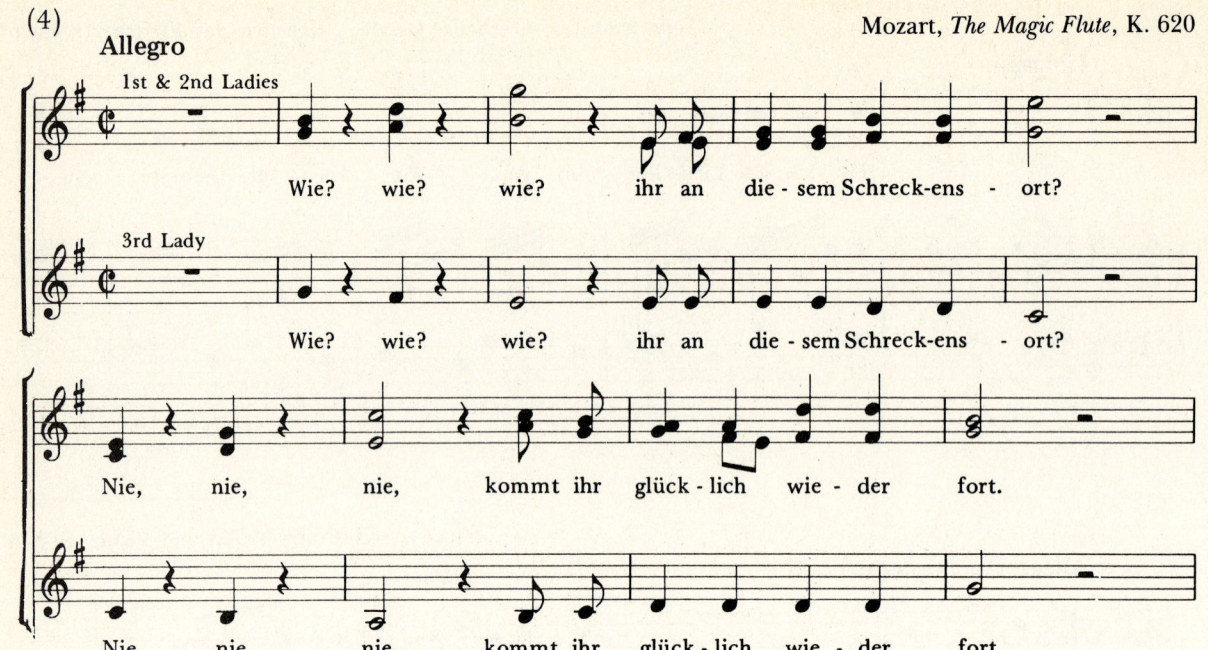

(5) This excerpt, the beginning of the chorale prelude, does *not* begin in G minor as it appears, even though the accidentals usually found in the G minor scale occur for the duration of the G minor triad. Find the cadence before determining the identification of the first triad. Also note several nonharmonic tones prepared by a rest. The melody is from chorale number 79.

Bach, *Orgelbüchlein*, "Triumphiret Gottes Sohn," BWV 640

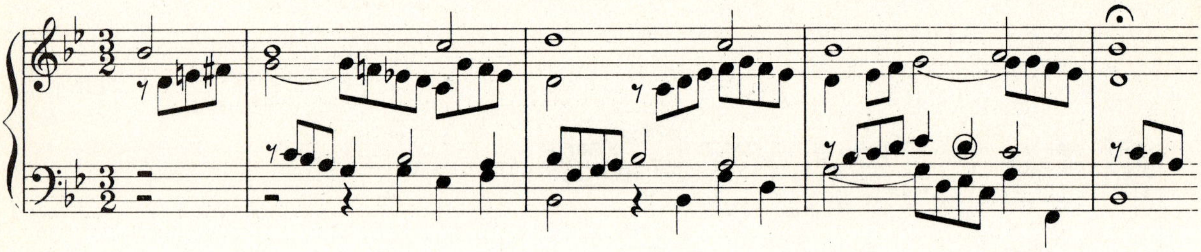

(6) Mozart, Quintet for Clarinet and Strings, K. 561

Allegretto

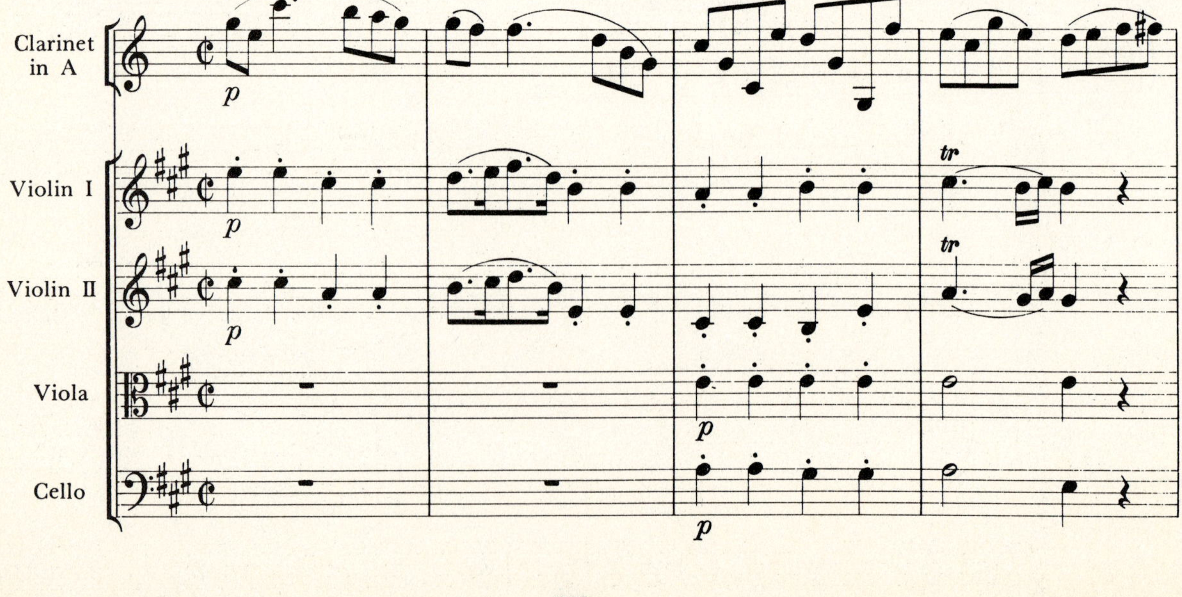

(7) Tempo di Menuetto Dvořák, *Slavonic Dances*, Op. 46, No. 4

(8) The violone grosso is a predecessor of the present-day double bass. *Continuo* indicates a bass line played by the melodic instruments indicated and by a keyboard instrument whose player improvises upon the given bass line.

Bach, *Brandenburg Concerto*, No. 1

Hrn.
Ob.
Vl. I
Vl. II
Vla.
Fg. Vc.
Vl. gr.
and C.

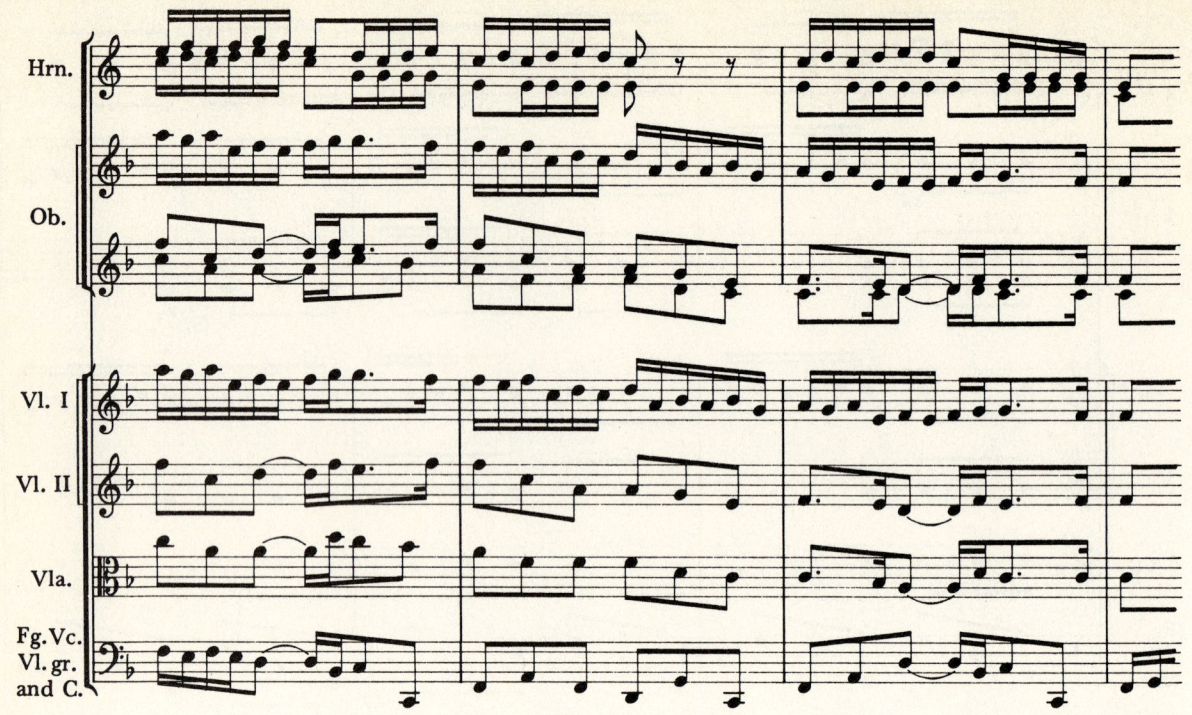

Assignment 14.3. (*EH*, p. 319). Part-writing the submediant triad. These short exercises show a wide variety of the uses of this triad. Include an harmonic analysis with your solution.

(1)

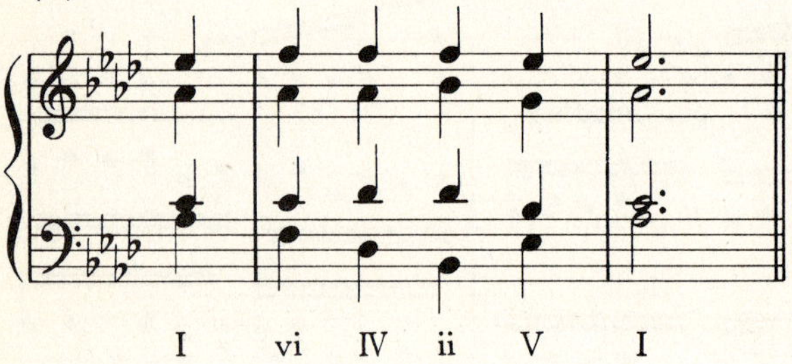
I vi IV ii V I

(1)

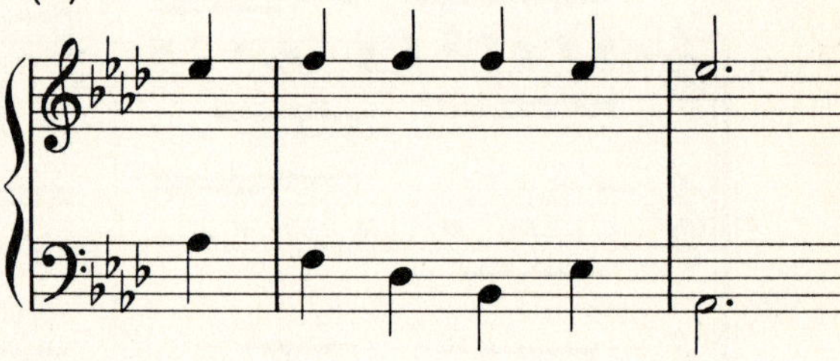

(2)

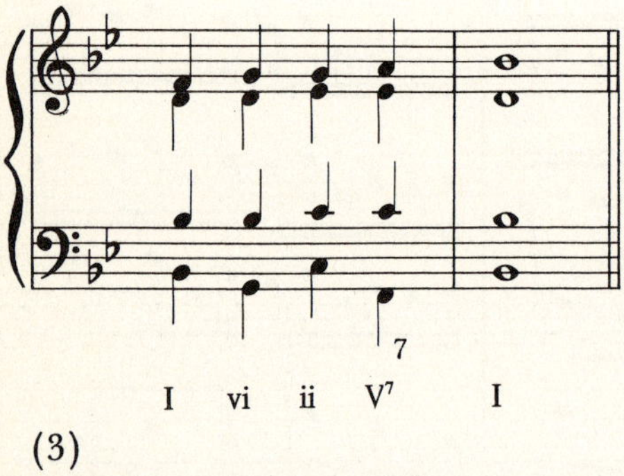
7
I vi ii V7 I

(2)

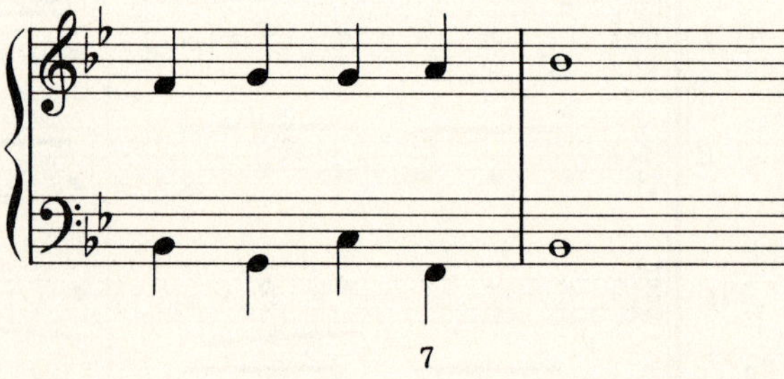
7

(3)

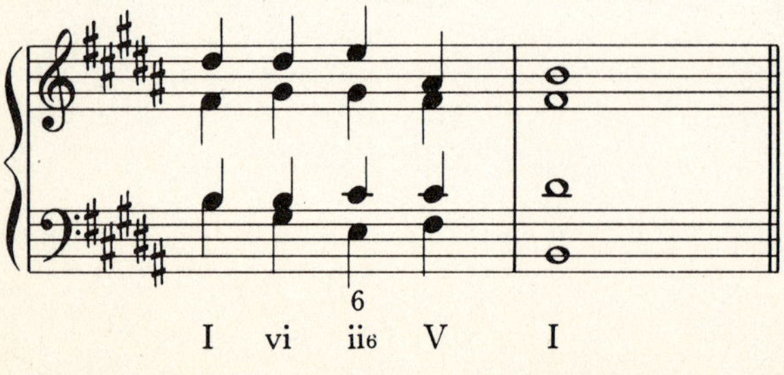
6
I vi ii6 V I

(3)

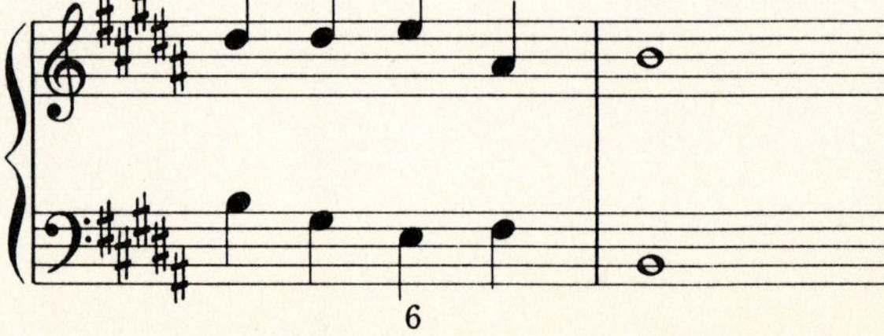
6

(9)
6 6 6 4 3
i VI ii6 i6 V4 3 i
(9)
6 6 6 4 3
(10)
♯ ♯
V i VI V i
(10)
♯ ♯
(11)
7 ♯
i VI ii7 V VI
(11)
7 ♯
(12)
♮ 6 ♮ 6
i VI V i6 IV vii6 i
(12)
♮ 6 ♮ 6
(13)
♯ 6 5 ♯
i V VI ii6 5 V i
(13)
7 ♯ 6 5 ♯

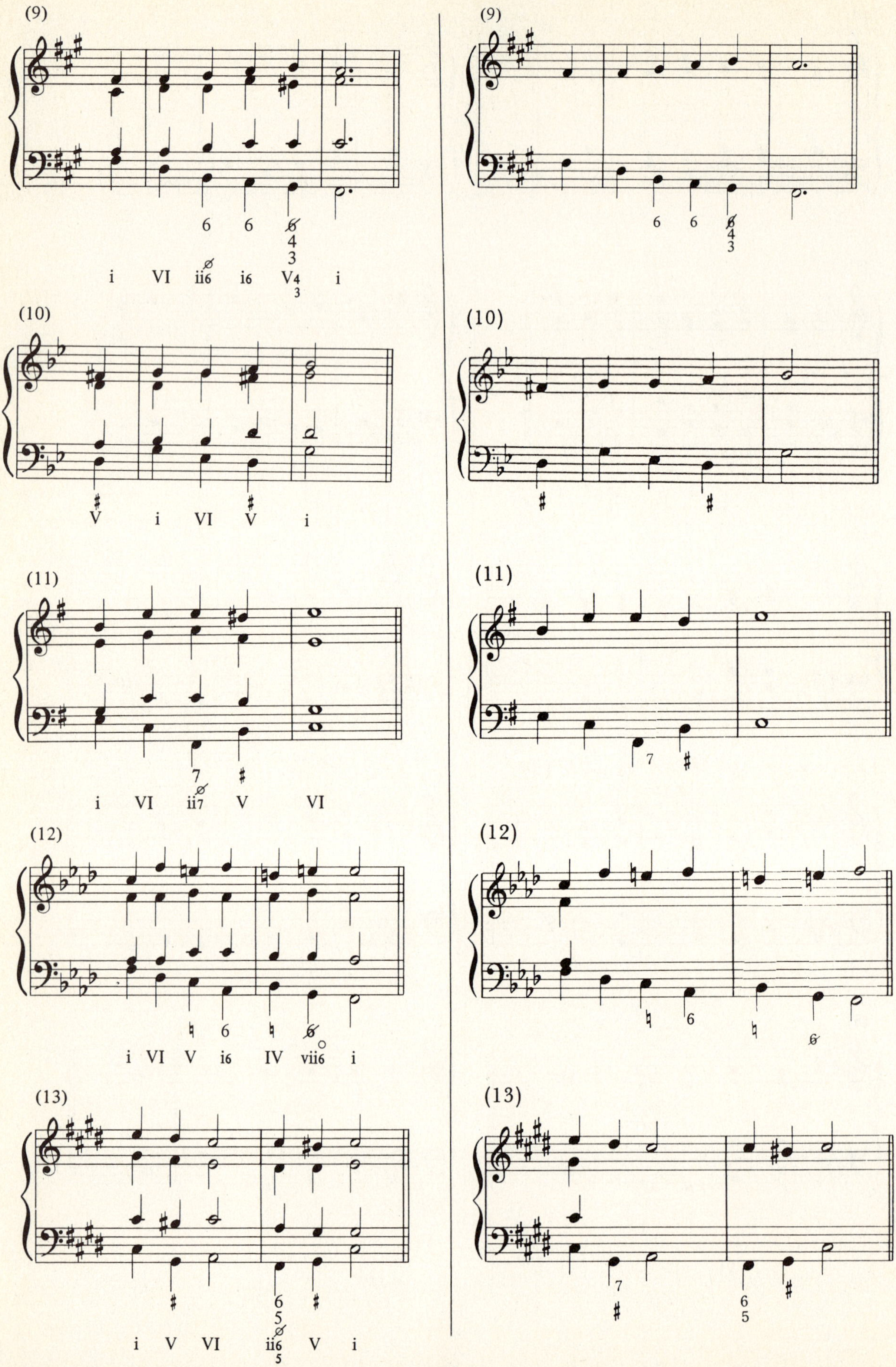

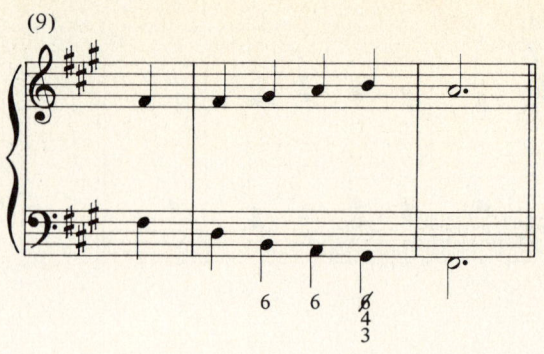

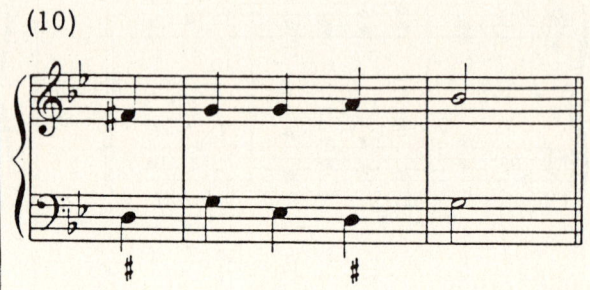

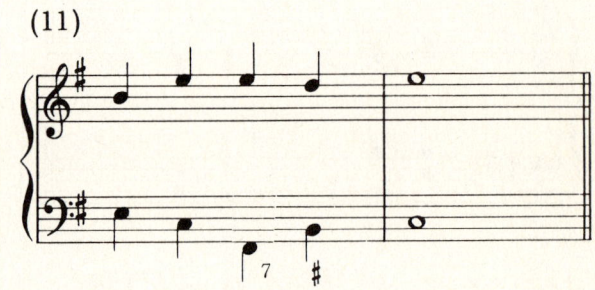

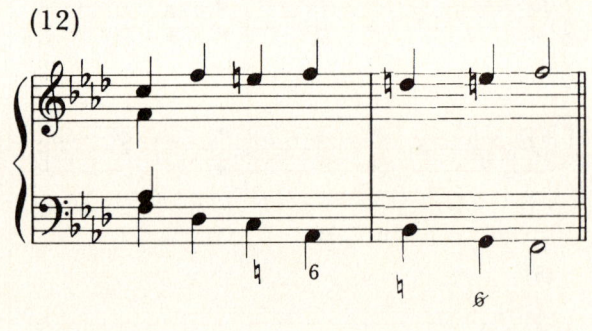

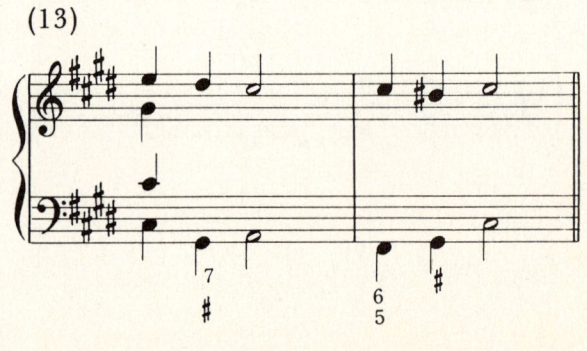

(14)

(14)

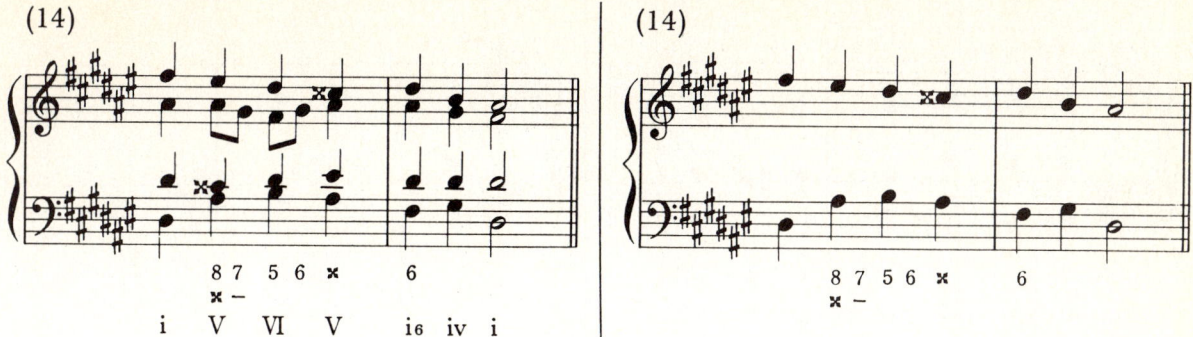

Assignment 14.4. (*EH*, p. 320). Part-writing the mediant triad. Proceed as in the previous assignment.

(1)

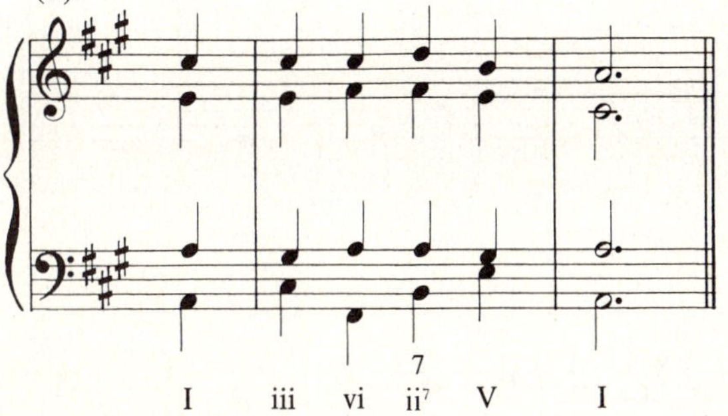

(1)

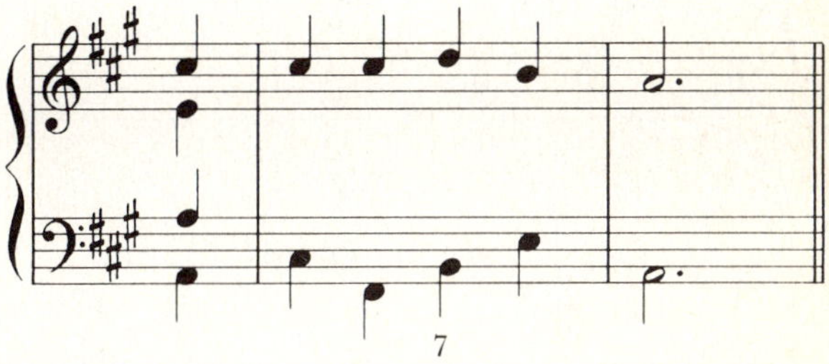

(2)

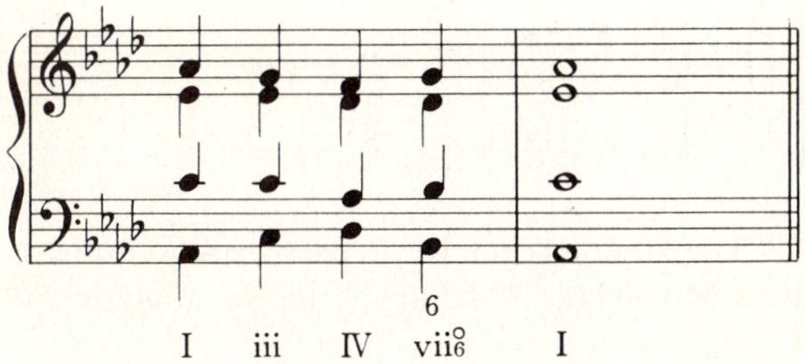

(2)

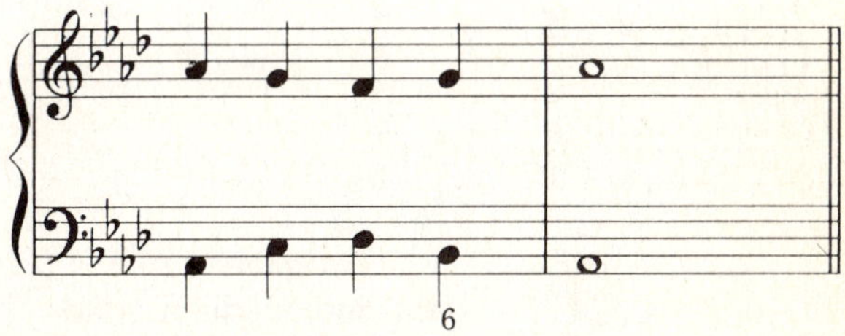

(3)

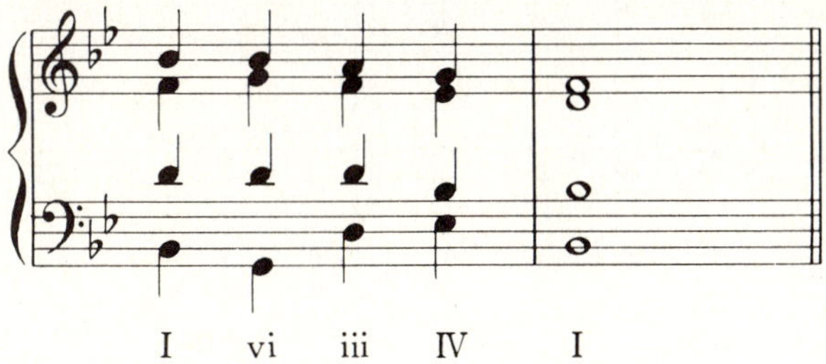

(3)

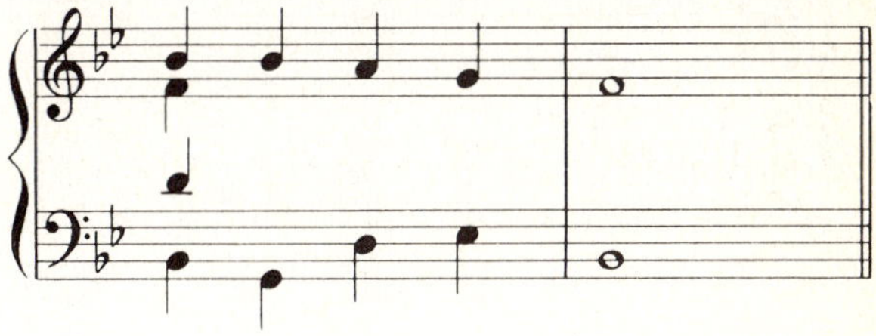

(4)

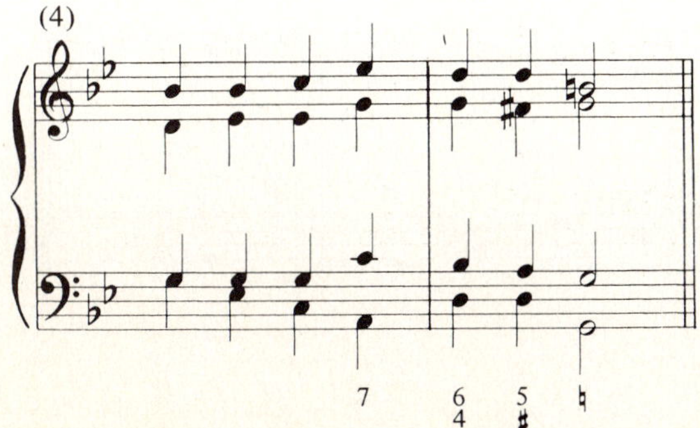

(4)

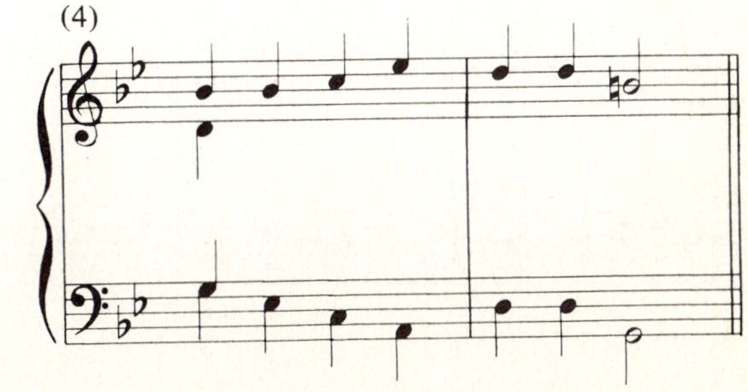

(5)

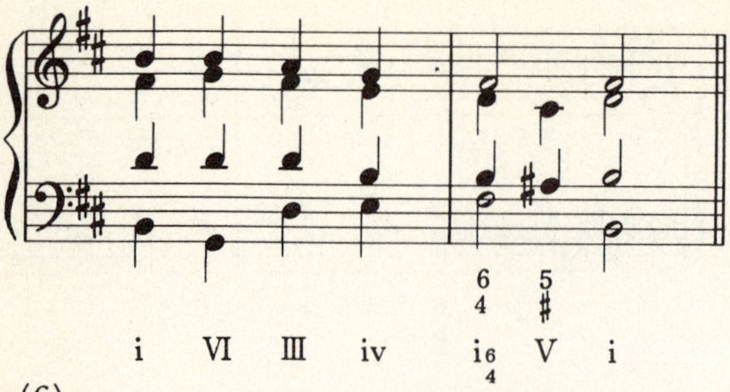

(5)

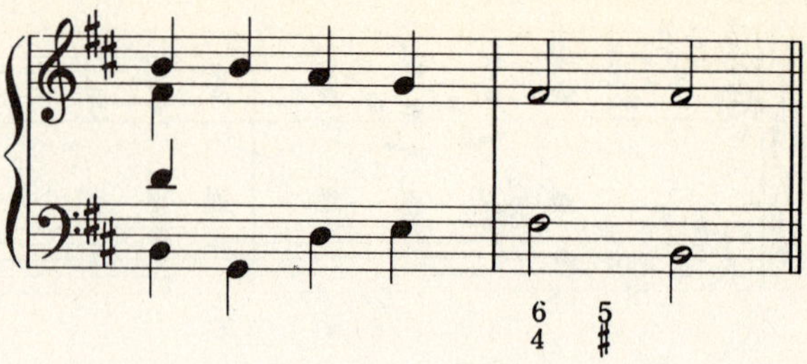

(6)

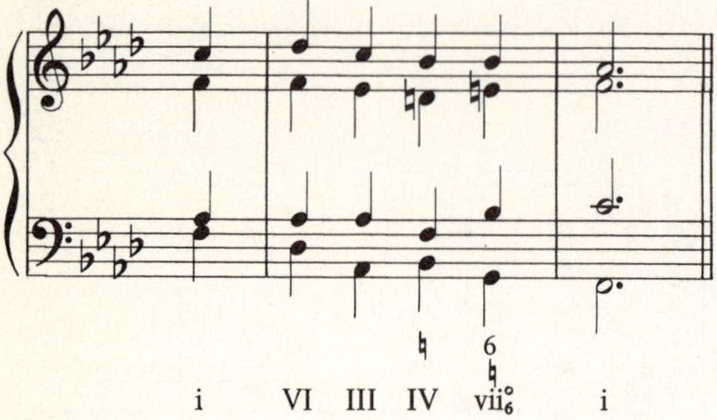

(6)

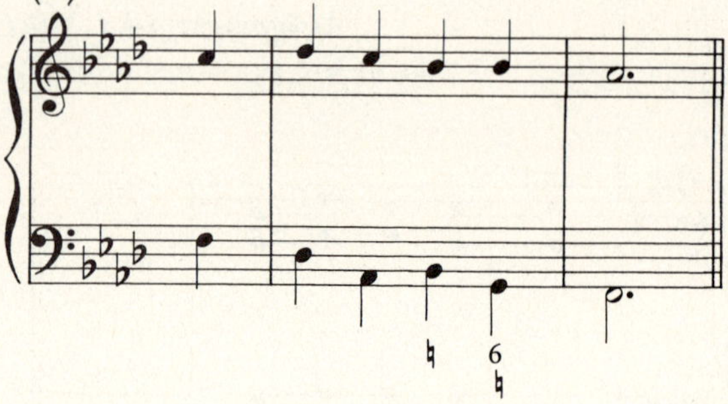

(7)

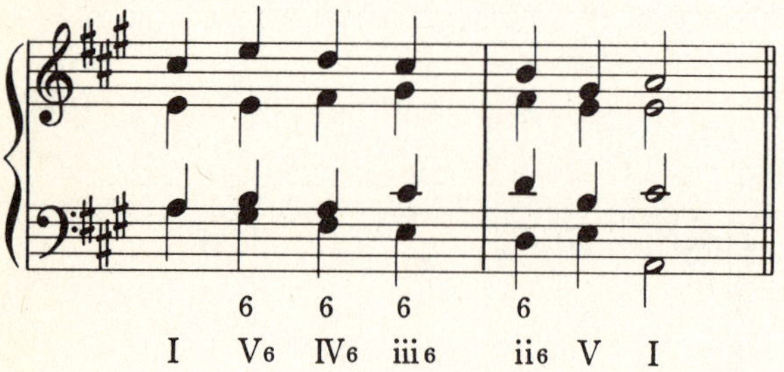

(7)

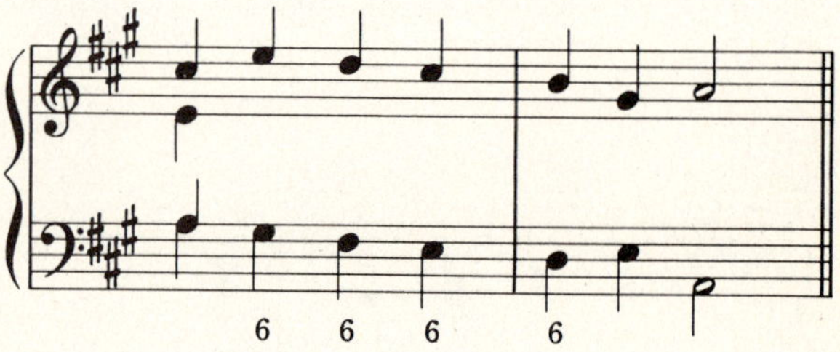

Assignment 14.5. (*EH*, p. 321). Extended exercises in part-writing: submediant and mediant triads. Fill in inner voices. Make an harmonic analysis and identify all nonharmonic tones.

(1)

(2)

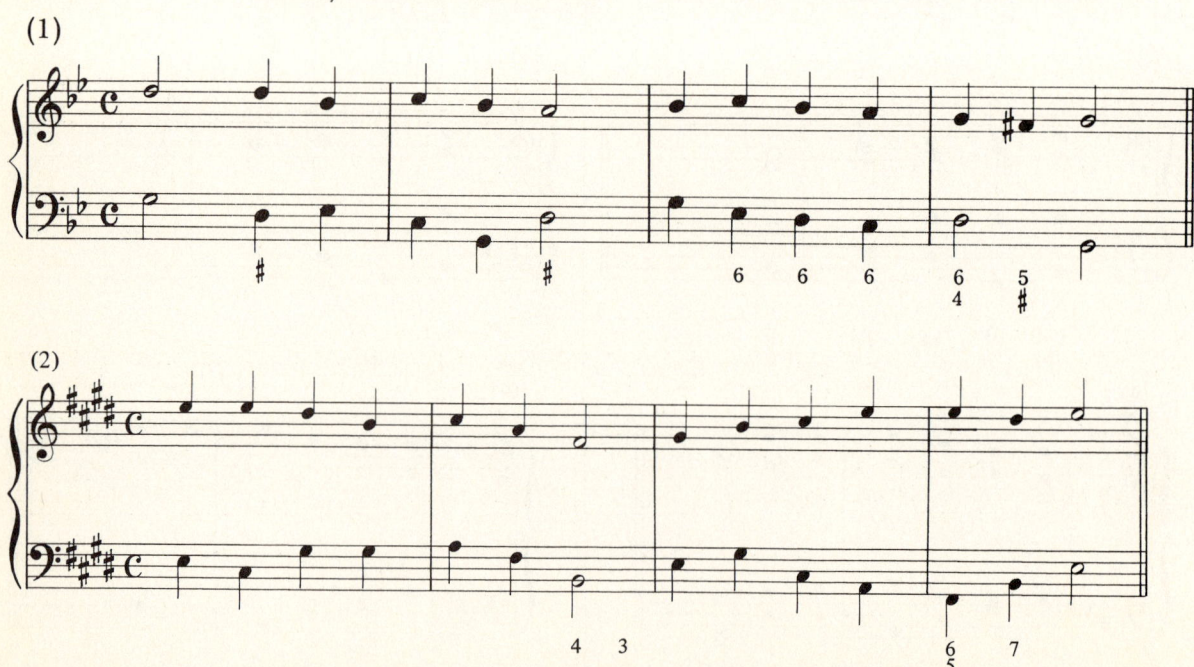

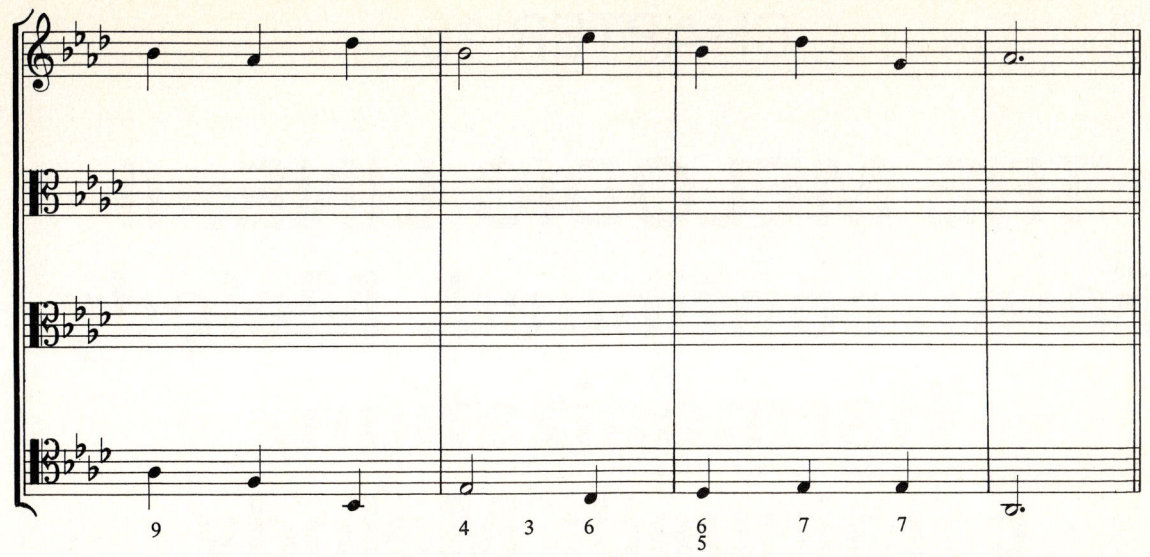

CHAPTER 15

THE MELODIC LINE: II Form, continued; Melody Harmonization, continued; Melody Writing

	Elementary Harmony	*Workbook*
Assignment 15A	—	168
Assignment 15.1	334	—
Assignment 15.2	343	—
Assignment 15B	—	172

Assignment 15A. Extending given phrases. Figures 15.1–15.8 in *EH* have shown you that in many cases a phrase length greater than four measures is simply a normal four-measure phrase with an added measure or measures. For this assignment, we will begin with four-measure phrases and add extensions as described in *EH*, pages 326–329.

Study each given example, then rewrite each phrase that follows, using a similar technique.

a) Repeating part of a phrase.

Example: U.S.A.

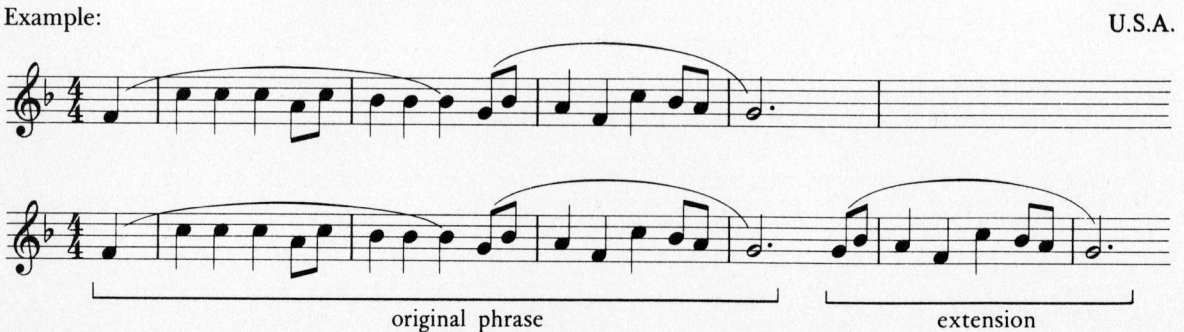

c) Adding a melodic sequence. The sequence may be very short, two or three notes, or it may be an entire motive.

d) Lengthening a motive.

Example:

Spain

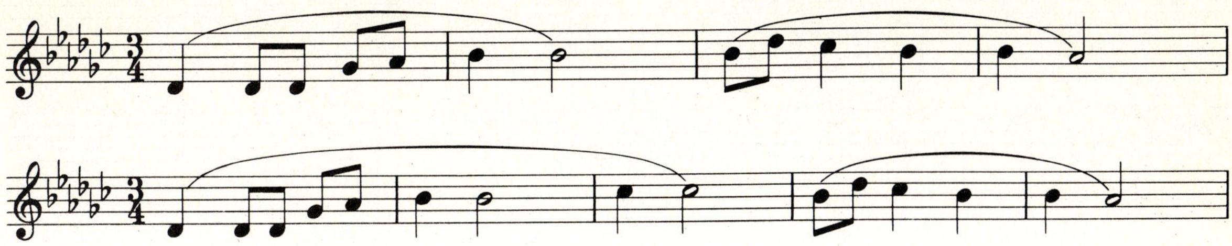

(1)

Fr. Silcher

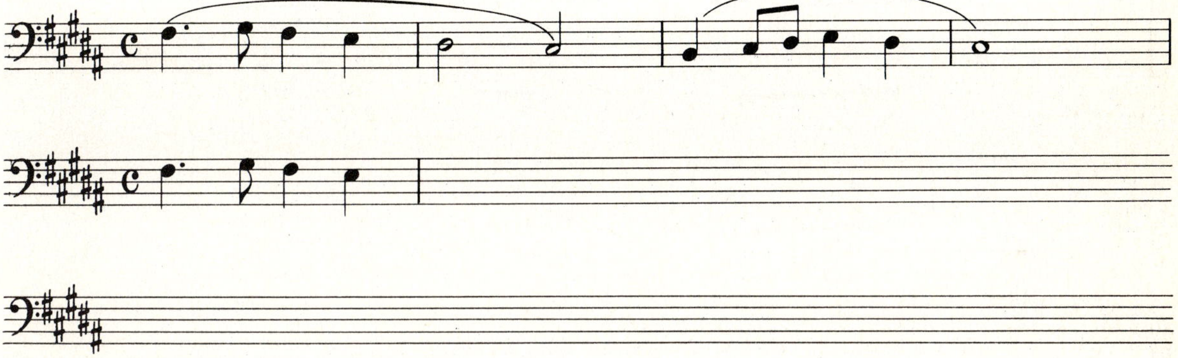

(2)

Czechoslovakia

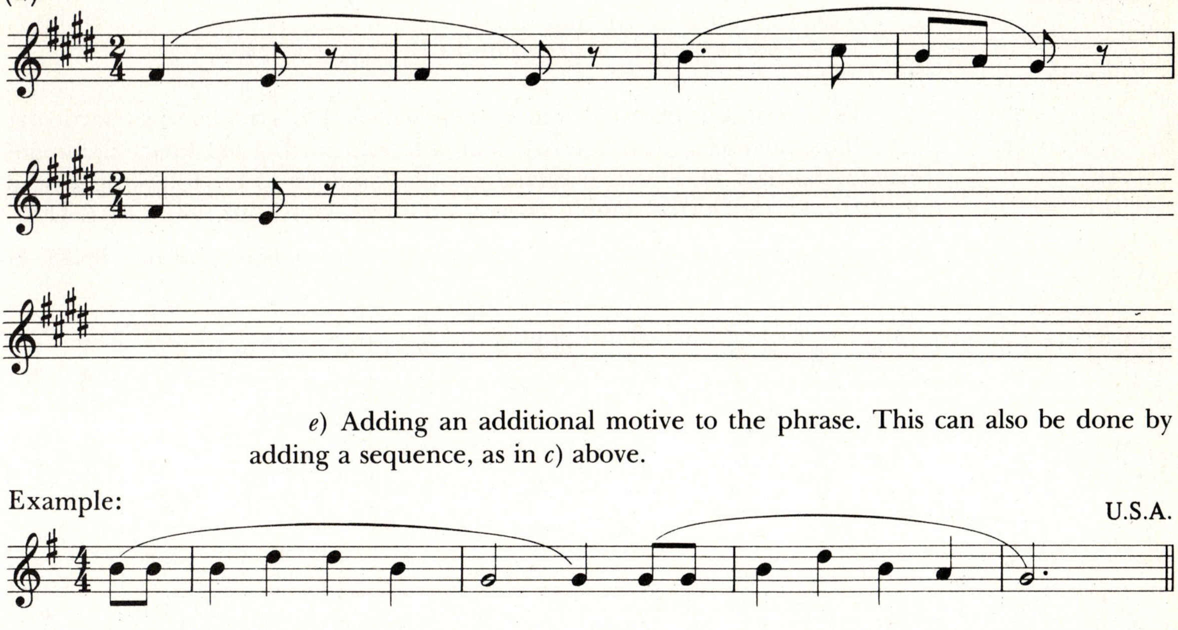

e) Adding an additional motive to the phrase. This can also be done by adding a sequence, as in *c*) above.

Example:

U.S.A.

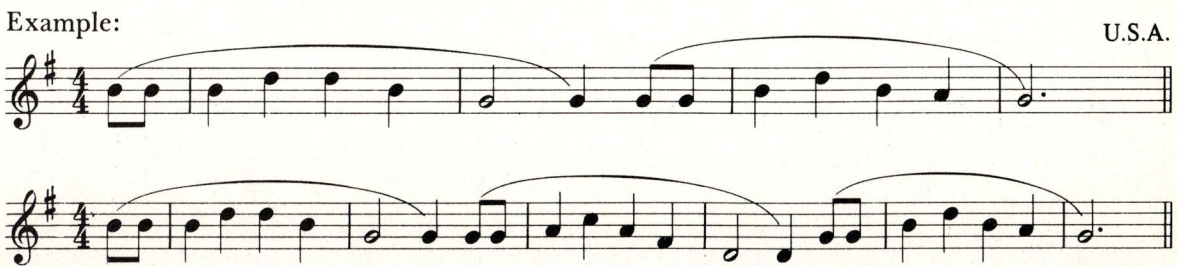

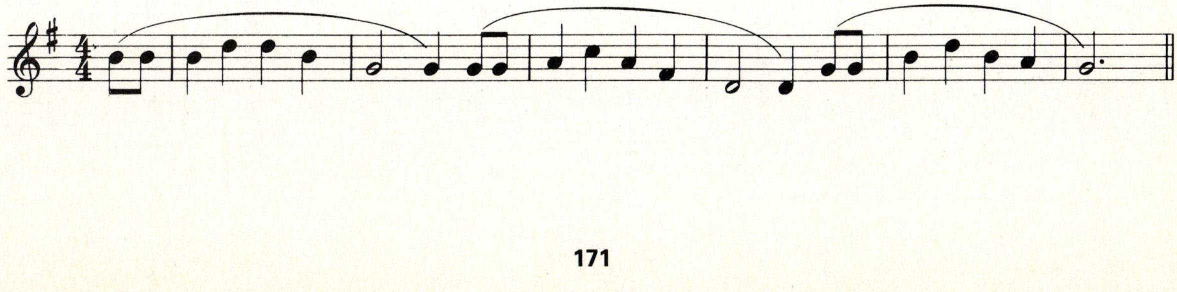

(1) Germany

(2) Mexico

Assignment 15B. Harmonic and form analysis. Make a complete analysis of each of the following compositions or excerpts:
 a) analysis of harmony;
 b) analysis of nonharmonic tones;
 c) analysis of form, as illustrated in *EH*, Figure 15.14.

(1) This short, complete, and well-known work is a model of its particular form. The harmony at the asterisk is an altered chord, a secondary dominant seventh chord, V^7/ii or VI^7. It functions as a dominant to the following ii triad (see Chapter 18). At the double asterisk we find ninth chord, V^9, E G♯ B D F♯.

(1) Chopin, Prelude, Op. 28, No. 7

Mozart, *Cosi fan tutte*, K.588

Beethoven, Symphony No.8, Op.93

Rameau, *Les Sauvages*

(6) This extended excerpt from a string quartet, though it contains a few harmonies not yet studied, is an excellent example of several form structures: the extended period, the extended double period, and a normal period. Be sure first to locate each perfect cadence; then identify the form leading up to that point. New harmonic devices are these:

Measures 36–37: An altered chord C♯ E G B♭ progressing to D F A.
Measures 38–39: An altered chord B D F A♭ progressing to F A C.
These two altered chords in measures 36–39 are diminished seventh chords. The triads (C♯ E G and B D F) from these chords act as leading tone triads to their respective following chords, just as vii° does to I.
Measure 46: the vii° triad with its seventh added: E G B♭ D.

Mozart, Quartet, K.458

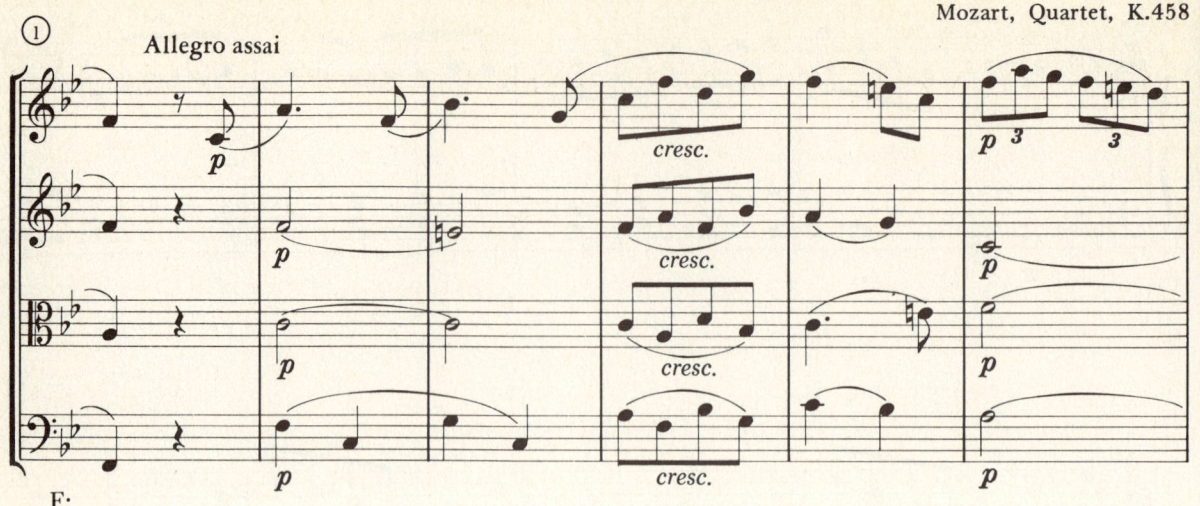

CHAPTER 16

THE v AND VII TRIADS; THE PHRYGIAN CADENCE

	Elementary Harmony	Workbook
Assignment 16.1	360	181
Assignment 16.2	360	182
Assignment 16.3	363	188
Assignment 16.4	364	189
Assignment 16.5	364	190
Assignment 16.6	366	191
Assignment 16.7	367	192

Assignment 16.1. (*EH*, p. 360). Spell the v and VII triads in each minor key.

a) Answers given.

	v	VII		v	VII
A	E G B	G B D	A	— — —	— — —
E	B D F♯	D F♯ A	E	— — —	— — —
B	F♯ A C♯	A C♯ E	B	— — —	— — —
F♯	C♯ E G♯	E G♯ B	F♯	— — —	— — —
C♯	G♯ B D♯	B D♯ F♯	C♯	— — —	— — —
G♯	D♯ F♯ A♯	F♯ A♯ C♯	G♯	— — —	— — —

	v	VII		v	VII
D♯	A♯ C♯ E♯	C♯ E♯ G♯	D♯	— — —	— — —
A♯	E♯ G♯ B♯	G♯ B♯ D♯	A♯	— — —	— — —
D	A C E	C E G	D	— — —	— — —
G	D F A	F A C	G	— — —	— — —
C	G B♭ D	B♭ D F	C	— — —	— — —
F	C E♭ G	E♭ G B♭	F	— — —	— — —
B♭	F A♭ C	A♭ C E♭	B♭	— — —	— — —
E♭	B♭ D♭ F	D♭ F A♭	E♭	— — —	— — —
A♭	E♭ G♭ B♭	G♭ B♭ D♭	A♭	— — —	— — —

b) Answers not given.

	v	VII		v	VII
B	— — —	— — —	E	— — —	— — —
G	— — —	— — —	F♯	— — —	— — —
C♯	— — —	— — —	E♭	— — —	— — —
F	— — —	— — —	D♯	— — —	— — —
B♭	— — —	— — —	A♯	— — —	— — —
A	— — —	— — —	C	— — —	— — —
G♯	— — —	— — —	D	— — —	— — —
A♭	— — —	— — —			

Assignment 16.2. (*EH*, p. 360). Harmonic analysis. Analyze the harmonic movement and nonharmonic usages in these excerpts.

For each v or VII, observe the use of $\hat{7}$ and state the relationship between that tone and the chord to which it is a member.

(1) Bach, *Wer nur den lieben Gott lässt walten* (#104)

(2)   Bach, *Jesu, du mein liebstes Leben* (#243)

Examples (3) and (4) show the v triad and the Phrygian cadence as commonly found together in a rather stereotyped cadence formula in compositions of the Baroque era. It is often found at the end of a slow movement in instrumental works, such as sonatas and concertos, and is followed, in the subsequent fast movement, by any one of several keys, commonly the key of the Phrygian cadence, or the relative major.

These two examples also illustrate the metric device known as a "hemiola." Read the discussion in *EH*, Article number 12, on page 395, and then analyze each of these examples.

(3) This first of these is from a Trio Sonata, so named because it is written in three voices. It is performed by four players, the bass line on the cello and on a keyboard instrument. The figured bass included in the continuo line serves as a guide to the keyboard player who improvises an accompaniment.

Corelli, Sonata, Op. 3, No. 4

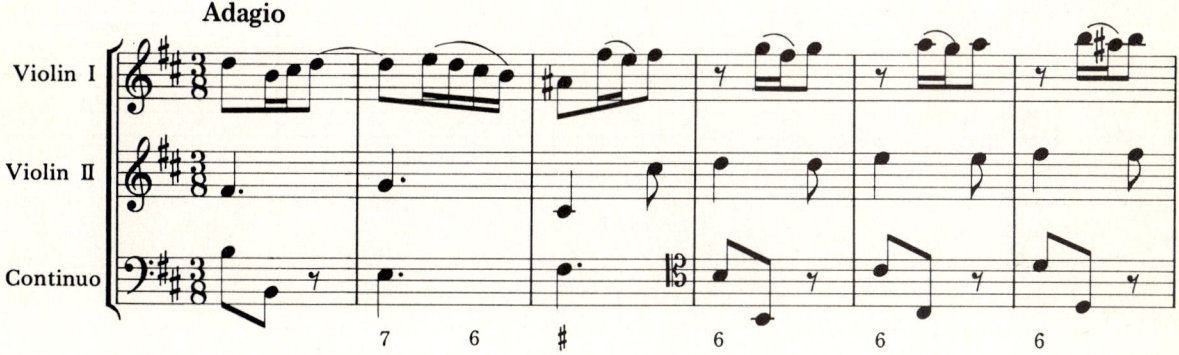

183

(4) Handel, Concerto Grosso, Op. 6, No. 5

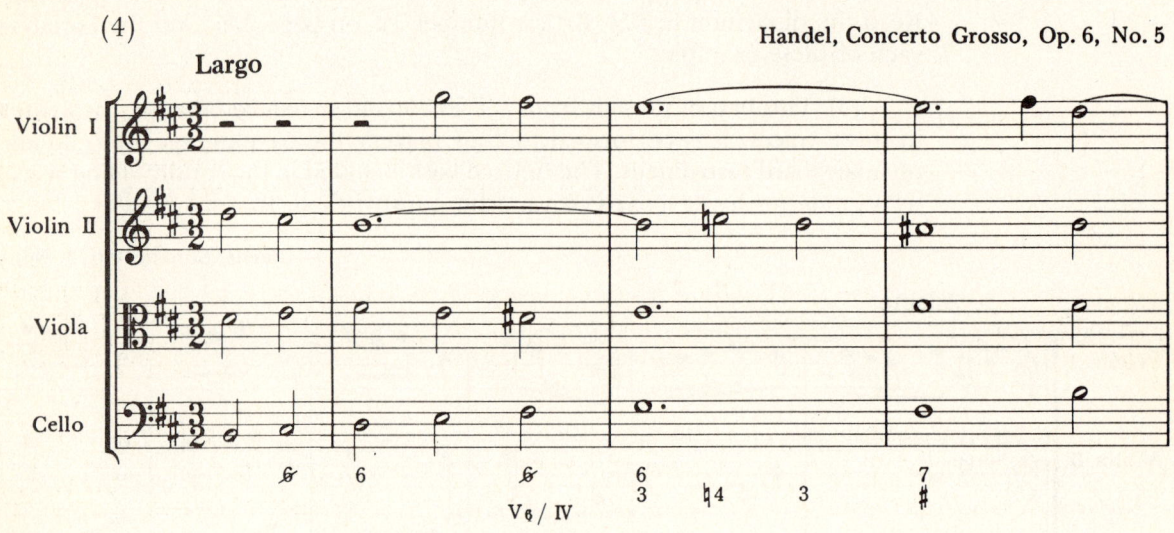

(5) The chord progression comprising the Phrygian cadence appears, in this example, other than at the cadence point.

Schumann, *Dichterliebe*, Op 48, "Im wunderschönen Monat Mai"

Im wun - der, schö - nen Mo - nat Mai, als

(6) At measure 5, "N_6" means "Neapolitan sixth," a major triad with its root on the *lowered* $\hat{2}$, and usually found in first inversion. (There is no known reason for the name "Neapolitan.")

Schumann, Quartet, Op. 41, No. 3

N_6

(7) In this excerpt, VII is found with a seventh added, making it a secondary dominant to its following chord.

Sullivan, *H. M. S. Pinafore*

(8) Here are less conventional uses of v and VII. Try to arrive at a good reason for each use of these chords.

Brahms, *Ein deutsches Requiem*, Op. 45

d minor:

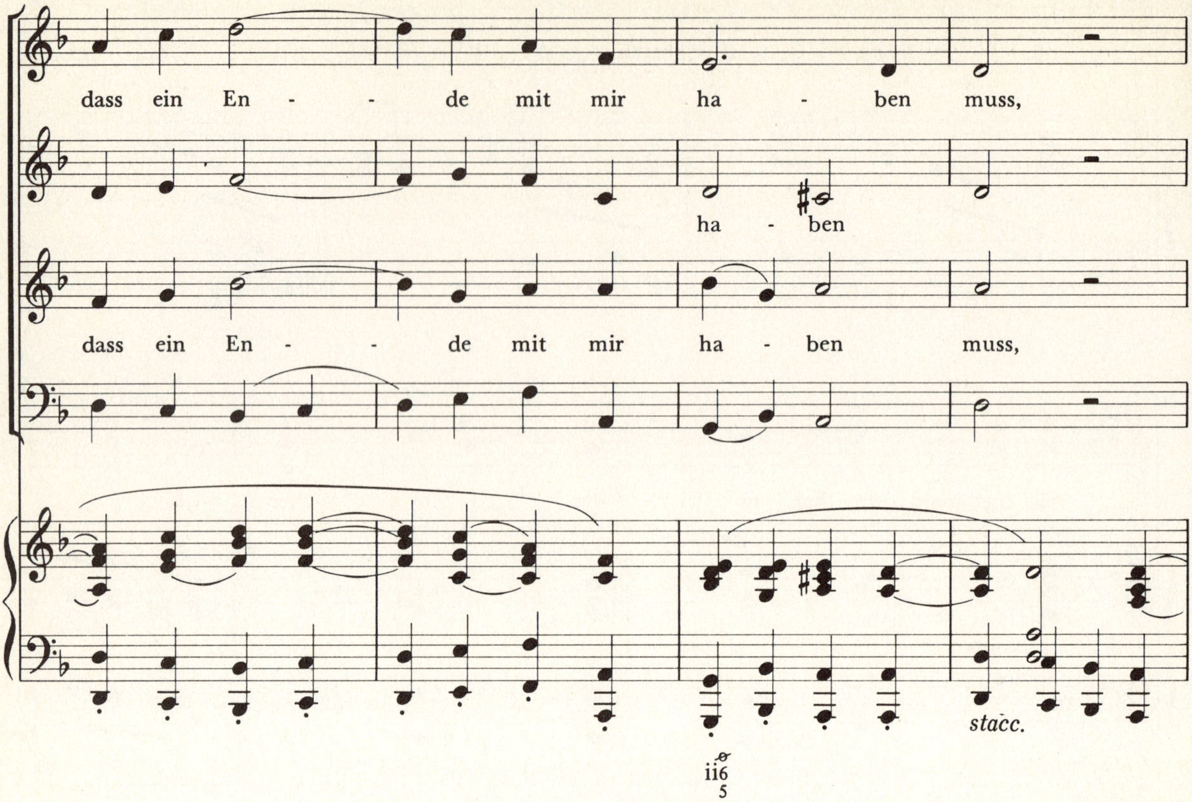

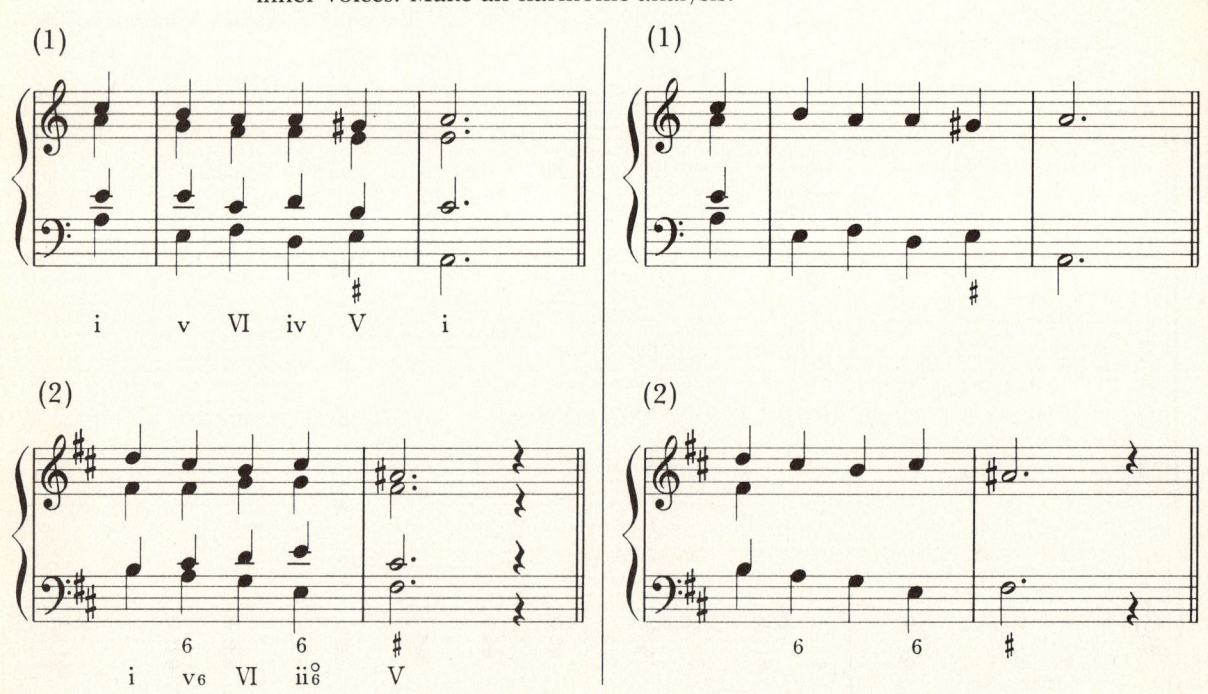

Assignment 16.3. (*EH*, p. 363). Part writing the v and VII triads. Fill in inner voices. Make an harmonic analysis.

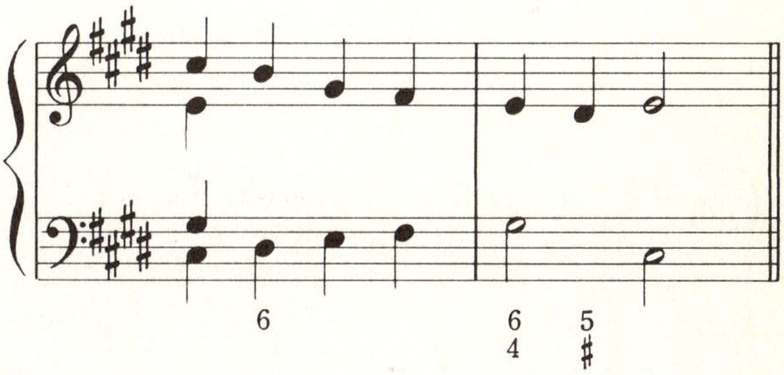

Assignment 16.4. (*EH*, p. 364). Part-writing the Phrygian cadence. Fill in inner voices. Make an harmonic analysis.

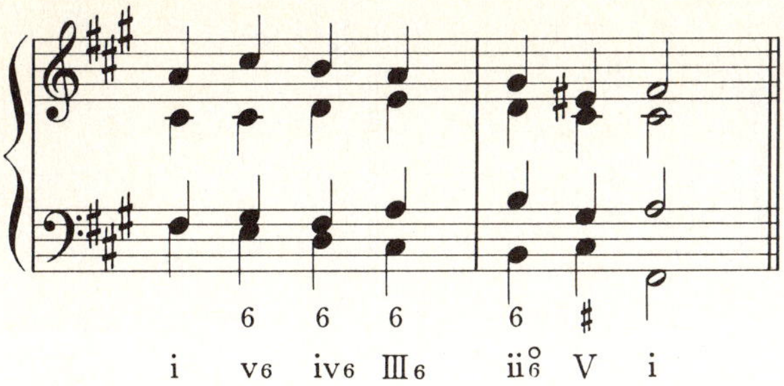

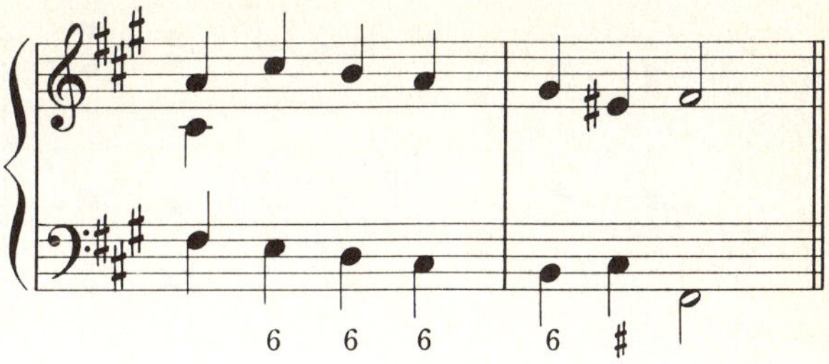

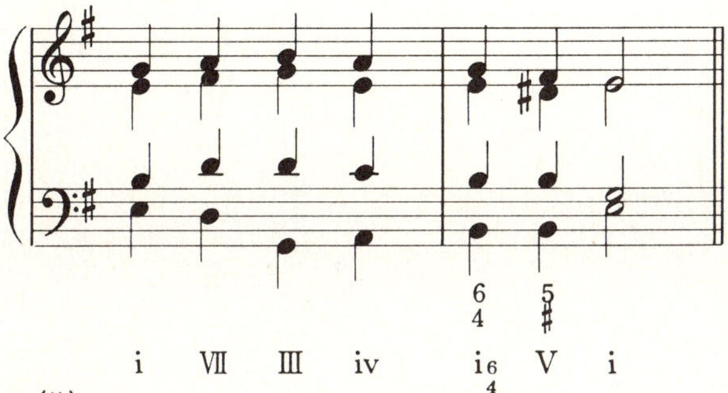

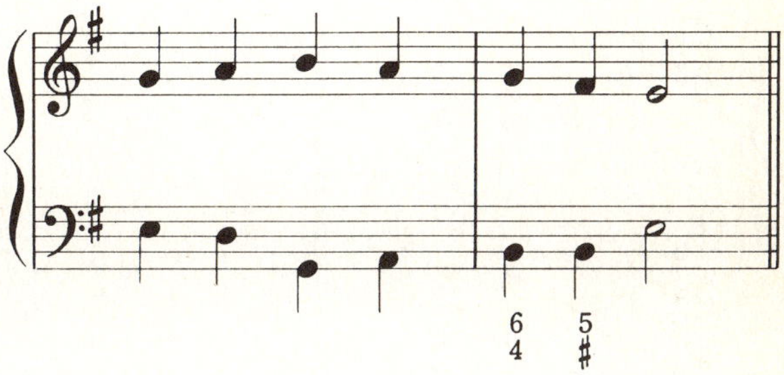

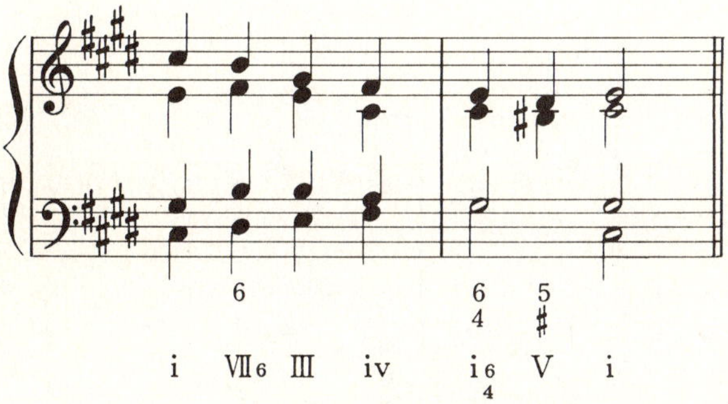

Numbers 1–3 have identical outside voices. Double the iv₆ differently in each as follows (and as illustrated in *EH*, Fig. 16.13):

(1) Double the root in the iv₆.
(2) Double the fifth in the iv₆.
(3) Double the third in the iv₆.

Assignment 16.5. (*EH*, p. 364). Part-writing. Fill in inner voices. Make an harmonic analysis.

(4) Number 2 from *EH*, page 364, transposed to E minor.

(5)

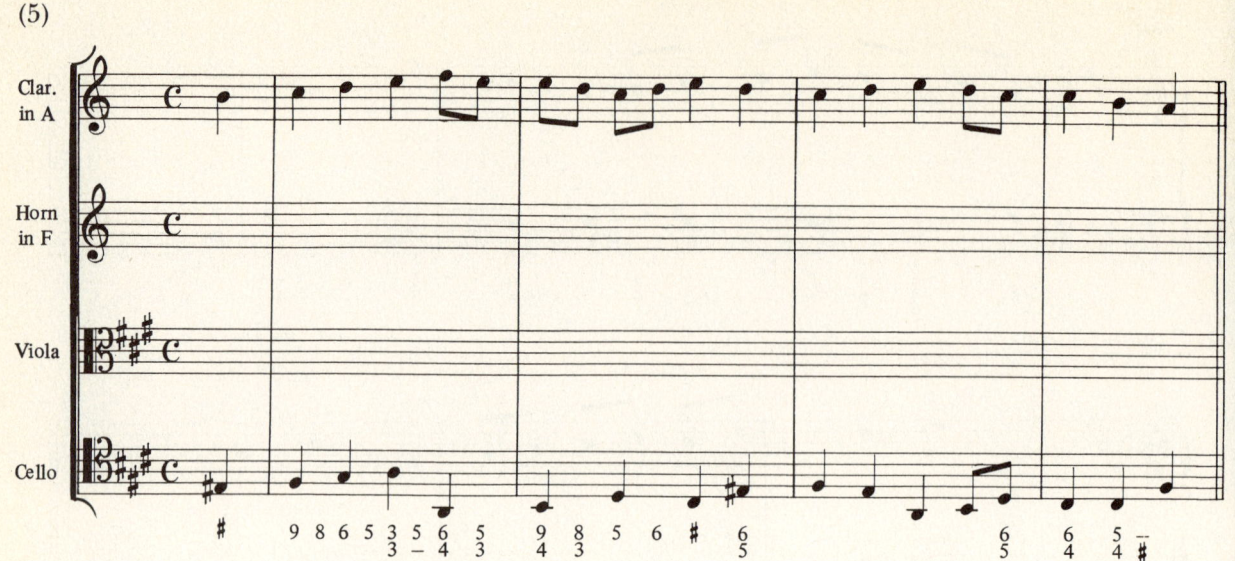

Assignment 16.6. (*EH*, p. 366). Part-writing, bass voice only given. Add soprano, alto, and tenor voices. Make an harmonic analysis.

(1)

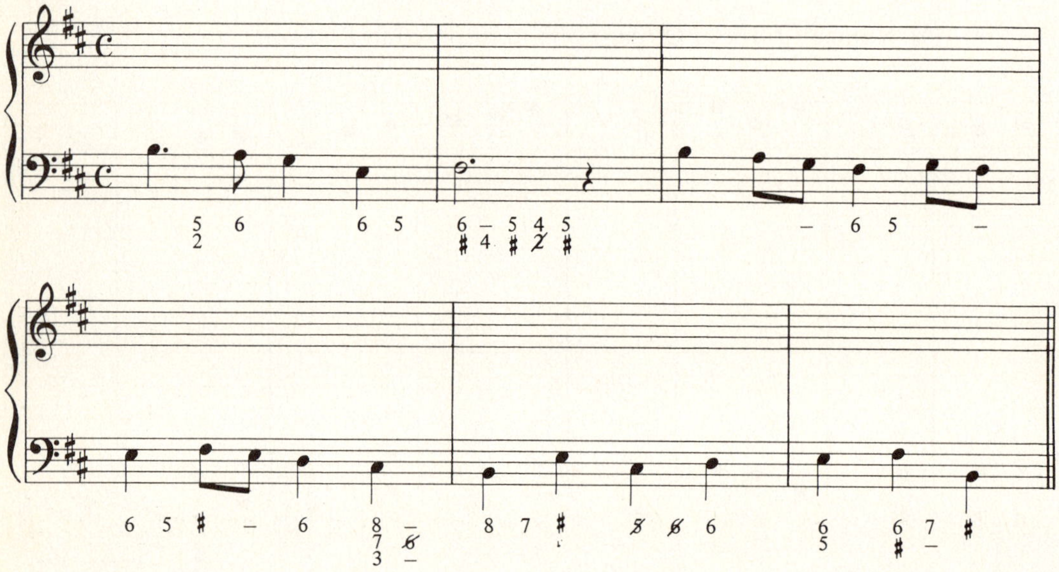

(2)

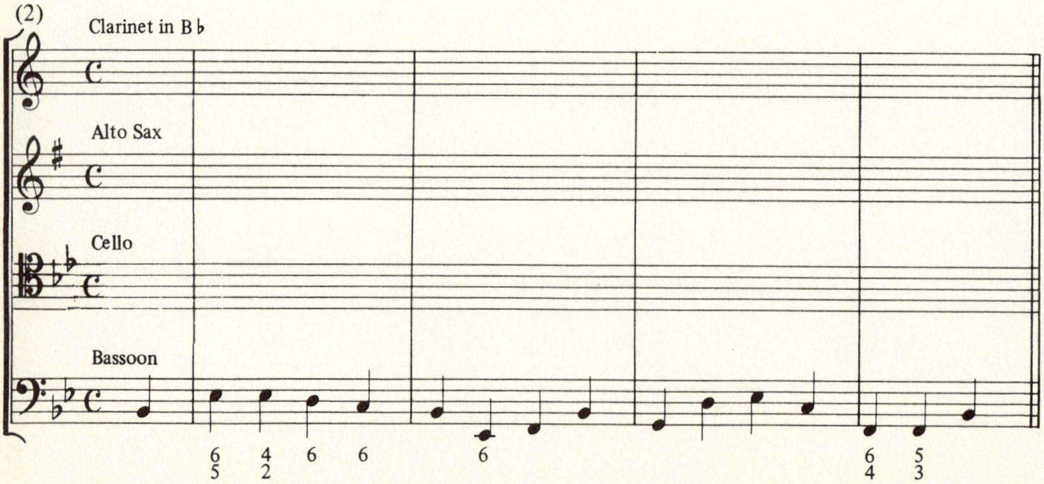

Assignment 16.7. (*EH*, p. 367). Part-writing an unfigured bass. Read full directions in *EH*.

(1)

(2)

(3) Number 4 from EH, page 368, transposed to D minor. Use a different melody line and different nonharmonic tones.

CHAPTER 17

HARMONIC SEQUENCE

	Elementary Harmony	*Workbook*
Assignment 17.1	382	194
Assignment 17.2	387	—
Assignment 17.3	387	197
Assignment 17.4	388	—

Assignment 17.1. (*EH*, p. 382). Analysis of harmonic sequences. Make an harmonic analysis and state the type of sequence as determined by its root movement (↑ **5** ↓ **4**, etc.)

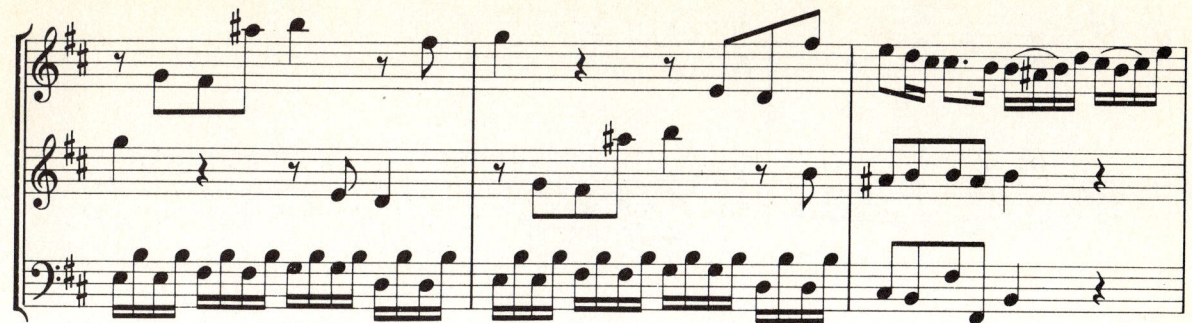

(3) Note the displacement of the melody by one half beat in relation to the left-hand accompaniment. Should the melody be moved forward one half beat or back one half beat when making an harmonic analysis?

Root movement ―――

Schumann, *Davidsbündlertänze*, Op. 6, No. 4

(3) Ungeduldig (Impatiently)

Root movement ―――

Mozart, Concerto in A Major for Piano and Orchestra, K.488

(4)

(6) The third beat of measure 1 is the tonic of a cadence in C♯ minor. But it is also the first chord in a new key, and the first in a sequence leading to a cadence in E major. This C♯ minor triad functions in two keys simultaneously and is called a *pivot chord*, a device to be considered in Chapter 18 and in *Advanced Harmony*.

At the E major cadence in measure 3, another device appears. Review *EH,* page 382, Figure 17.17, if the analysis eludes you.

(7) Using only the lower of each pair of notes in the bass clef, what common device is produced? How was the sequence manipulated to produce this effect?

Root movement _____

Beethoven, Sonata for Piano, Op. 109

Assignment 17.3. (*EH*, p. 387). Writing harmonic sequences. Continue each sequence until a cadence is reached. If the tonic falls on a weak beat, add another cadential progression, such as IV–V–I or ii–V–I.

In a minor key, observe these special considerations.

(1) $\hat{6}$ and $\hat{7}$ are usually lowered until arriving at a cadential V–I or vii–I.
(2) To continue through and past the dominant-tonic progression, use v–i or VII–i.

(2) Same as (1), but in G minor.

(3) Same as (1), but alternate root position and first inversion.

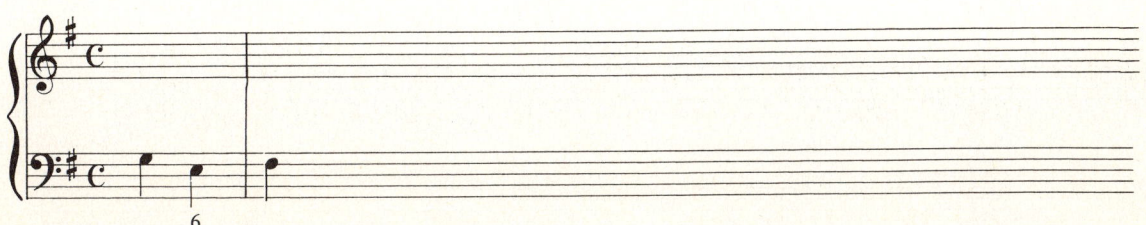

(4) ↓ 4 ↑ 2

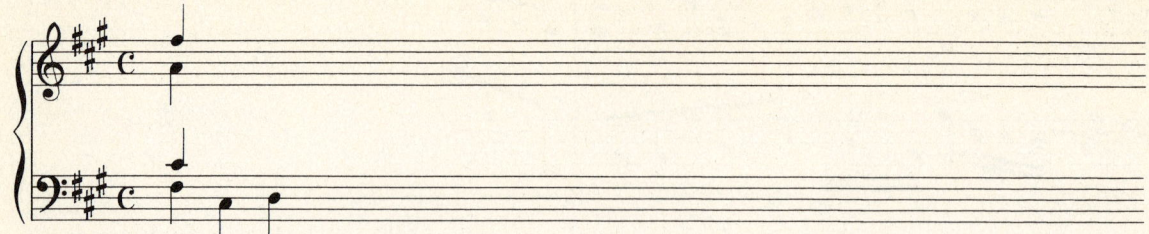

(5) ↓ 4 ↑ 2 with suspensions. Continue suspensions to the end of the sequence.

(6) ↓ 3 ↑ 4

(7) ↓ 3 ↑ 2. Sequence begins at the *.

(8)

CHAPTER 18

SECONDARY DOMINANT CHORDS; ELEMENTARY MODULATION

	Elementary Harmony	*Workbook*
Assignment 18.1	393	200
Assignment 18.2	393	—
Assignment 18.3	407	201
Assignment 18.4	407	203
Assignment 18.5	407	—
Assignment 18.6	407	205
Assignment 18.7	414	218
Assignment 18.8	416	219
Assignment 18.9	417	220
Assignment 18.10	419	222

Assignment 18.1. (*EH*, p. 393). Spelling secondary dominant chords. Having spelled each secondary dominant triad and seventh chord from Assignment 18.1 in *EH*, spell here a random selection of these chords. At *a*, answers are given; at *b*, no answers are given.

a) Answers given.

| E G♯ B | D major, V/V | __ __ __ |
| D F♯ A C | B♭ major, V^7/vi | __ __ __ __ |

E G♯ B D	E minor; V⁷/iv	___	___	___
B D♯ F♯	F♯ minor, V/VII	___	___	___
F A C E♭	A♭ major, V⁷/ii	___	___	___
A C♯ E G	A major, V⁷/IV	___	___	___
A♯ C𝑥 E♯ G♯	G♯ minor, V⁷/V	___	___	___
F A C	D minor, V/VI	___	___	___
D♯ F𝑥 A♯ C♯	F♯ major, V⁷/ii	___	___	___
B♯ D𝑥 F𝑥	A♯ minor, V/V	___	___	___

b) No answers given.

A major	V/ii	___	___	___ ;	V⁷/ii	___	___	___ ___
D minor	V/V	___	___	___ ;	V⁷/V	___	___	___ ___
E♭ major	V/vi	___	___	___ ;	V⁷/vi	___	___	___ ___
C minor	V/iv	___	___	___ ;	V⁷/iv	___	___	___ ___
B major	V/V	___	___	___ ;	V⁷/V	___	___	___ ___
C♯ minor	V/VI	___	___	___ ;	V⁷/VI	___	___	___ ___
A♭ major	V/ii	___	___	___ ;	V⁷/IV	___	___	___ ___
D♭ major	V/iii	___	___	___ ;	V⁷/iii	___	___	___ ___
F♯ major	V/ii	___	___	___ ;	V⁷/ii	___	___	___ ___
G♭ major	V/iii	___	___	___ ;	V⁷/iii	___	___	___ ___

Assignment 18.3. (*EH*, p. 407). Spelling pivot chord progressions in modulating from a major key to the key of the dominant. Given is an example of a modulation from the key of C to its dominant, G.[1] Below this example, other tonic triads are listed. Fill in chord spellings to effect modulation to the dominant from these tonics.

---

[1] Since these short examples are not found in the context of a complete formal structure, each could be equally well analyzed as a secondary dominant progression (I–I–V/V–V, etc.). For instructional purposes, they are considered modulatory progressions in this assignment.

a) Answers given.

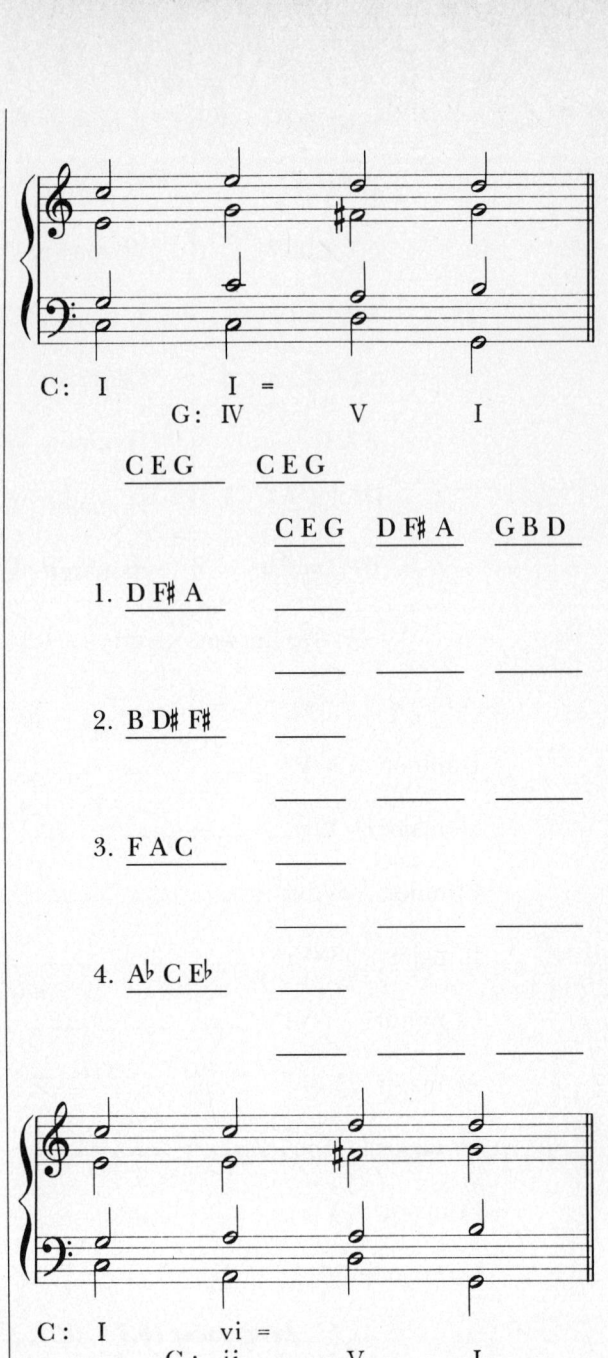

```
                            C E G     C E G

                                 C E G   D F♯ A   G B D

1. D F♯ A    D F♯ A         1. D F♯ A   ____    ____

             D F♯ A    E G♯ B    A C♯ E
2. B D♯ F♯   B D♯ F♯        2. B D♯ F♯  ____    ____

             B D♯ F♯   C♯ E♯ G♯  F♯ A♯ C♯
3. F A C     F A C          3. F A C    ____    ____

             F A C     G B D     C E G
4. A♭ C E♭   A♭ C E♭        4. A♭ C E♭  ____    ____

             A♭ C E♭   B♭ D F    E♭ G B♭
```

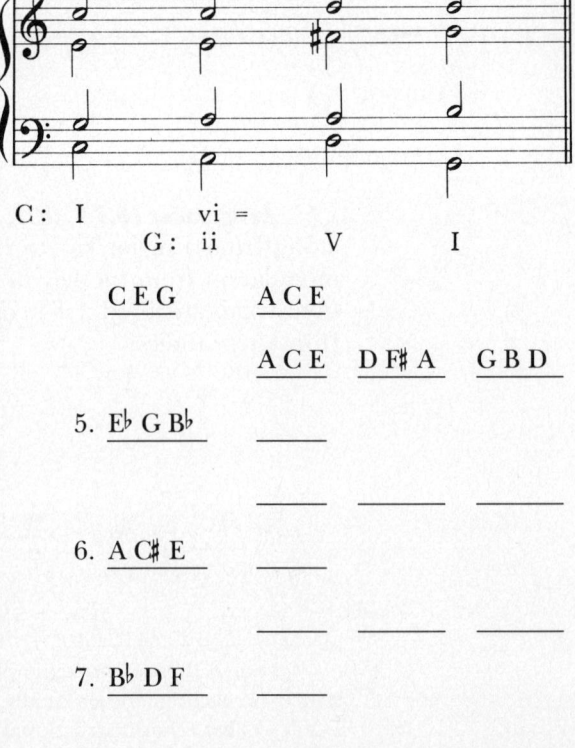

```
                            C E G     A C E

                                 A C E    D F♯ A   G B D

5. E♭ G B♭   C E♭ G         5. E♭ G B♭  ____    ____

             C E♭ G    F A C     B♭ D F
6. A C♯ E    F♯ A C♯        6. A C♯ E   ____    ____

             F♯ A C♯   B D♯ F♯   E G♯ B
7. B♭ D F    G B♭ D         7. B♭ D F   ____    ____

             G B♭ D    C E G     F A C
```

8. D♭ F A♭   B♭ D♭ F

   B♭ D♭ F   E♭ G B♭   A♭ C E♭

b) Answers not given.

	I	I =					I	vi =		
			IV	V	I				ii	V	I
1. GBD						5. FAC				
2. A♭ C E♭						6. E G♯ B				
3. E G♯ B						7. B D♯ F♯				
4. G♭ B♭ D♭						8. F♯ A♯ C♯				

Assignment 18.4. (*EH*, p. 407). Spelling pivot chord progressions in modulating from a minor key to the key of the mediant (relative major). Follow the directions given in Assignment 18.3.

a) Answers given.

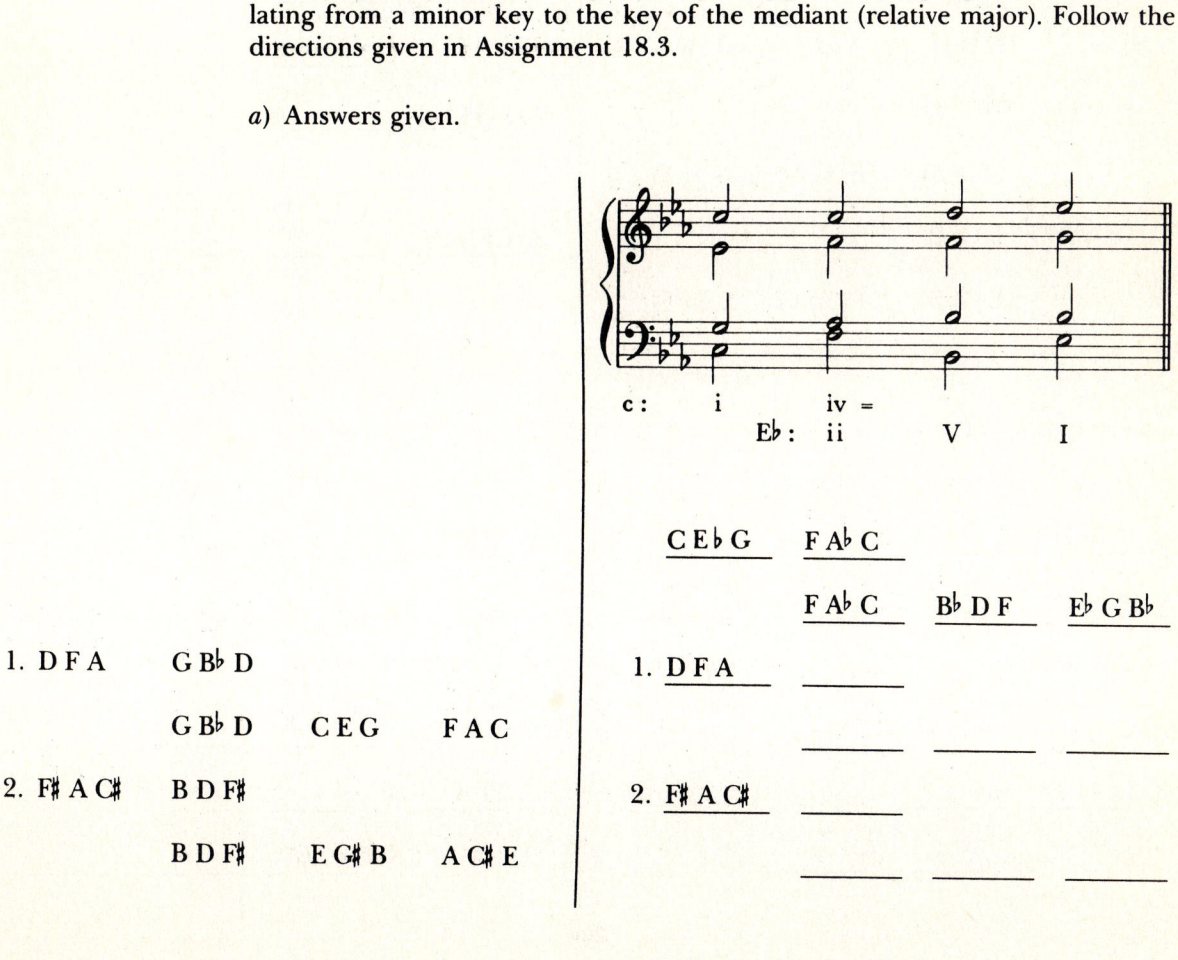

c: i   iv =
Eb: ii   V   I

             C E♭ G   F A♭ C
                      F A♭ C   B♭ D F   E♭ G B♭

1. D F A   G B♭ D   1. D F A

           G B♭ D   C E G   F A C

2. F♯ A C♯   B D F♯   2. F♯ A C♯

             B D F♯   E G♯ B   A C♯ E

3. B♭ D♭ F   E♭ G♭ B♭

                E♭ G♭ B♭   A♭ C E♭   D♭ F A♭

4. C♯ E G♯   F♯ A C♯

                F♯ A C♯   B D♯ F♯   E G♯ B

5. G B♭ D   E♭ G B♭

                E♭ G B♭   F A C   B♭ D F

6. B D F♯   G B D

                G B D   A C♯ E   D F♯ A

7. F A♭ C   D♭ F A♭

                D♭ F A♭   E♭ G B♭   A♭ C E♭

8. G♯ B D♯   E G♯ B

                E G♯ B   F♯ A♯ C♯   B D♯ F♯

3. B♭ D♭ F   _____

          _____   _____   _____

4. C♯ E G♯   _____

          _____   _____   _____

c: i   VI =
              E♭: IV   V   I

    C E♭ G   A♭ C E♭

    A♭ C E♭   B♭ D F   E♭ G B♭

5. G B♭ D   _____

          _____   _____   _____

6. B D F♯   _____

          _____   _____   _____

7. F A♭ C   _____

          _____   _____   _____

8. G♯ B D♯   _____

          _____   _____   _____

b) Answers not given.

    i   iv =
             ii   V   I

1. G B♭ D   _____

          _____   _____   _____

2. E G B   _____

          _____   _____   _____

3. E♭ G♭ B♭ _____

          _____   _____   _____

    i   VI =
           IV   V   I

5. D F A   _____

          _____   _____   _____

6. B♭ D♭ F   _____

          _____   _____   _____

7. F♯ A C♯   _____

4. D♯ F♯ A♯ _____   8. C♯ E G♯ _____

_____ _____ _____   _____ _____ _____

Assignment 18.6. (*EH*, p. 407). Harmonic analysis. These excerpts include examples of secondary dominant chords, modulation to the dominant, and modulation to the relative major. In several instances, interpretation of a given passage as a dominant of the dominant progression or as a modulation to the dominant may be equally logical. Be prepared to furnish either analysis, or to provide good reasons why you believe the progression is definitely one or the other.

Bach, *Ach Gott, wie manches Herzeleid* (#217)

(1)

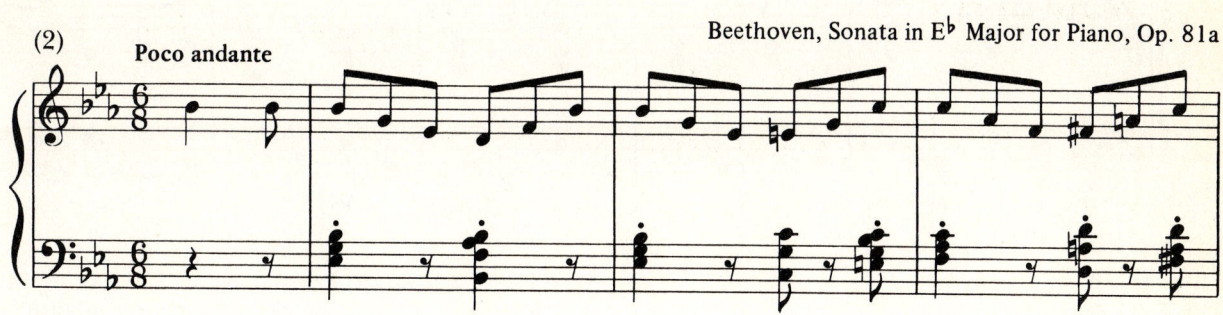

(2) Poco andante

Beethoven, Sonata in E♭ Major for Piano, Op. 81a

Haydn, Sonata in D Major for Piano, Hob XVI:37

(6) Larghetto Handel, *Messiah*

(7) The harmonic progression in this example is I–ii–V–I V/V–V. All other tones are conventional nonharmonic tones.

Andantino, teneramente Brahms, Intermezzo, Op. 116, No. 6

(8) Molto vivace Weber, *Der Freischütz*, Overture

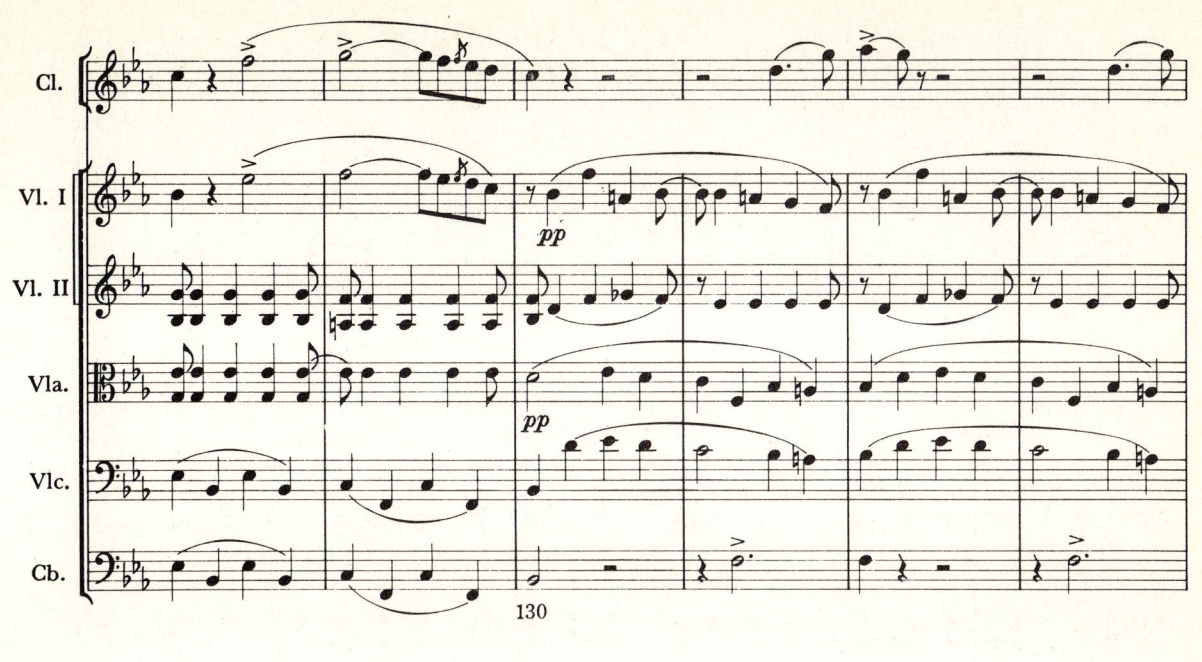

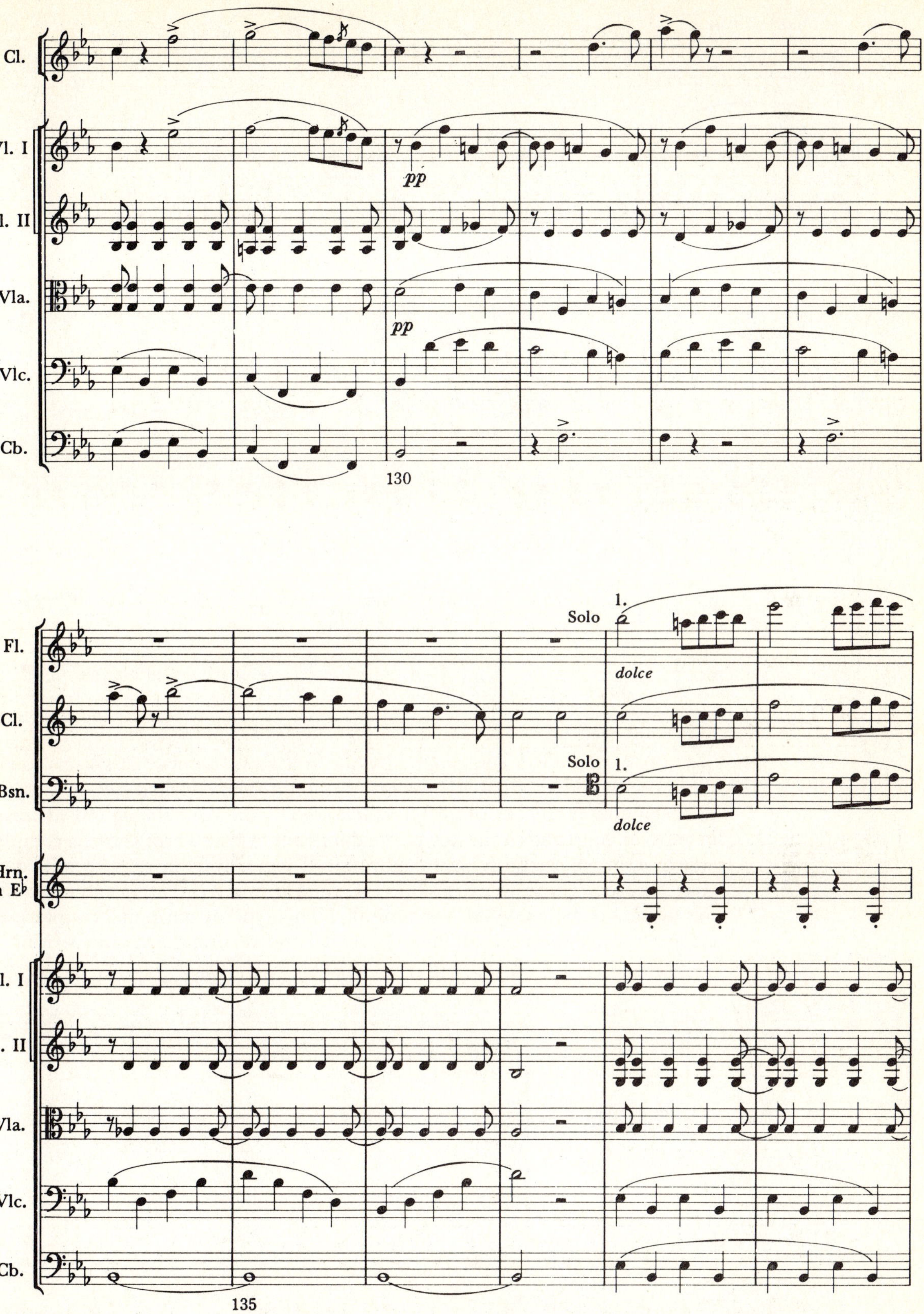
Cl.
Vl. I
Vl. II
Vla.
Vlc.
Cb.
pp
pp
130
Fl.
Cl.
Bsn.
Hrn. in E♭
Vl. I
Vl. II
Vla.
Vlc.
Cb.
Solo
1.
dolce
Solo
1.
dolce
135

(9) A fugue is a contrapuntal work in a given number of voices, usually three or four, that is based principally upon a theme, called *subject*, stated at the beginning in the key of the tonic, followed by the same theme, called *answer*, in another voice and in the key of the dominant. This excerpt shows a complete *exposition*, in which the subject is introduced successively in each of four given voices: subject (C), answer (G), subject (C), and answer (G). Though contrapuntal, the music can be analyzed harmonically. This type of harmonic counterpoint is a perfect juxtaposition of linear (melodic) and vertical (harmonic) writing.

Bach, Fugure in C Major for Organ, BWV 545

Schumann, *Fantasiestücke*, Op. 12, "Aufschung"

Grieg, *Solvejg's Song*, Op. 23, No. 1

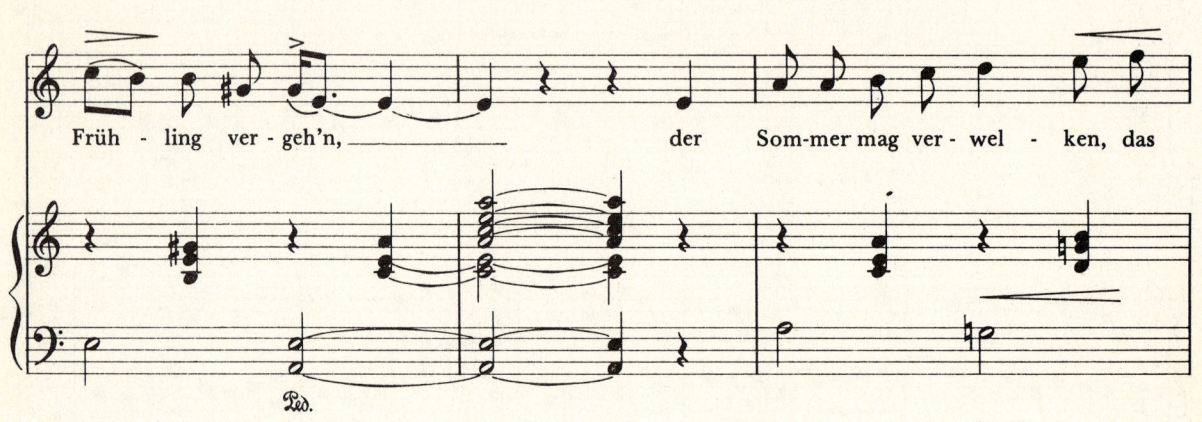

(12) Mozart, Quintet for Piano and Winds, K. 452

(13) Mozart, Serenade, *Eine kleine Nachtmusik*, K. 525

214

Assignment 18.7. (*EH*, p. 414). Analysis of modulation and secondary dominants in a melodic line. Below the staff, write the chord symbols that express the harmony implied by the melody. Circle and identify each nonharmonic tone.

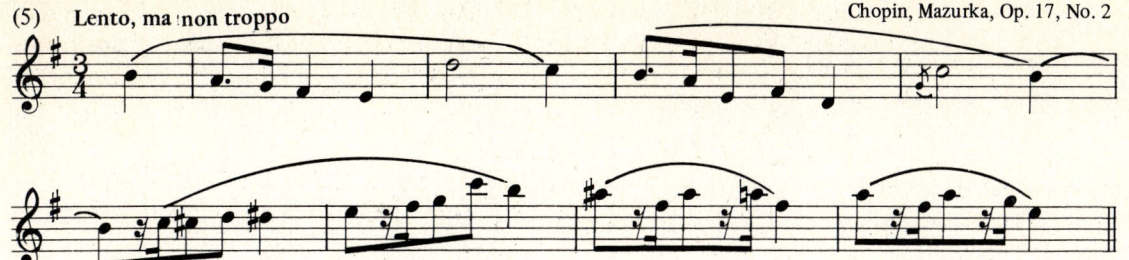

(5) Lento, ma non troppo

Chopin, Mazurka, Op. 17, No. 2

Assignment 18.8. (*EH*, p. 416). Writing the V/V chord. Add alto and tenor voices. Make an harmonic analysis.

(1) (2)

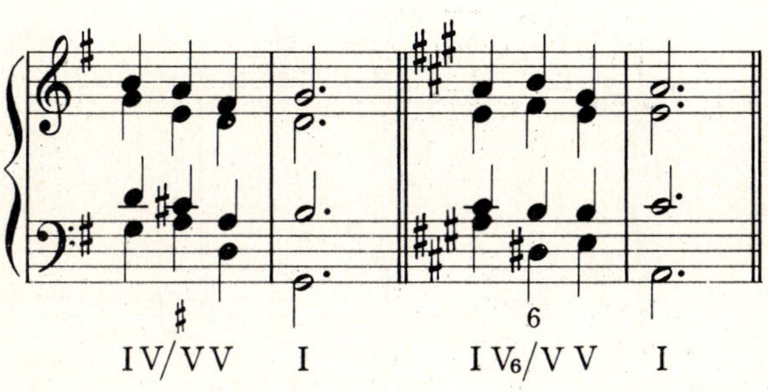

(1) (2)

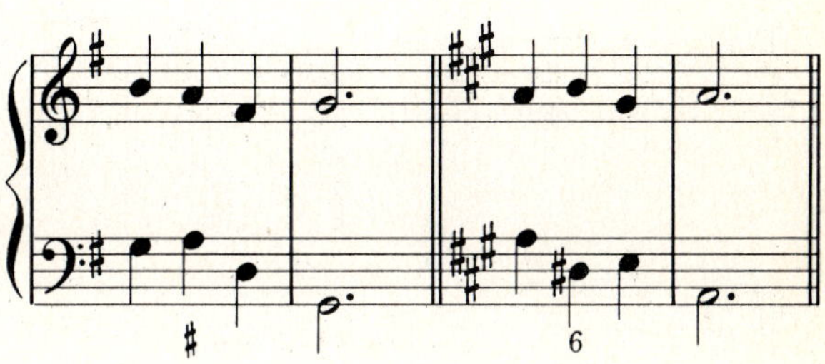

(3)

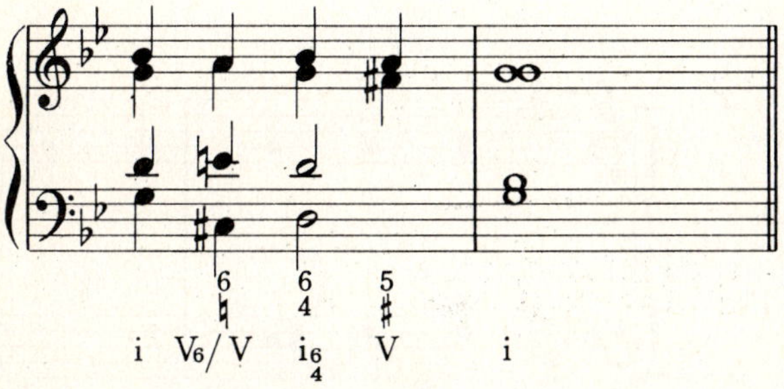

(3)

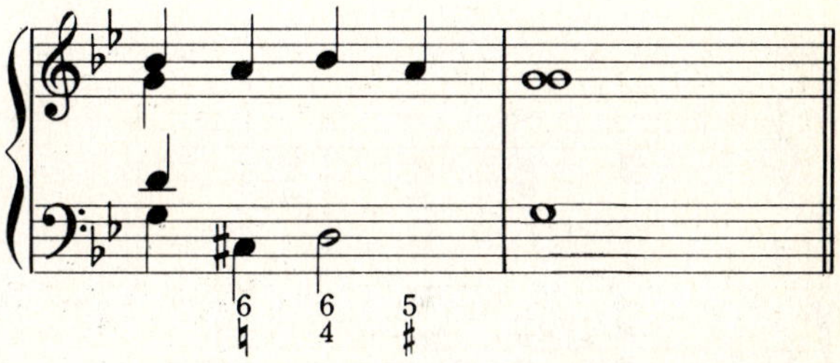

(4) (5)

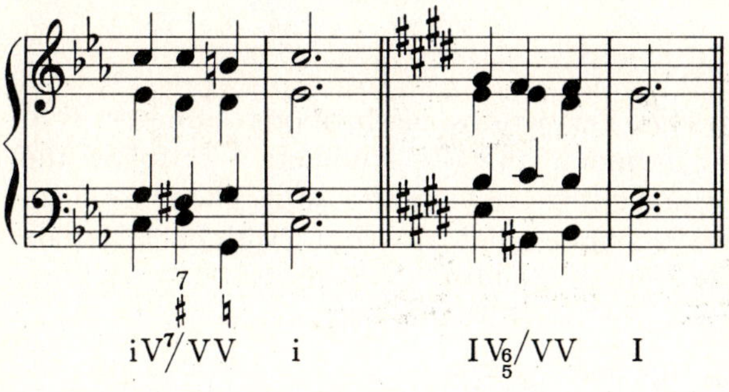

(4) (5)

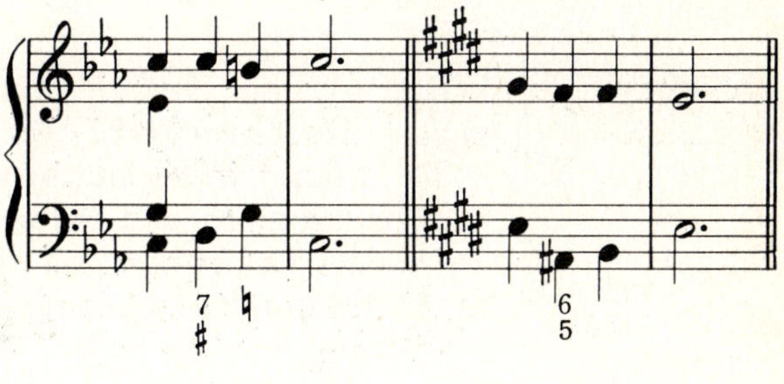

(6)

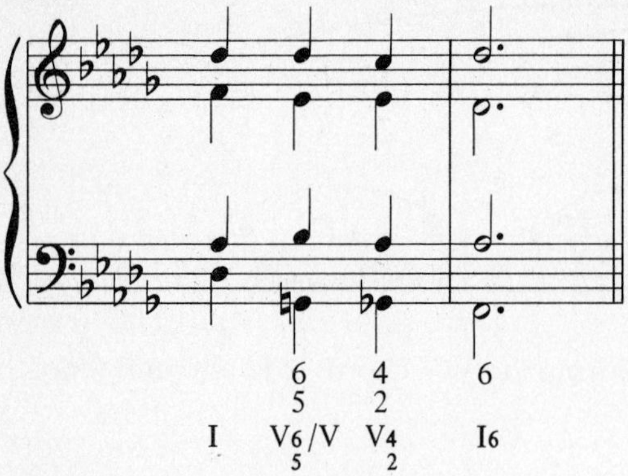

(6)

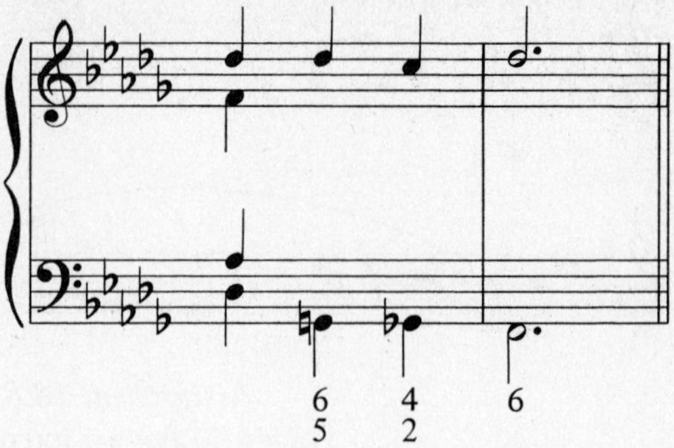

(7)

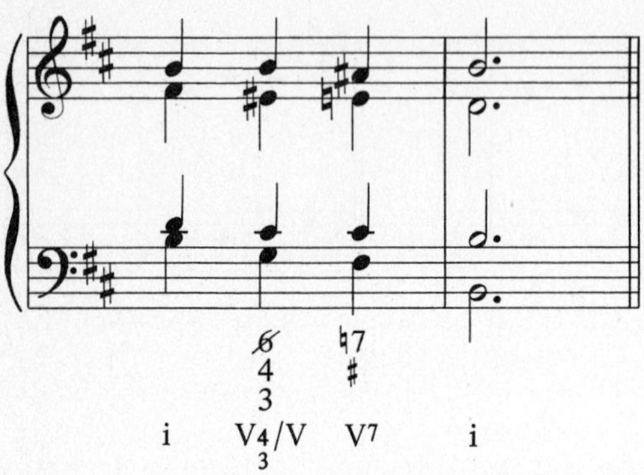

(7)

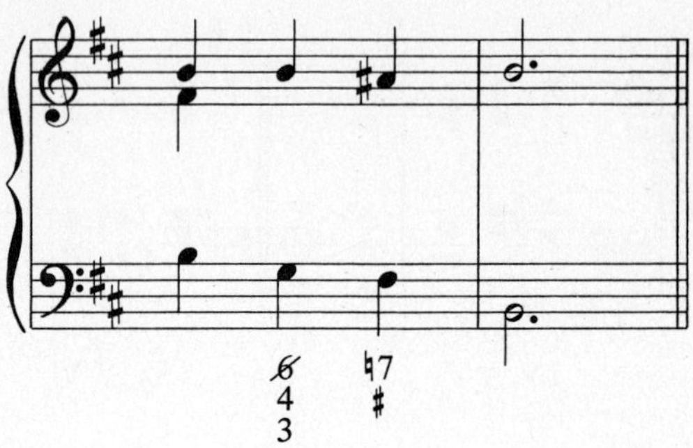

(8)

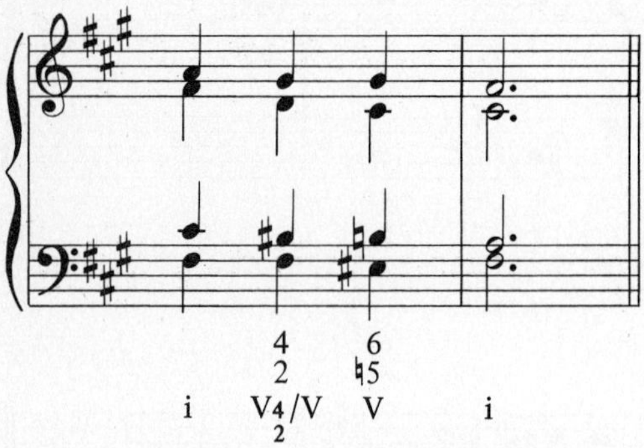

(8)

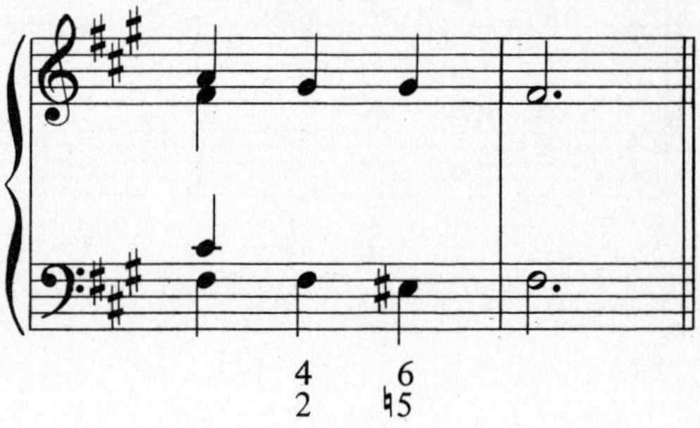

Assignment 18.9. (*EH*, p. 417). Part-writing modulations. Numbers 1–3: fill in inner voices and make an harmonic analysis. Numbers 4–5: follow the same directions, and add nonharmonic tones of your choosing. These are Bach chorales. Compare your 4 with Bach chorale #192, and your 5 with Bach chorale #281, phrases 1, 2, 3, and 6 only.

(1)

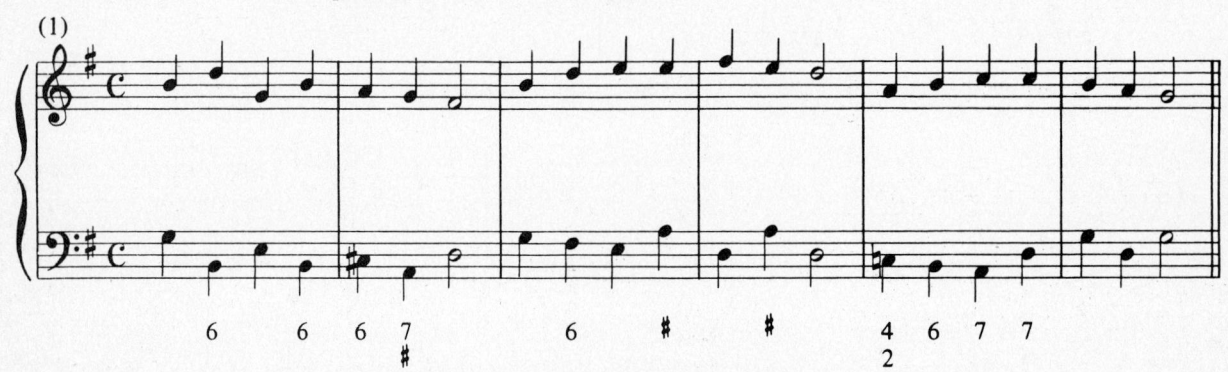

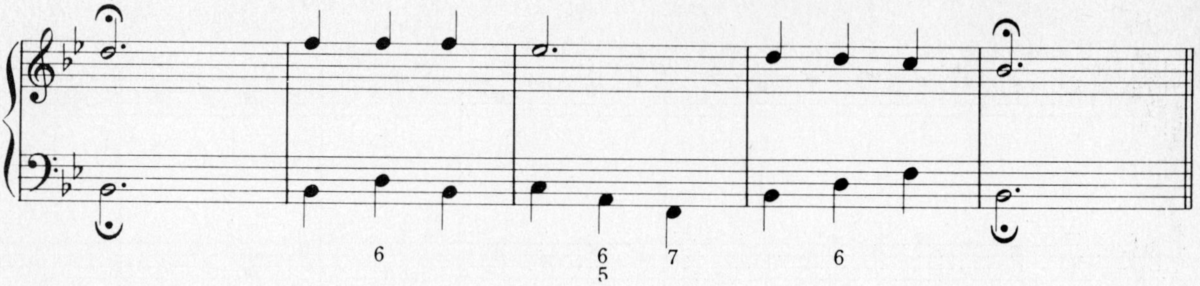

(5) Unfigured

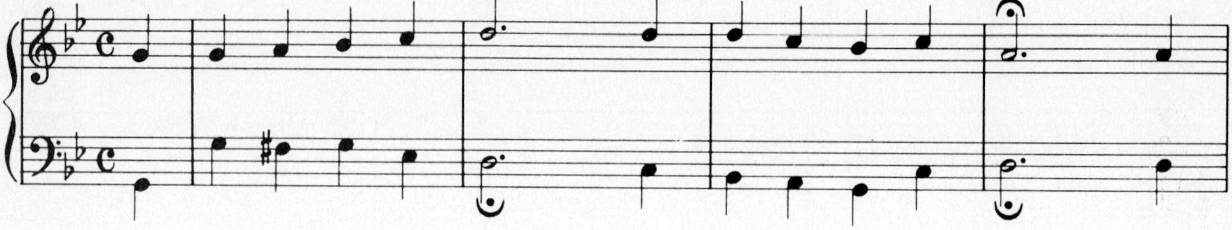

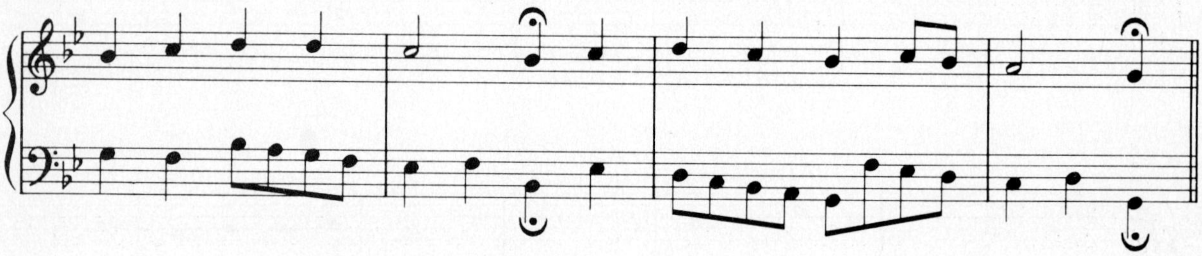

Assignment 18.10. (*EH*, p. 419). Part-writing secondary dominant harmony other than V/V.

(1) (2)

(3) (4)

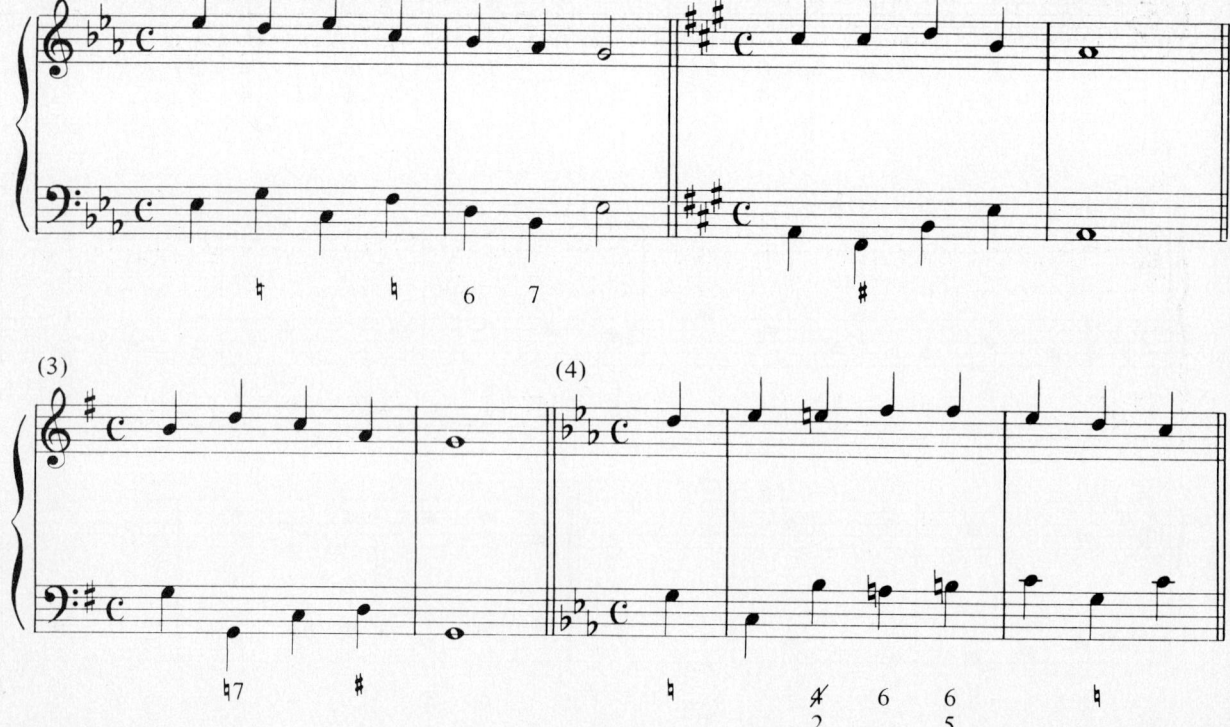

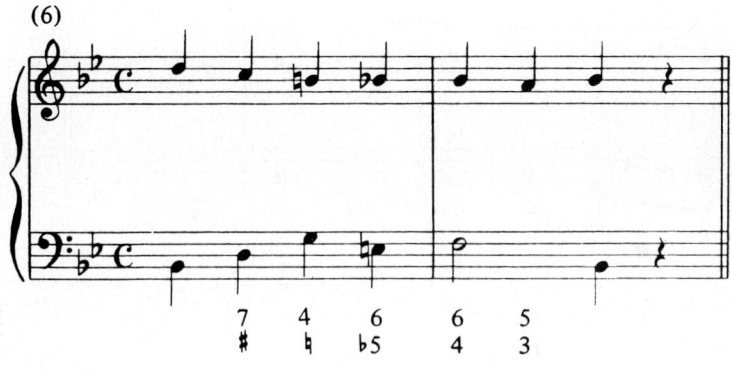
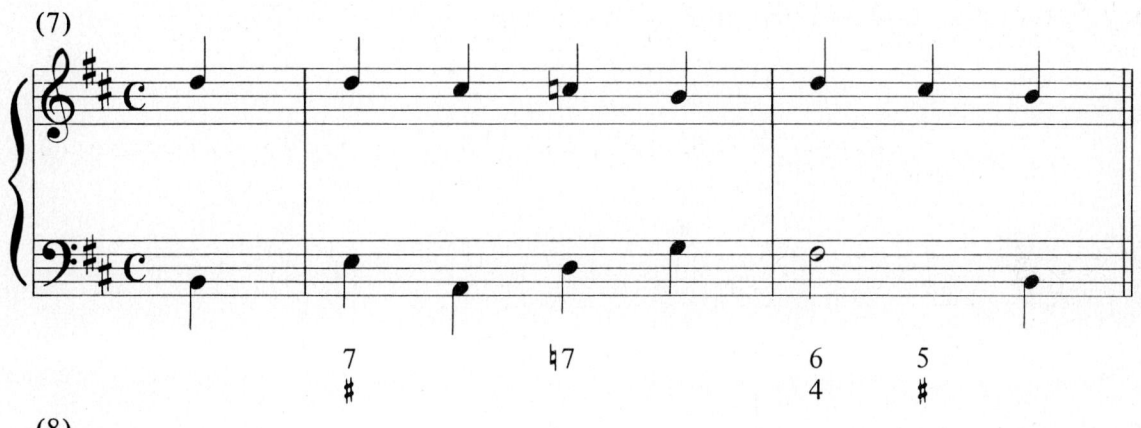
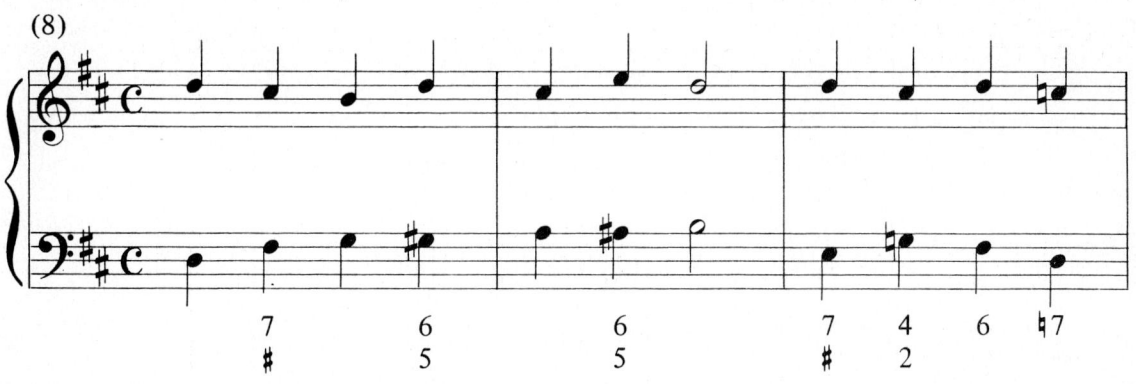

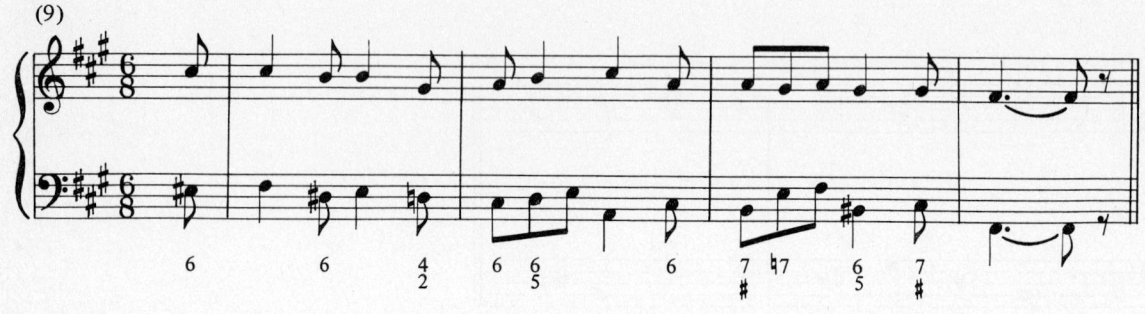